'The LORD is your rock, your ~~fortress~~
and your ~~deliverer~~
your rock, in w...
He is your shield...
salvation, your s...
PS 27:1

Restoration

A direction for prayer

Kjell Sjöberg

For in the day of trouble He will
keep you safe in His dwelling place, He
will hide you in the shelter of His
tabernacle and set you high upon a rock...
PS 27: 5 + 6

To Sylvia with love from Jean
6 MARCH 1996

New Wine Press

New Wine Press
PO Box 17
Chichester
England PO20 6YB

ISBN: 1 874367 44 2

Typeset by CRB Associates, Norwich.
Printed by Clays Ltd, St Ives plc, Bungay, Suffolk.

Contents

Chapter 1	Lord, Restore us Again!	5
Chapter 2	Prayer for Restoration	29
Chapter 3	Restoration of the Individual	63
Chapter 4	The Glory of the Lord	89
Chapter 5	Restoration of the Family	103
Chapter 6	The Second Fall of Man and the Flood	127
Chapter 7	Restoring the Church	157
Chapter 8	The Third Fall of Man and the Restoration of Society	185
Chapter 9	The Battle for Restoration	225
Chapter 10	Come, Lord Jesus!	257

Chapter 1

Lord, Restore us Again!

One of the themes of God's Word that holds special significance for me at the present time is this: that one day everything is going to be restored.

The vision of restoration has been born in me at a time when Sweden has been proceeding from one low point to another even lower. For example, we became the third country in the world to accept homosexual marriages. The prophets in Israel were given experiences of the Lord just at the time their hopes were being shattered, for example when Jerusalem was captured and the people were carried away as prisoners. It was the same prophets who lived through Israel's lowest moments that were given visions and prophetic messages of hope and restoration.

A prayer of faith has been born in my spirit: 'Lord, restore us again!' I write as an intercessor so that other intercessors may be given faith to pray for restoration. Prayer for restoration is a prophetic prayer ministry in the End Time. In order to enter into this ministry, we need to know everything in God's Word that can strengthen our faith that restoration is going on in all those areas where man has fallen from God's original plan.

Restoration is the Lord's programme for raising up individuals who have fallen, and reinstating them in the Lord's service.

I have been a preacher for 43 years, and have worked as a pastor, as a missionary, and as a national prayer leader. As the years have gone by, I have worked with many different friends and colleagues. I am always glad when things go well for them spiritually in the Lord's service, but some of them have gone off course. This has caused much hurt, but has also been a challenge to intercession. During the past two years, some of those who were very close to me both in Sweden and in Pakistan, have come back into their ministry again. While the teaching about restoration was forming and growing in my heart, the Lord was demonstrating his grace by granting restoration in the lives of my friends.

The times of restoration of all things

> *'Repent therefore and be converted, that your sins may be blotted out, so that times of refreshing may come from the presence of the Lord, and that He may send Jesus Christ, who was preached to you before, whom heaven must receive until the times of restoration of all things, of which God has spoken by the mouth of all his holy prophets since the world began.'*
>
> (Acts 3:19–21, NKJV)

The background to Peter's message of restoration was that a lame man had been so healed by the power of Jesus, that he could get up and walk. I have learnt from experience that the Holy Spirit is a skilful drama director who makes certain that an important message from God is clarified and illustrated in power before those who listen to it. The healing of sick bodies is an expression of restoration. Restoration means lifting up someone who has fallen down. Here was someone who from his birth had been unable to stand on his feet. As Peter was preaching restoration, so the man who had been lame was walking and jumping among those who were listening. It was against this background that Peter could declare that Jesus' power of restoration can act in such a way that everything is restored again. Times of refreshing can come for a whole nation, if they repent and turn to God. Peter preached about restoration for Israel, so that they might obtain the blessing that had been promised when the Lord made his covenant with Abraham.

The power that produces restoration is the power of Jesus' resurrection

Peter spoke in Solomon's colonnade to startled people who wanted to know how it was that the lame man was able to walk and jump. Peter's explanation was a testimony to the power of Jesus' resurrection:

> *'But you ... put to death the Prince of life, the one whom God raised from the dead, a fact to which we are witnesses. And on the basis of faith in His name, it is the name of Jesus which has strengthened this man whom you see and know.'* (Acts 3:14–16, NASB)

If you believe that God raised Jesus from the dead, then you can also believe that everything can be restored: even dead bodies, even dead churches, even cities and nations where death rules and the culture of the kingdom of death has taken over.

We learn from Peter's sermon that preaching about restoration must be accompanied by a demonstration of Jesus' resurrection power through signs and wonders, healing and raising of the dead. Otherwise, people are not going to believe it possible for everything to be restored, even when the lowest point has been reached.

Healing, in the Gospels, is represented as restoration. The Greek word used for restoration is also one of the words used to describe Jesus' healing of the sick.

> *'And the prayer offered in faith will make the sick person well; the Lord will raise him up.'*   (James 5:15)

Restoration means that he who has fallen will get up again; here it is applied to the sick person whom the Lord raises up.

Simeon said of Jesus:

> *'This child is set for the fall and rising again of many in Israel.'*   (Luke 2:34, KJV)

Here the phrase 'rising again' is used as a synonym for restoration. Jesus is set for the rising again of many. When Israel is restored, it will be like life from the dead:

> *'What will their acceptance be but life from the dead?'*
> (Romans 11:15)

The condition for restoration is repentance and conversion

Peter's message of restoration contained a challenge to his hearers to be converted. Restoration is God's gracious invitation because of man's fallen state. It is sin that prevents us from attaining the level that we were created for. Anyone who wants to experience restoration in his life must ruthlessly come to terms with sin in his life, without trying to plead any extenuating circumstances and without seeking to blame anyone else.

> *'Repent therefore and be converted, that your sins may be blotted out, so that times of refreshing may come*

> *from the presence of the Lord ... until the times of restoration of all things.'* (Acts 3:19, 21, NKJV)

When intercessors pray for awakening and restoration for the church and the community, their prayers must be characterized by contrition and repentance and they must identify themselves with the sin that has caused the downfall. If we want to liberate people, we have to confront the enemy who holds them bound, but when we pray for restoration, it is sin that is the enemy we must deal with, in order that God can act in restoration.

> *'Brothers, if someone is caught in a sin, you who are spiritual should restore him gently. But watch yourself, or you also may be tempted.'* (Galatians 6:1)

Our task is to restore those who have sinned, but I have learnt that it is no use restoring a minister of the Lord who has fallen into sin, so that he can regain the confidence of men and the goodwill of God and be reinstated in his position, as long as there still remains unconfessed sin in his life. Yet anyone who is totally open and honest and truly wants to put everything right, receives forgiveness.

Times of refreshing

Peter spoke of times of refreshing which would come in connection with the restoration of all things before the return of Jesus. This is what we are experiencing at the present time in many places in the world (Acts 3:19–21). It is happening in the form of various manifestations of God's Spirit. Jeremiah described it as waking up from a pleasant sleep.

> *'"I will refresh the weary and satisfy the faint." At this I awoke and looked around. My sleep had been pleasant to me.'* (Jeremiah 31:25–26)

Jeremiah had this experience of refreshing just before he was taken into custody in the courtyard of the guard (Jeremiah 37:21), and before Jerusalem was destroyed. The Church of God is even now experiencing a higher level of glory, so that we can be strengthened for walking the last stretch of the road before the coming of Jesus.

Tired, burnt-out, exhausted servants of God are being touched by God's power and are returning to their churches transformed. Many who have experienced refreshing say that Jesus revealed himself to them. He revealed what had been hidden in their lives. One pastor prayed, 'Lord, show me my heart.' Those who were praying for him pointed out three areas in his life where he needed to repent. He had failed in his faithfulness to the Lord and his friends; he had compromised, and he had spoken untruthfully.

The Lord has promised:

> *'For the earth will be filled with the knowledge of the glory of the Lord, as the waters cover the sea.'*
>
> (Habakkuk 2:14)

But before the Lord can fill the earth with his glory, he has to deal with the sins of the people. He can cleanse the world by his judgments, or else he can work together with his intercessors, who pray on behalf of their people that they might be forgiven for their unforgiveness, their hatred and their blood-guiltiness, and lay the sins of the people upon the Lamb who takes away the sin of the world. The Spirit of God has concentrated the intercessors upon dealing with those sins that have grieved God's Spirit and obstructed God's glory. The Lord is crushing and softening hard hearts; reconciliation is taking place between races where ethnic conflicts have occurred over a long period. Where sin is washed away through prayer for reconciliation, times of refreshing follow. There is a perceptible increase in this kind of intercession in many countries, and the Lord is answering these prayers by sending wave after wave of his presence, which in the end will fill the whole earth with his glory.

What is going to be restored?

It is the image of God in man, deformed by the Fall, that is going to be fully restored again in righteousness. God's plan for restoration implies a reinstatement of the quality of life on earth that God had in his mind from the beginning. God created us to live in Paradise. We ruined Paradise by our sin and by allowing Satan to exploit us. God's plan of salvation looks forward to a restoration of everything that God offered to man in Paradise, every-thing that was there at the start of creation.

But there is also evidently a limit to what Peter preached about restoration. That which is to be restored consists only of those areas that God has revealed through the prophets. The teaching about the restoration of all things has for some extended so far that they declare that no one should ever be condemned, but that every one will ultimately be restored, even Lucifer and the fallen angels.

All the prophets spoke with one voice about restora-tion. They were given visions of a re-gathered Israel and a restored Paradise – a kingdom of peace on earth. Jerusalem will be the praise of the earth. The ruined cities will be rebuilt. The desert will flower. Family relation-ships will be restored, as Malachi foretells. The prophets all speak of restoration for the nations of the Middle East. When Peter was summing up all that the prophets had said about restoration, he expressed it by saying:

> '... *until the times of restoration of all things, of which God has spoken by the mouth of all his holy prophets since the world began.'* (Acts 3:21, NKJV)

11

A prophetic ministry that prepares for the coming of Jesus

The restoration process is part of the preparation for Jesus' return. Acts 3:21 tells us that Jesus will stay in heaven *'until the times of restoration of all things.'* The disciples asked Jesus, after the revelation on the Mount of Transfiguration, why the 'teachers of the law' said that Elijah must come first, before Messiah could appear.

> *'Jesus replied, "To be sure, Elijah comes and will restore all things. But I tell you, Elijah has already come, and they did not recognize him, but have done to him everything they wished."'*   (Matthew 17:11–12)

Jesus confirmed that Elijah would come first. Restoration must come first so that Jesus will be able to enter into his task as Messiah-King.

In Acts 3:19, restoration is a prophetic plan of action taking place in the period before Jesus' return. In Matthew 17:11, the accent lies on the actual human agent who will carry out the prophetic acts before Jesus comes.

Elijah came on the scene at a moment when Israel was at a spiritually low point, and by doing powerful miracles he restored Israel's fear of God through manifestations of God's glory. He raised up an altar that had been broken down; he restored the prophetic ministry. Because he had given a dead son back to his mother, he became known as the prophet who healed family relationships. In himself he bore evidence that he was a restored man of God.

I do not believe that Elijah will return in the sense of being reincarnated. God brought Elijah, the man of God, through to a stage of maturity in his understanding of God's plan of restoration. There is nothing to prevent God from doing the same thing again, bringing the men and women of God through to a similar stage of maturity and understanding of God's purposes of reconciliation.

The return of Elijah, in this sense, and the restoration of all things, will be brought into being through intercessors who pray in the spirit and power of Elijah. I see the Elijah ministry as a stage in the maturing of the Body of Christ all over the world; this is why we need to have a deeper understanding of restoration as a prophetic area of prayer.

> *'Jesus said to them, "I tell you the truth, at the renewal of all things, when the Son of Man sits on his glorious throne, you who have followed me will also sit on twelve thrones, judging the twelve tribes of Israel."'*
> (Matthew 19:28)

The word here translated 'renewal' is the Greek word *paliggenesia*, literally 'becoming again', meaning the renewal of the whole of creation, with the same implication that everything will be restored again. The complete restoration comes with the return of Jesus:

> *'Behold, I am making all things new.'*
> (Revelation 21:5, NASB)

The Greek word for 'new' here is *kainos*, meaning new in character or quality. There is another Greek word, *neos*, meaning new in the sense of youthful or fresh. When Paul urges, *'Be transformed by the renewing of your mind'* (Romans 12:2), his word for 'renewing' derives from *kainos*.

From something that is old, God can create something that is entirely new in character and quality – that is restoration. What God says from the throne means: See, I am making all things new in character. Gone is all decay, all ageing, all that has become worn-out by time, circumstances, or the attacks of the enemy. Just as it was all good at the beginning, so it becomes again, so that it is as fresh as when it was first created.

The threefold Fall that has affected mankind

If we look upon the Fall of man as a step-by-step downward progress, it becomes easier to see restoration as an upward climb from glory to glory. In restoration, mankind is on the way upwards by stages. We begin our upward journey from the cross and the resurrection, and we make our way step-by-step upwards from there to the return of Jesus.

The principal Fall of man was the fall of Adam and Eve in the Garden of Eden; I will refer to this as the first Fall. The second Fall took place during the time before the Flood, and the third Fall was when the Tower of Babel was built. The first Fall was the decisive one, with the others following from it, taking mankind on a gradual descent to bottom level.

For some time after the great nuclear disaster at Chernobyl, further destructive effects of the explosion came to light one by one, effects that could not be seen immediately after the disaster. For instance, after an interval there were sicknesses affecting children. Later, the effect of fallout could be seen in the destruction of forests near Chernobyl. It has been established that fish in Swedish rivers are still affected at the present time, and that the meat of the reindeer in the north of Scandinavia is still radio-active.

In the same way, the first Fall of man had subsequent effects like ripples on a pond, creating sin-active fallout that continues to destroy the spiritual environment. The Fall was something like a climbing accident where the climber falls from the top of a mountain, tumbling from rock-ledge to rock-ledge and incurring one terrible injury after another until he lies helpless at the bottom. But there, at the bottom where the fallen are lying, God raises up the Cross and offers us reconciliation. From the full atonement made for us by Jesus, the path to heaven is opened and we can make our way upwards step-by-step from one level to the next, until Jesus comes.

Restoration takes place as evil grows to maturity

All things will be restored before the coming of Jesus, in accordance with a programme of action that God has revealed to his servants the prophets, a programme that will be implemented at the same time that evil is developing to its full maturity, when it will be struck down by the judgment of God's wrath.

> *'Jesus Christ ... whom heaven must receive until the times of restoration of all things, of which God has spoken by the mouth of all his holy prophets since the world began.'* (Acts 3:20–21, NKJV)

There are going to be times of renewal. Israel is going to be gathered again from the four corners of the earth and renewed spiritually. Individuals will reach maturity and become like Jesus, families and family relationships will be restored through reconciliation and churches will be restored through spiritual growth, and we shall be able to see prophetic examples of the economy of the kingdom of heaven, freed from the curse of the Fall, and examples too of the restoration of peoples and nations right in the darkest time before Jesus comes.

Broken pottery can be repaired

What God created at the beginning was the Potter's masterwork in its beauty and its design. Our sin broke up this perfect, beautiful clay vessel.

Jeremiah was the prophet who was given the clearest visions of restoration, and was one of those who prophesied about God's restoration plan: see particularly chapters 29–33. He was also the one who demonstrated

15

for us the two spiritual principles that have affected the original creation: the breaking-up of the clay vessel and then the re-assembling of the broken pieces into a restored vessel.

Jeremiah was told by the Lord to buy a clay jar from the potter and to assemble some of the elders of the people outside the city of Jerusalem in the valley of Hinnom.

> *'Then break the jar while those who go with you are watching, and say to them, "This is what the Lord Almighty says: I will smash this nation and this city just as this potter's jar is smashed and cannot be repaired."'* (Jeremiah 19:10–11)

Before Jeremiah broke the clay jar into small pieces, he rebuked the elders for the sins that had caused God's judgment to fall on Judah and Jerusalem. They had forsaken God and had burnt sacrifices to foreign gods; they had even gone so far as to offer human sacrifices to Baal, burning their own sons in the fire.

> *'But the pot he was shaping from the clay was marred in his hands; so the potter formed it into another pot, shaping it as it seemed best to him.'* (Jeremiah 18:4)

Jeremiah came to learn that God in his grace is willing to begin all over again; but he can first do it with individuals or nations that are willing to repent.

> *'If at any time I announce that a nation or kingdom is to be uprooted, torn down and destroyed, and if that nation I warned repents of its evil, then I will relent and not inflict on it the disaster I had planned.'* (Jeremiah 18:7–8)

The law of the smashing of the clay pot remains in force right up to the moment when a person turns from his evil ways; that is the moment when restoration begins.

The breaking of the clay pot was a symbolic act that showed the destruction that sin causes. The Jewish mystics see the whole story as a message in which two different laws are in force: *sheverit hakelim* means the smashing of the pot; *tikkun* means the restoring and repair of the broken pot.

The destruction of Jerusalem and the dispersion of the Jewish people are an expression of the law of the smashed pot, while the reinstatement of Israel as a nation and the regathering of the Jews from the nations are *tikkun*, the repair of the broken pot.

Paul was conscious of these two laws at work in God's creation. The law of sin and death affects everything since the Fall, but the law of the Spirit of life is in force from the moment that Jesus rose from the dead. When the law of sin and death is at work in our bodies, we work together with that law and by our thoughts and acts we cause one disaster after another. Our way of life is surrounded by destruction. Living in disobedience to God leads to constant failure, from broken marriages to ruined cities. But when the law of the Spirit of life is at work in us, there is restoring and healing of the broken vessel.

A thirty-three-year-old man lies lifeless in a tomb. His heart begins to beat again, and his eyelids, which have been lifeless, begin to flutter and open. The power that awakens a dead body is present, and the grave-clothes are thrown off from the body that is now pulsating with life and recovering all its powers.

The law of sin and death, the law that the Jews call the broken pot, was at work when Jesus' heart broke. Blood and water came out when the soldier pierced his side with a spear as he hung on the cross. At the institution of the Lord's Supper, Jesus took bread and broke it, to demonstrate what would happen to his body when he gave it up as a sacrifice for us. Jesus' body was the clay vessel broken for us. But then, the law of the Spirit took over, with the Father as the Potter repairing the smashed jar. Jesus' heart, the broken vessel, was healed and began to beat again, made whole from its wounds.

The condemning judgment is set aside through Jesus' atonement

> *'Therefore, there is now no condemnation for those who are in Christ Jesus.'*   (Romans 8:1)

Restoration cannot begin until God sets aside his condemning judgment, which he pronounced in connection with the Fall of man.

Every phase of the Fall carries with it a judgment of rejection and condemnation, which we consequently bear in our own sinful nature. It is like a computer virus, programmed to cause chaos and destruction. These lie barring the way for us when we want to come back into fellowship with God and to regain what we once enjoyed in Paradise.

God's Word tells us clearly that there is no condemnation for those who are in Christ Jesus, but many people have imagined this statement to mean that God's condemnation of us was so superficial that it was really only a feeling of being condemned. People can indeed imagine themselves to be damned, but God's condemnations are real, not imaginary; they are judgments pronounced by him over Adam and Eve, over Cain, over the generation who lived before the Flood, and the people who built the Tower of Babel.

The condemning judgments over Adam and Eve

Adam and Eve were expelled from their home in the Garden of Eden, banished by order of the Judge, and angelic guards were placed to prevent them from ever going back:

> *'So the Lord God banished him from the Garden of Eden ... After he drove the man out, he placed on the east side of the Garden of Eden cherubim and a flaming sword flashing back and forth to guard the way to the tree of life.'* (Genesis 3:23–24)

Now, when I stand at the checkpoint on the road back to the Garden, I can proclaim that there is now no condemnation for me, because I am in Christ Jesus, and therefore I have entry into fellowship with God.

As a consequence of the Fall, God pronounced condemning judgments on childbearing, the earth, farming and the working life:

> *'To the woman he said, "I will greatly increase your pains in childbearing; with pain you will give birth to children."'* (Genesis 3:16)

The images of childbirth and labour pains are used in Scripture to describe the time when evil reaches its peak, just before Jesus returns; but God's first reference to these things was in his judgment against Adam and Eve:

> *'Cursed is the ground because of you; through painful toil you will eat of it all the days of your life ... By the sweat of your brow you will eat your food.'* (Genesis 3:17, 19)

There is going to be a restoration of working life, a stream of blessing in which we shall not feel God's condemning judgments over the ground and over labour – a rest, not in the sweat of our brow. You can proclaim: there is now no condemnation over the work of my hands, over my tilling of the soil, because I am in Christ Jesus. In order that everything can be restored again, we need to be loosed from one after another of these condemning judgments which are still at work in our sinful nature and in a fallen world.

> *'For dust you are and to dust you will return.'*
>
> (Genesis 3:19)

This judgment leads to death.

Adam lost his walk with God, his fellowship with God. He lost the harvest; he was driven out of a garden full of fruit. He was excluded from the blessing of fruitfulness.

The condemning judgment over Cain

> *'Now you are under a curse and driven from the ground, which opened its mouth to receive your brother's blood from your hand. When you work the ground, it will no longer yield its crops for you. You will be a restless wanderer on the earth.'*
>
> (Genesis 4:11–12)

Cain was the first murderer, and for the rest of his life he remained under condemnation because of the bloodguilt that he bore. He could not support himself by tilling the soil, because the ground was for him under a curse; from the ground, his brother's blood cried for vengeance. The work of his hands was condemned to be unfruitful and unprofitable. His personality contained many elements: he was the restless, stressed, hunted fugitive; he could never be settled in one place; he could not maintain deep, secure relationships; and he was forever frightened that his sin might catch up with him. Cain's rejection remains over anyone who goes the way of Cain and bears hatred and bitterness towards his brother. Yet all these judgments cease to have any effect on such a person as soon as he or she turns away from his sin and receives Jesus.

Let me go back once more to that powerful statement of Paul in Romans 8:1. Therefore there is now no Cain-condemnation of restlessness, unfruitfulness, unprofitability and relationships constantly breaking, because I am in Christ Jesus. The condemning judgments remain and block the way to new levels of restoration for you, but you need to discover new dimensions of the grace that has been given to you through the atonement offered by Jesus, saving you from God's judgments of wrath.

One result of restoration is being received back into God's family.

> *'I will receive you. I will be a Father to you, and you will be my sons and daughters, says the Lord Almighty.'* (2 Corinthians 6:17–18)

To be received is the opposite of being thrown out. Israel was rejected but will be restored again.

> *'For if their rejection is the reconciliation of the world, what will their acceptance be but life from the dead?'* (Romans 11:15)

The condemning judgments over the second Fall

God's judgment over the second Fall of man, before the Flood, struck at two areas. There was a judgment over the length of man's life. Before that judgment was pronounced, mankind lived for 700 to 800 years, even up to nearly 1000 years like Methuselah. Now, the length of man's life became limited to 120 years, and at the same time the Lord withdrew his Spirit:

> *'My Spirit will not contend with man for ever, for he is mortal; his days will be a hundred and twenty years.'* (Genesis 6:3)

David prayed, *'Do not cast me from your presence or take your Holy Spirit from me'* (Psalm 51:11). Sin causes the Lord to withdraw his Spirit from man. I believe that Adam at the beginning was filled with the Spirit. It is God who gives life, spirit and everything to man. He formed Adam from the dust of the ground, and then breathed into him the breath of life, so that he became a living being. When God the Father carried out this artificial respiration on Adam, Adam indeed received air in his lungs, but he also became filled with the Holy Spirit. But the second Fall resulted in God withdrawing his Spirit, shortening the life of man and limiting man's capacities in all areas.

In theory, man can live to 120 years, but not many attain that age nowadays. It was reported [1] that on 21st February 1995, Jeanne Calment of Arles in the south of France celebrated her 120th birthday, but that was very exceptional.

Moses established that:

> *'The length of our days is seventy years – or eighty, if we have the strength; yet their span is but trouble and sorrow, for they quickly pass, and we fly away.'*
>
> (Psalm 90:10)

This length of life is not the result of any express judgment of God; it is caused by man's fear and anxiety about what the morrow will bring. Fear and stress have taken away 40 to 50 years from man's life.

Among people in Siberia who live in the area where the testing of nuclear weapons took place under the Soviet régime, the average length of life is 41 to 43 years, a figure that also applies among other groups of people exposed to poverty, hunger, undernourishment and destruction of the environment.

Owing to the devastating Aids epidemic in Africa, it is reckoned that the average length of life in Uganda by the year 2010 will be 31.5 years, in Zambia 33.4 years and in Malawi 32.7 years. [2]

In certain villages in Uganda, the average life expectancy is already down to 25 years. The middle generation dies out, leaving only the children and the old people.

We were created to live in eternity, if the Fall had not occurred. We became limited to 120 years because of our continuing sin. This judgment means that no man can any longer live to his full capacity for which God originally created him. We are only a shadow of what God intended us to be.

One of the judgments from the second Fall of man has been cancelled through the Lord sending his Holy Spirit on the day of Pentecost. He who earlier withdrew his Spirit from men made the decision, as he recognized the atoning death of Jesus, to give his Spirit once more to men.

The second judgment, affecting the length of life, has not yet been cancelled. It will continue until the time that Jesus comes and his kingdom of peace begins. I believe we have the right to pray: Lord, restore us to our full capacity; and to ask the question: Father in heaven, on what conditions will you agree to alter the decision that you made before the Flood? What is needed in order that you will reverse your judgment which reduced the length of man's life to 120 years? It is the Father who decides exactly when he will send his Son back to the earth. When the Father makes that decision, he must alter his previous decision from his judgment over the second Fall of man.

> '*I will wipe mankind, whom I have created, from the face of the earth ... I am going to put an end to all people ... I am surely going to destroy both them and the earth.*' (Genesis 6:7, 13)

With this terrible judgment, we have to read the

prophecy in 2 Peter 3:5–13 about the day of the Lord. God has promised that he will never again cut off all life by the waters of a flood; but he is going to do it by fire before the Kingdom of God comes in.

God's judgment over the third Fall of man

> '"*Come, let us go down and confuse their language so they will not understand each other.*" *So the Lord scattered them from there over all the earth, and they stopped building the city.*'
>
> (Genesis 11:7–8)

The judgment of condemnation over the third Fall has caused the multiplication of languages on the earth. As well as the many different languages, it sometimes happens that even those who speak the same language have difficulty in understanding one another. It is a consequence of the Fall that frequent misunderstandings arise in communication between people, and that people talk past one another. The Lord scattered the people of Babylon, and ever since that time large numbers of refugees have left their native lands and wandered abroad to be dispersed around the world. That is why there are so many refugees today.

The judgment over the communication between people comes to an end in Christ. We are going to see miracles in the restoration of new dimensions of communication and deep understanding between people in the kingdom of God. When the kingdom of peace comes in, refugees will no longer wander about the world, but instead:

> '*Every man will sit under his own vine and under his own fig-tree, and no-one will make them afraid.*'
>
> (Micah 4:4)

Examples of restoration: prayer for restoring colours

During the Swedish midsummer holiday period in 1985, we were holding a conference in southern Sweden on praise and artistic creativity. The Swedish people were at that time still much influenced by the protest movements of the 60s against the Vietnam war, by Mao's 'Little Red Book', and by the 'grey' rule of the Social Democrat party which had lasted for more than 40 years. Many came wearing jeans; at that time, even a university professor was quite likely to wear jeans so as to be accepted by his students. I had recently visited Vienna, and had noticed the people's clothes there, colourful and cheerful, in contrast to us Swedes, who seemed to be a grey people and to have lost our sense of colour. This applied particularly to the men, who lacked the boldness needed to wear bright coloured clothing; and the greyest of all were to be seen in the churches.

The conference concluded with prayer for the restoring of colours to our land. Some artists who were present made fourteen flags and held a flag parade, with seven of the flags painted in different strong colours, and the other seven bearing various patterns. When the flags came up to the podium, we took hold of each in turn, and showed that red had been the colour adopted by the communists, blue by the political moderates, green by the party concerned with the environment, yellow by the Tibetan Buddhists and the yoga people, and black by the punks and the Freemasons. The only colour left over for the Christians was grey.

The Lord gave instructions on what colours were to be used in the adornment of the Tabernacle in the desert. It was his desire that the place where men would come to meet their God should be beautifully rich in colours. The colours were white, dark blue, purple, scarlet and gold (Exodus 26). What a sparkling harmony of colours results from this combination! Our God, the creator, has a sense of colour, but it is the enemy who wants our lives and surroundings to be grey.

Our prayer at the conference was for the recovery and restoring of colours. Since that time, great changes have taken place in our fashions in Sweden. Grey Stockholm suburbs have been transformed and become brightly coloured. Men have become bold enough to wear colourful clothes. Ties are more garish. Colours are a part of praise. The Lord heard our prayers and gave us back our colours; it was part of our prayer for restoration.

On my travels, I have visited a number of sad grey residential areas. I saw them in East Germany before unification; more recently I have seen them in Glasgow and in Moscow. Whenever I see men in grey clothes in grey residential areas, it reminds me of how we prayed to get back our colours that had been stolen from us.

Australia – recovering a Christian festival

The following account appeared in *Prayer Track News* in September 1993. [3]

'AUSTRALIANS MOBILIZED FOR PUBLIC PRAYER: A spiritual phenomenon called the "Aussie Awakening" began at the dedication of the new Parliament House in Canberra, Australia, in 1988 ... 50,000 from all denominations flooded into Canberra to physically surround the new Parliament House for the largest prayer meeting the nation had ever seen. This began what Christian leaders see as a "Christian people-power movement". It is an informal network of believers who have discovered a unity in the Spirit, a God-given love for their country, and the power of prayer.

'RECLAIMING EASTER: A powerful initiative was then begun, called "Reclaiming Easter". The idea is for Christians all over the nation [Australia] to take to the streets in praise marches and prayer rallies on Easter Sunday, the traditional day for Christian festivals. What has happened?

'In 1990, 18,000 gathered to march in Sydney, plus 6 smaller places.

'In 1991, 60,000 participated in 31 cities.

'In 1992, 150,000 reclaimed Easter in 105 locations.

'In 1993, 250,000 celebrated publicly in population centers throughout the nation, including 90,000 unchurched people.

'Furthermore, in 1993, 10,000 participated in an all-night prayer meeting on Good Friday night.'

Notes

1. *The Times*, 22 February 1995.
2. *Newsweek* magazine, 9 May 1994.
3. *Prayer Track News*, a news-letter published by Global Harvest Ministries, Pasadena, California, Vol. 2, No. 3, September 1993, p. 2.

Chapter 2

Prayer for Restoration

When God's time comes for restoration, the Lord will want to co-operate with the intercessors. Prayers are of various kinds, but I believe there is a particular kind that is a restoration prayer. David, Nehemiah and Daniel are examples of those who prayed for the restoration of their people.

The prayer in Psalm 126:4, *'Restore our fortunes, O Lord,'* is rendered in the Swedish Bible simply as *'Lord, restore us again.'* That prayer has so moved me that I have chosen to approach this subject from an intercessor's point of view, and it is to intercessors that I am writing. We have held intercessors' conferences in recent years with restoration as the theme. We see families breaking up, and we pray for healing of family relationships. We see the Lord's servants weary and giving up, and we pray, 'Lord, raise up the fallen heroes.' We pray for churches that have had a history of awakening. When we pray for awakening, that is a restoration prayer; but restoration also includes reaching out further than we have reached before. We pray for restoration to God's highest purposes and intentions for us and for his Church, far beyond anything that happened in the time of the first Christians.

Prayers, songs and proclamations of restoration

There are several visions, prayers, songs and proclamations of restoration in the Bible. Psalm 126 is one example of how a people prayed to be brought out of captivity.

In order to be able to recognize these prayers, we need to learn the language of restoration. Those who pray for restoration use expressions such as these: Lord, return to us now. Release us from captivity. Lord, gather us together again. *'For your sake, O Lord, look with favour on your desolate sanctuary'* (Daniel 9:17).

Psalm 80 is a cry for help from Asaph. He was remembering how the Lord had brought Israel out of Egypt, like a vine that had been planted and had taken root and filled the land. But now, he said, the vineyard lies unprotected, because its walls have been broken down. Wild boars from the forest and the creatures of the field are ravaging what the Lord has planted. Asaph is aware that the Lord's anger has been kindled against his people, and asks, *'O Lord God Almighty, how long will your anger smoulder against the prayers of your people?'* (Psalm 80:4). The prayer of restoration is born when things have reached the bottom, when everything is going badly for God's people. Four times the prayer for restoration is repeated in this psalm: *'Return to us, O God Almighty!'* (verse 14); *'Restore us, O God; make your face shine upon us, that we may be saved'* (verses 4, 7, 19).

Psalm 85 is another restoration prayer:

> *'You showed favour to your land, O Lord; you restored the fortunes of Jacob. You forgave the iniquity of your people and covered all their sins. You set aside all your wrath and turned from your fierce anger. Restore us again, O God our Saviour, and put away your displeasure towards us. Will you be angry with us for ever? Will you prolong your anger through all generations? Will you not revive us again, that your people may rejoice in you?'* (Psalm 85:1–6)

Restoration in a song of praise

'Who is like the Lord our God, the One who sits enthroned on high, who stoops down to look on the heavens and the earth? He raises the poor from the dust and lifts the needy from the ash heap; he seats them with princes, with the princes of their people. He settles the barren woman in her home as a happy mother of children. Praise the Lord.' (Psalm 113:5–9)

Proclaiming restoration

'The Lord upholds all those who fall and lifts up all who are bowed down.' (Psalm 145:14)

Job was restored when he prayed for his friends

The accuser had demanded to be allowed to test Job, who was now at the end of his time of testing. His friends had not spoken rightly of him, nor of the Lord.

'And the Lord turned the captivity of Job, when he prayed for his friends: also the Lord gave Job twice as much as he had before.' (Job 42:10, KJV)

Job's restoration implied that he was cleared of all the unjustified accusations that had been made against his godly conduct. He was restored to health and wealth (twice as much as before) and was given a new family. Restoration comes in accordance with God's grace and generosity, and he gives double recompense, even when we ourselves have become indebted and ended up in trouble. When the Lord restores Israel, he says:

'Instead of their shame, my people will receive a double portion, and instead of disgrace they will rejoice in their inheritance; and so they will inherit a double portion in their land, and everlasting joy will be theirs.'

(Isaiah 61:7)

New Testament prayers for restoration

Paul's prayer for the church in Ephesus was:

> *'I keep asking that the God of our Lord Jesus Christ,*
> *the glorious Father, may give you the Spirit of wisdom*
> *and revelation, so that you may know him better.'*
>
> (Ephesians 1:17)

And when he prayed for the church in Philippi, he thanked God for them and prayed in the confidence:

> *'That he who began a good work in you will carry it on*
> *to completion until the day of Christ Jesus.'*
>
> (Philippians 1:6)

Restoration ministry

When I was a young preacher, I knew very little about the way that people in our own day can be freed from evil spirits. It was Derek Prince who came to Sweden and taught us about these things. Today there are people with a ministry of deliverance. The fruit of their confident prayer ministry is that prisoners are set free from the influence of evil spirits.

The restoration ministry is a distinctive ministry like the ministry of deliverance. It is a form of prophetic prayer ministry.

Prophetic prayer ministry

As we study how God puts his plans into action to restore his people, we see that it is done through cooperation between prophets and intercessors.

It was the prophets who carried the visions of hope for restoration. Each prophet, however hopeless the situation in which he found himself, as he brought the Lord's message even though there was no one listening to it, nevertheless had a message of good news, of how the Lord would bring restoration. Even the prophets whose message was concerned with the destruction of Israel and her dispersion into captivity had a vision of the Lord rebuilding the ruined cities and gathering his people together again. They grasped God's programme of action for restoration and it became their message of good news.

> *'But in the days when the seventh angel is about to sound his trumpet, the mystery of God will be accomplished, just as he announced to his servants the prophets.'*   (Revelation 10:7)

John uses the Greek verb *euaggelizo*, here translated 'announce', a word that is usually associated with the Gospel – bringing the good news. The good news was proclaimed to his servants the prophets.

When the time came for God's plans for restoration to be put into action, it was the turn of the intercessors to come on the scene. This co-operation between prophets and intercessors is what I call prophetic prayer ministry.

The prophet comes to know God's plans for restoration

Jeremiah learned by revelation that the Lord had plans for peace for his people, and would therefore restore them after seventy years of captivity. The Lord announced through him:

> *'I will ... bring you back to this place ... Then you will call upon me and come and pray to me, and I will listen to you ... I will be found by you, declares the Lord, and will bring you back from captivity [I will restore your fortunes]. I will gather you from all the nations and places where I have banished you, declares the Lord,*

> *and will bring you back to the place from which I carried you into exile.'* (Jeremiah 29:10–14)

When the seventy years had passed, the time came for praying for restoration. Daniel and his praying friends took hold of Jeremiah's prophecy about the appointed time for restoration. Daniel is an example of one who exercises prophetic prayer ministry leading to restoration. He prayed for fulfilment of the prophecy when the time came for the people to be freed from captivity. This is the way that we shall pray before the coming of Jesus, when everything will be restored in accordance with the prophetic word. Daniel discovered the prophetic word that would be fulfilled in his time, and it was this discovery that provoked him to prayer. We for our part need to discover what the prophets have said about restoration in our own time, and that discovery will initiate our prayer.

Praying for fulfilment of the prophetic message

Prophetic intercession is praying for the fulfilment of prophecy. The prophetic word of the elders had been spoken over Timothy when he was separated for his ministry, and Paul encouraged Timothy to use these prophetic words as a weapon in fighting the good fight (1 Timothy 1:18). On the night that I came into faith in Jesus, prophetic words were uttered over me: 'Within fourteen days you will be filled with the Holy Spirit.' Fourteen days later, I lay and waited. I had put my light out. If the prophet were a true one, then his word would be fulfilled. At a quarter to midnight, my passive waiting attitude changed to an active faith for the fulfilment. I woke my brothers and sisters and asked them to help me in prayer. 'I have had a prophetic word spoken over me. Before midnight, I am to be filled with the Holy Spirit. Lay hands on me and pray.' Before midnight I was filled with the Spirit and received a prayer language. I learned that nothing happens through passive waiting for the fulfilment of the prophetic word. The prophet is the intermediary in God's programme of action, to let us know how we should be praying.

The prophetic word is not given to us so that we can speculate about it and discuss it and draw up timetables for the end time. David *'served God's purpose in his own generation'* (Acts 13:36). He worked together with the Lord in the prophetic plan that applied in his time. I put the question: What prophetic words is the Lord planning to fulfil during my time on earth? There are particular words that are important for me, that I need to know so that I can pray for their fulfilment. The promises that the Jews will return from the land of the north: these I have been praying about since 1983. For Egypt too, I am praying because there is a programme of restoration for her in Isaiah 19.

Prayer for restoration is marked by breaking and repentance

Praying for restoration is to confront the consequences of the Fall of man. It is always sin that causes us to live below the standard that God has planned for us in his creation, and therefore, we must pray for forgiveness and grace before restoration can take place.

For someone who has fallen into sin and a broken marriage, there is always a way back to God. The condition is honesty in confessing the sin that caused the fall.

When Peter preached about the times of restoration and refreshing, he challenged his listeners:

> *'Repent, then, and turn to God, so that your sins may be wiped out.'* (Acts 3:19)

Since this is the way to restoration, so it must characterize our prayers: Psalm 51 shows us how David repented of his sin.

The prayer of identification

Prayer for restoration is a deep prophetic identification with those who have fallen, who are down in the mud at the bottom.

God sometimes creates circumstances in which the prophet, in his own life and on a small scale, experiences what the people are going through on a much wider scale. The officials of king Zedekiah accused Jeremiah of discouraging the people and of seeking their ruin instead of their welfare, and he was thrown into a cistern in the courtyard of the guard. There was no water in the cistern, but only mud, and Jeremiah sank down into the mud (Jeremiah 38:1–6). This experience of being thrown into an empty cistern by his own people helped Jeremiah to identify himself with his nation when it was at its lowest point. In his book Lamentations, he converses with God and remembers the cistern, praying:

> *They tried to end my life in a pit and threw stones at me; the waters closed over my head, and I thought I was about to be cut off. I called on your name, O Lord, from the depths of the pit. You heard my plea: "Do not close your ears to my cry for relief." You came near when I called you, and you said, "Do not fear."'*
>
> (Lamentations 3:53–57)

Jeremiah was rescued from the cistern by a Cushite, a man from Africa, who with the king's permission took thirty men and lifted Jeremiah out of the pit. Then the king sent for Jeremiah and secretly swore to spare his life in return for giving the king advice (Jeremiah 38:7–16).

This identifying of himself with the people affected Jeremiah deeply in his spirit, as he could see sin increasing and judgment coming nearer:

> *'Oh, my anguish, my anguish! I writhe in pain. Oh, the agony of my heart! My heart pounds within me, I*

cannot keep silent. For I have heard the sound of the trumpet; I have heard the battle cry.' (Jeremiah 4:19)

'Oh, that my head were a spring of water and my eyes a fountain of tears! I would weep day and night for the slain of my people ... for they are all adulterers, a crowd of unfaithful people.' (Jeremiah 9:1–2)

Nehemiah received a report from Jerusalem about the distressing state of affairs in Jerusalem. The Jewish survivors there were in great trouble and disgrace, the city walls were broken down and the gates burned with fire (Nehemiah 1:1–3). This report became for Nehemiah his call to a ministry of restoration. He became the one who built up the broken-down walls. The immediate effect on him of the message of distress was a deep emotional identification which gave birth to a prayer for restoration:

'When I heard these things, I sat down and wept, For some days I mourned and fasted and prayed before the God of heaven.' (Nehemiah 1:4)

Nehemiah's prayer was first and foremost a confession of sin on behalf of himself and his people:

'I confess the sins we Israelites, including myself and my father's house, have committed against you. We have acted very wickedly towards you.'
(Nehemiah 1:6–7)

In the latter part of his prayer, Nehemiah reminds God of his promise of restoration:

'Remember the instruction you gave your servant Moses, saying, "If you are unfaithful, I will scatter you among the nations, but if you return to me and obey my commands, then even if your exiled people are at the farthest horizon, I will gather them from there and

*bring them to the place I have chosen as a dwelling for
my Name.'''*   (Nehemiah 1:8–9)

We live in a place of tension. We see people rebelling
against God and going still deeper into sin, and at the
same time we know that God's judgment over sinners is
coming ever nearer. There are not enough words to
express how this tension makes us feel. We need a much
stronger language in order to identify ourselves with
sinners who are moving ever further away from God. In
the End Time we shall need the Bible's way of expressing
sorrow, repentance and conversion. There we can read
how people tore their garments, strewed ashes on their
heads and went about mourning in sackcloth. Ezekiel
came to the exiles in Babylon and sat there among them,
quite silent and overwhelmed with deep sorrow, for seven
days (Ezekiel 3:14–15). Daniel made himself ready to pray
for forgiveness for Israel's sin by fasting in sackcloth and
ashes (Daniel 9:3).

When Ezra heard of the sin and disobedience of the
people of Israel against God's Word, he tore his tunic and
cloak, pulled hair from his head and beard, and sat down
appalled until the time of the evening sacrifice, when he
began to pray for forgiveness for the sin of the people
(Ezra 9:3–4).

When Moses saw the people dancing around the golden
calf, he was moved so deeply that he threw down the two
stone tablets of the Testimony, breaking them to pieces
(Exodus 32:19).

*'Then once again I fell prostrate before the Lord for
forty days and forty nights; I ate no bread and drank
no water, because of all the sin you had committed,
doing what was evil in the Lord's sight and so provok-
ing him to anger. I feared the anger and wrath of the
Lord, for he was angry enough with you to destroy you.
But again the Lord listened to me.'*

(Deuteronomy 9:18–19)

In my distress I tore my own garments

When the news came that Sweden, the third country in the world to do so, had passed a law legalizing homosexual marriages, I was standing in the pulpit in the City Church, a large Pentecostal meeting-place in Stockholm. About 150 intercessors were assembled in the church's 'Mahogany Hall'; we had all gathered there for a day of prayer from nine in the morning until four in the afternoon, while the debate was proceeding in the Riksdag, the Swedish parliament. I stayed there in the pulpit for many hours, and meanwhile, through the wife of a member of the Riksdag, we had telephone contact with her husband who was present in the debate. She reported to us what was going on during the debate, and we prayed all day. She informed me about the decision as I stood in the pulpit.

My usual way of expressing grief and anger was insufficient. I was compelled to make use of the Bible's strongest expression of anguish. Standing there in the pulpit, I tore the clothes I was wearing. I tore the jacket in two from the bottom up to the collar, and I slit open the trouser-legs from the bottoms up to the knees. By passing this law, Sweden crossed a spiritual frontier. We went over into the community of Antichrist by making this outright breach of God's word.

God's Spirit is grieved for Sweden. Ezekiel was able to identify himself with the anguish in God's heart:

> *'The Spirit then lifted me up and took me away, and I went in bitterness and in the anger of my spirit, with the strong hand of the Lord upon me.'*   (Ezekiel 3:14)

Ezekiel sat there among the exiles for seven days in deep grief. As for myself, I went about in mourning for seven days, wearing black clothes; and when the days of mourning were over, I started a long period of fasting.

Tearing our clothes can be an act of faith, that is, a

statement distancing ourselves from unbelief and denial. Joshua and Caleb tore their garments as a mark of the distance separating them from the unbelief of the people who were saying, *'We should choose a leader and go back to Egypt'* (Numbers 14:4–6). Joshua and Caleb received a renewed promise that they would enter into the Promised Land, but none of those who tempted God by their unbelief would be allowed to enter the Land.

Ezra tore his garments in sorrow over his people's unbelief, but it was the beginning of a reformation, as we read in Ezra 9 and 10.

King Josiah heard God's word read to him, and tore his robes because he understood that:

> *'Great is the Lord's anger that burns against us because our fathers have not obeyed the words of this book; they have not acted in accordance with all that is written there concerning us.'* (2 Kings 22:13)

Interceding with God on behalf of the people

The foundation of prayer for restoration, is knowledge of the sin that has caused us to fall. If an individual has committed a sin, it is up to him to confess his sin; but if a sin has been committed by a church, a city, or a nation, then an intercessor can come before God as the representative of the people and confess the collective sin.

We are a kingdom of priests. The Old Testament priest represented the people, when he presented sacrifices for sin and exercised a ministry of reconciliation on their behalf. The high priest bore a breastpiece on which the names of the twelve tribes of Israel were written:

> *'Whenever Aaron enters the Holy Place, he will bear the names of the sons of Israel over his heart on the breastpiece of decision as a continuing memorial before the Lord.'* (Exodus 28:29)

My own life has a frame of reference which enables me to represent certain groups in a natural way when I come before God in prayer ministry. I can represent my nation, the place where I live, my church, the Nordic Vikings, married men, fathers, the older generation, pastors and intercessors.

When the Holy Spirit enables me to identify myself with the sin of my country, then I have no need to hesitate in believing that God has chosen me to come before God on behalf of the people and to pray for forgiveness as Daniel did; but I need to seek the Lord in order to know exactly how we should go about it. There are occasions when I feel God instructing me that I need to have leaders from all the churches in the city so that the confession can be properly made. Sometimes we feel the call for a national day of prayer so that Christians from all over the nation can confess the nation's sin and pray for restoration. Nehemiah prayed for forgiveness for his nation's sin, but as a next step he led the whole nation in doing the same:

> *'The Israelites gathered together, fasting and wearing sackcloth and having dust on their heads ... They stood in their places and confessed their sins and the wickedness of their fathers.'* (Nehemiah 9:1–2)

There are times when we feel it right to encourage the mayor of the city, the president of the country, or a member of the royal family, to confess the sin of the people. My friend Gunnar Olsson went to the King of Tonga with a prayer of confession that he had received from the Lord. He asked the King if he was willing to step down from his throne, bow his knees and confess the sin of the nation's leaders, and the King of one of the world's smallest nations bowed his knees and prayed a prayer of confession, which I know bore fruit.

The President leads a confession of sin in a TV talk to the nation

Immediately after President Frederick Chiluba of Zambia took office, he led the people in a prayer of confession in a TV speech to his nation. On 29th December 1991, the President declared Zambia to be a Christian nation. He shouted, as the people cheered triumphantly, 'Jesus is the Lord of my life, Jesus is Lord in the government, Jesus is Lord over Zambia.' President Chiluba had studied in God's Word how King Josiah gave himself to leading a radical cleansing of his nation from worship of false gods, witchcraft and every other occult practice. In 2 Kings 23:3 it is described how Josiah *stood by the pillar and renewed the covenant in the presence of the Lord'* on behalf of the people. On the night before President Chiluba spoke to the nation, there was a night of prayer in the Presidential palace, from seven o'clock in the evening until five in the morning, when a hundred or so Christian leaders from various churches gathered to pray.

This is what the President said in his TV speech:

'As you might remember, my first function after I was sworn in as the President of Zambia was to pray to my heavenly Father. That was not just a part of the ceremony, but it was a prayer of thankfulness born out of my personal convictions that the change we have witnessed in Zambia in 1991 has only been possible because of grace of God. It is therefore only natural that we have this solemn occasion here today, whereby I – on behalf of the Zambian nation – enter into a covenant with the one true God, whose love and saving grace is revealed in God the Son, Jesus Christ.

'I personally testify to the mighty saving power of Jesus Christ, who said in John 14:6, *"I am the way, the truth and the life. No one comes to the Father except through me."*

'When we talk about entering into a covenant with God as a nation then, it is only possible because God took the first initiative by sending Jesus to die for the sins of the world. Jesus established a new covenant through the shedding of his blood. Jesus says in Luke 22:20, *"This cup is the new covenant in my blood, which is poured out for you."* It is only on the basis of the blood of Jesus atoning for our sins that we can approach God today.

'The Bible, which is the Word of God, abounds with proof that a nation is blessed, whenever it makes a covenant with God and obeys the Word of God. The opposite is also true. Any nation that turns its back on God and turns to idolatry and wickedness will come under the judgment of God and suffer. God says in Jeremiah 7:23, *"I gave Israel this command: Obey me, and I will be your God, and you will be my people. Walk in all the ways I command you, that it may go well with you."*

'In a covenant there are certain things we have to do, and there are other things that God promises to do. We have to humble ourselves and repent from our wicked ways. Then God promises to forgive and heal the land. God told King Solomon in 2 Chronicles 7:14: *"If my people, who are called by my name, will humble themselves and pray and seek my face and turn from their wicked ways, then I will hear from heaven and will forgive their sin and will heal their land."*

'...You have heard me before compare the nation with a sick person. I have said, "We are sick and weak, but we are still alive, and we are determined to get well again." Today I want to say to all of you: We need God to heal our land!

'I will therefore now do my part of the covenant, as I will identify myself with the Zambian nation in the following prayer:

"Dear God, as a nation we now come to your throne of grace, and we humble ourselves and admit our guilt. We repent from all our wicked ways of idolatry, witchcraft, the occult, immorality, injustice and corruption and all other sins that have violated your righteous laws. We turn away from all this and renounce it all in Jesus' name. We ask for your forgiveness, dear Father, and cleansing through the blood of Jesus. Therefore we thank you that you will heal our land. We pray that you will send healing, restoration, revival, blessing, and prosperity to Zambia. In the name of Jesus, Amen."

'On behalf of the nation, I have now entered into a covenant with the living God, and therefore I want to make the following declaration:

"I declare today that I submit myself as President to the lordship of Jesus Christ. I likewise submit the Government and the entire nation of Zambia to the lordship of Jesus Christ. I further declare that Zambia is a Christian nation, that will seek to be governed by the righteous principles of the Word of God. Righteousness and justice must prevail in all levels of authority, and then we shall see the righteousness of God exalting Zambia."

'My fellow Zambians, let this message reach all civil servants in all Government departments. The time of corruption and bribery is over. For too long these wicked practices have been destroying and tearing down the nation. Now the hour has come for building up. The hour has come for stability. For Proverbs 29:4 declares that one who is greedy for bribes tears down a nation, but by justice a king – or a president – gives the country stability.

'The book of Romans chapter 13 verse 11 urges us to understand the present time, as the hour has come for us to wake up from our slumber, because our salvation is near. The night is nearly over and the day is almost here. So let us put aside the deeds of darkness and put on the armour of light.

'My fellow Zambians, a new dawn has come to Zambia. May God bless and help us all to live according to his righteous laws.'[1]

Reformation begins by raising up the broken-down altar

The Garden of Eden was the first meeting-place between God and man, but through the Fall, this meeting-place was lost, and Adam and Eve were driven out of the Garden. God has since come with fresh invitations to meeting-places. The altar where the atoning sacrifice was given for sins became the new meeting-place where a holy God could meet sinners, and then the Cross of Jesus became, and is still for us, the meeting-place where God and man can meet in peace. Now we do not need to repeat the sacrifice on the altar day after day; we can come boldly to the throne of grace and relate to God in prayer. The prayer altar is an expression of the restored meeting-place between God and man.

The first stage in reformation is the building-up of the altar. When the first group of exiles returned from the Babylonian captivity, the rebuilding of Jerusalem was begun by building the altar on the same spot where it had been before:

> '*Then Jeshua ... and his fellow priests and Zerubbabel ... and his associates began to build the altar of the God of Israel to sacrifice burnt offerings on it, in accordance with what is written in the Law of Moses the man of God ... they built the altar on its foundation.*'
>
> (Ezra 3:2–3)

The altar was rebuilt before the foundation was laid for the new temple. At a later stage, Nehemiah built up the walls around the city.

Whenever there were times of decline in Israel, and the Lord raised up a king or a prophet or a spiritual leader to call the people back to God, reformation always began with the rebuilding of the altar.

King Hezekiah gave a command that the Levites should clean up and purify the Temple.

> *'Then they went in to King Hezekiah and reported: "We have purified the entire temple of the Lord, the altar of burnt offering ... We have prepared and consecrated all the articles that King Ahaz removed in his unfaithfulness while he was king. They are now in front of the Lord's altar."'* (2 Chronicles 29:18–19)

On the day that the Lord restores Egypt, there will be a sign:

> *'In that day there will be an altar to the Lord in the heart of Egypt ... It will be a sign and witness to the Lord Almighty in the land of Egypt. When they cry out to the Lord because of their oppressors, he will send them a saviour and defender, and he will rescue them.'* (Isaiah 19:19–20)

And when Elijah came to Mount Carmel:

> *'He repaired the altar of the Lord, which was in ruins. Elijah took twelve stones, one for each of the tribes descended from Jacob ... With the stones he built an altar in the name of the Lord.'* (1 Kings 18:30–32)

When I came to faith in the Lord as an eighteen-year-old in Stockholm, there were one or two churches in the city that used to open their buildings for prayer at midday. I was working in an office in the city centre, and I used to eat my lunch quickly so that I could spend half an hour in prayer with about 150 others who gathered there. There are churches in Stockholm that formerly had their buildings so full when they held evangelistic campaigns that people had to stand in a queue for an hour before the meeting to be sure of getting a seat. In the summer, a tent was put up holding 5,000 people, and that was filled. One church was well known for its summer outreach 'Juliaden' during the month of July, when hundreds of young people were out on the streets and squares of the city, evangelizing. Three years ago, the Lord called me to raise up a prayer altar in my home city of Stockholm. The vision was to restore the prayer-place of my youth. The City Church welcomed this initiative, and every Tuesday midday about 150 intercessors, from about twenty different churches in Stockholm, meet for two hours. By means of this rebuilt prayer altar we have recaptured lost ground and regained the initiative.

Intercessors confess their own and the people's sins

Whenever I lead prayer meetings around the world, I invariably lead to the Cross, in repentance and confession of sin, all those who are praying. I count the intercessors as my best friends and as the best members in the churches. Yet confession of sin and prayer for cleansing are always necessary. There is no short-cut to avoid this preparation. In our own lives we can find a sample selection of the sins prevailing in the community, and as we humble ourselves and turn away from our evil ways, so the Lord can come in with his healing and restoration. It is equally dramatic every time the Lord puts our lives under his searchlight. In my experience, when there has been an honest dealing with sin, that is when we have had the strongest and most lasting answers to prayer, leading to spiritual breakthrough.

Vitoria – a town full of scrawling and graffiti

The first thing you notice when you come into the town of Vitoria, in northern Spain, is all the scribbling on the walls. I have never seen a town with so much graffiti. On one wall we saw INTIFADA written in large letters. We realized that we were in the chief town of the Basque people, and Basque terrorists are struggling to obtain independence from Spain. Behind all the scribblings, we were able to discern three driving powers: rebellion, rejection and pride.

We went to speak at a young people's centre where several hundred Christian young people were assembled, and saw that the wall at the back of the platform was painted to look like a brick wall covered with graffiti. We have often found that the problems existing in a town have infiltrated into the church. Here it was obviously so, as we could see in this young people's centre, where the young people had written their names on the brick wall behind the platform.

I challenged them to repent of scribbling on walls. About twenty young folk came forward, in tears, and confessed that they had written graffiti on the city walls and walls of houses. The man who had painted the wall at the front of the hall confessed that when he was nine years old he had drawn a pagan nude picture of Jesus. Ever since that time he had been tempted to draw pornographic pictures. Now he was an artist and an illustrator for a Christian periodical. He shook with sobbing as he came forward in front of all the young people and confessed this.

Among the abandoned street children of São Paulo

São Paulo is an enormous city of 17 million inhabitants. Every great city has a personality of its own, and God's Spirit can give us a picture of that personality. A leader of

Youth with a Mission said that the heart of São Paulo is like an unwanted, abandoned child's. The pain has brought a hardness. The child trusts no one and shares his secrets with no one.

Is there any description of such a city in the Bible? Yes, Jerusalem is described in this way by the prophet Ezekiel, who in chapter 16 of his book shows us the Lord addressing the city as an unwanted child of mixed parentage, the father an Amorite and the mother a Hittite:

> 'On the day you were born your cord was not cut, nor were you washed with water to make you clean, nor were you rubbed with salt or wrapped in cloths ... Then I passed by and saw you kicking about in your blood, and as you lay there in your blood I said to you, "Live!"' (Ezekiel 16:4–6)

At one meeting, I asked how many of those present had grown up on the street as abandoned children. About fifteen came forward. Some of them had been homosexuals and prostitutes, but salvation had transformed them. Others were still marked as the result of their abandonment. Then I asked whether there were those in the conference who had abandoned a child: men who had fathered children outside marriage and had never been concerned with them since, or mothers who had abandoned their children. A second large group of people came forward on the other side; among the others there was a woman who was full of bitterness against preachers. I had been compelled to challenge her seriously about her hard attitude, by saying to her: 'I do not want you to come with us to the night of prayer in the city centre.' Now I understood the reason. The hardness that had come in when she abandoned her child was now directed against pastors. She was transformed and filled with love. After we had prayed for each of those who had come forward, the two groups joined together in reconciliation: members of families who had abandoned children were united with those who had been abandoned.

Later we held a night of prayer, with 150 taking part, on the streets of São Paulo, lasting until 5 am. We began on the Plaza de Sue, the true heart-centre of the city. Abandoned children were lying there, sleeping on the square or in the park. In the previous year, 86 children had been killed on this square. Businessmen find the children a nuisance because they steal in order to survive, so they pay retired policemen to kill them. One man who worked among the street children told me how one day he was able to win a child's trust, but the next day he attended the child's funeral.

A group of boys were gathered on the steps of the Catholic cathedral. A little way away from them lay a lonely little lad, about seven years old, like my own grandson Simon – no pillow, no covering, wearing tattered clothes. He was sleeping on a grating where warm air was blowing out from the underground railway. Seeing this boy touched me deeply, and I still think of him and the city of São Paulo. There are 8 million street children in Brazil.

Tamils and Sinhalese reconciled

In Sri Lanka, a civil war has been going on for many years between the two principal groups of people: the Sinhalese, who are Buddhists, and the Tamils, of whom the majority are Hindus. In the churches there are often both Tamils and Sinhalese, so that a visiting speaker has to be interpreted into two languages. During our prayer conference there in 1994, we were directed to seek the help of the Holy Spirit in bringing about a deep process of reconciliation between Sinhalese and Tamils. I suggested to them that there were seven areas where they should examine themselves, and in each of the areas that I named, confessions followed.

1. Pride in one's own group heritage.

2.   Racism and discrimination in the church between Tamils and Sinhalese.

3.   Racism and discrimination in language against the other group. Deep-seated conflicts set their marks on the language and one's manner of speaking of the other group. There are humiliating words and phrases of abuse, proverbs and jokes that discriminate against the other group. People came forward and described examples of racism in language, and confessed that they had recently used such prejudiced words.

4.   Economic discrimination. Pastors confessed that when they received donations of money from abroad for aid to refugees, they had not divided it fairly between Tamil and Sinhalese sufferers, but had unduly favoured their own group. When shopping, they went mostly to shops run by members of their own race. Employees too were likely to be members of their own people.

5.   Murder, blood-guilt, massacres and destruction of the other group's houses and property. In the morning when I was preparing for the conference, the Spirit of the Lord said, 'Today there are going to be people present in the meetings who have blood on their hands, people who have murdered others with their own hands.' I challenged those who had confessed to the Lord, but had never confessed openly before the church, to come forward publicly and confess their participation in Sri Lanka's civil war. Three men, two Tamils and one Sinhalese, came forward to the microphone and confessed that they had murdered people with their own hands. All three of them were taking a great risk. The 'Tamil Tigers' avenge themselves on their own people who tell them that they have taken part in killings, and the Sinhalese police torture those whom they suspect to have taken part in massacres, to get them to divulge further information. One of the men confessed that

he had been a guerrilla leader of the Tamil Tigers in a district, and that he had both given orders for killing, and killed personally. The Sinhalese man had taken part in killing Tamils, plundering their houses before burning them to the ground. 'I plundered their jewellery for hundreds of thousands of rupees.' These confessions were made in deep remorse; there was sobbing and weeping all over the hall. Pastors who were present said that on earlier occasions there had been people asking one another for forgiveness, but they had been touched only on the religious level and had used pious words wrapped up in religious packaging. This time, however, the confessions brought us right into reality and into concrete situations.

6. Broken peace agreements and political agreements. One pastor confessed that before he became a Christian he had been a very militant Buddhist; he had written newspaper articles and had opposed peace agreements with the Tamils, doing what he could to ensure such agreements were broken.

7. Confession of inability to rely on the other group. Long-drawn-out ethnic conflicts make people feel they no longer dare to trust the other group. God's generous love can never live together with suspicion and breaches of confidence. God's church is to be the bearer of hope for the future in our land.

In every area that I named, I received a response, and people confessed before the Lord and before the other group. Hatred and unforgiveness between groups of people grieve the Holy Spirit. When people have wept out loud over their hardness and have been cleansed by the blood of Jesus, the presence of the Holy Spirit always comes over God's people, and the result is a new openness for evangelization and church growth.

Bauro, Brazil

Bauro is a town of about 250,000 inhabitants, four hours'

drive from São Paulo. I was invited to a church with about 1,200 members.

The town was founded when the railway was built about 100 years ago. An Indian tribe opposed the building of the railway in their area, but the manager of the railway gave the order to shoot and murder the most militant of the Indians and the rest were driven away. I was told that because of this there remained a curse over the town. I asked if there were any Indians in the church, but there were none. When I came into the pedestrian street in the town's shopping centre, I saw an Indian selling natural medicines. I asked him to explain what his natural products were good for, and he demonstrated them and pointed to roots and various other natural products. When he had finished, I asked his forgiveness on behalf of the white race for the way that we had driven his people away from Bauro and for the murder and bloodshed they had been exposed to. 'No-one has ever spoken to me in that way before,' he said, deeply moved. He gave me some gifts of Indian handcraft. I invited him to our evening meeting, and said I would continue to encourage the people of the town to settle their blood-debt to the Indians. He brought a group of Indians to the meeting with him, and we gave them the place of honour on the front bench and invited them up on the platform. The whole meeting was affected; many people asked the Indians for forgiveness. They granted forgiveness and blessed the town. A man came into the meeting and spoke, saying that his great-grandfather had been the railway manager who had given the order to shoot and kill the Indians. 'There has been a curse on my family since that time.' In the name of Jesus we broke the curse. The Indians agreed among themselves that they, together with a delegation from the church, would travel to an Indian village and tell the people there of the reconciliation that had taken place. They would also report about it in a newspaper that looked after the interests of the Indians. After the reconciliation had taken place, the power of

God was poured out on the church, and we prayed until midnight.

'Operation Swift Cloud'

We called our action in Egypt 'Operation Swift Cloud' from Isaiah:

> *'See, the Lord rides on a swift cloud and is coming to Egypt. The idols of Egypt tremble before him.'*
>
> (Isaiah 19:1)

In the Egyptian temples, a varying trio of gods are worshipped: a father-god, Osiris; a mother-god, Isis, and a son of the gods, Horus. Before the Lord restores Egypt he will judge their gods. The gods of Egypt have had a great influence on all the secret orders, and can be found also in the occult outpourings of the New Age movement. In the houses of the Egyptian gods which are today the most important tourist attractions, there were New Age inspired *son et lumière* productions, held in the evenings, encouraging the tourists to open themselves up to the gods who live in these places. Our team consisted of 25 men from 11 different nations, aged from 25 to 83 years. Four of them were Messianic Jews from Israel.

'Blessed be Egypt my people'

We began with the assumption that Egypt is a land that belongs to the Lord; it has been stolen by the Egyptian gods and by Islam, but it will revert to God's ownership. We waged the spiritual battle for the freeing of Egypt particularly through the Pyramids, which the New Age movement look on as one of their most powerful strong-points, together with the three ancient priest-cities of Memphis, Thebes (Luxor or Noph), and Heliopolis (On).

In several of these places we were conscious of the spiritual battle and of confrontation with the power of death.

Just before we were about to pray at the Pyramids, one of the team nearly died. We found him bloody and unconscious, and had to take him to the hospital. We had a doctor with us in the team, and also a most energetic Israeli, who had taken part in the capture of the Golan Heights as a paratrooper. He was accustomed to treating the wounded on the battlefield, and he put his experience to good use in treating the wounded member of our team. I had warned the team not to accept any occult souvenirs when we visited the Egyptian temple sites. This particular team member had accepted a green good-luck stone, smeared with oil, from a souvenir-seller. Just after that, the incident occurred which could have cost him his life.

Alexandria

Praying for restoration is important in application to all the principal mission centres of the early Christian era, such as Antioch, Ephesus, Thessalonica, Alexandria and Carthage. We believe that these will one day again become mission centres, when the last harvest is brought in.

We took the desert road from Cairo to Alexandria. On that day, our prayer was directed towards the Body of Christ in Egypt. An Egyptian doctor in our team gave us information about what God is doing in Egypt. The Jewish brothers prayed for God's forgiveness for the persecution of the Christian church by the Jews in Alexandria; there were Jews from this city among those that persecuted Stephen (Acts 6:9). Also in Alexandria we can trace some of the roots of 'replacement theology', which teaches that the Christian church has taken the place of Israel, and denies that God has any future for Israel. Origen, one of the Church Fathers writing in Alexandria in the third century AD, interpreted all that is said about Israel in God's Word as if it applied to the Church. We prayed that North Africa, which historically had a strong Christian influence, would be retaken for the Kingdom of God.

By river-boat along the Nile

On the journey up to Aswan we travelled by the night train and held a whole night of prayer on the train. For the return journey we hired a river-boat and travelled down the river Nile for three days and nights, stopping to pray where we saw ancient temples along the river bank, for example at Kom Ombo where there is a temple to the crocodile-god. In this temple of Kom Ombo in ancient times young women were sacrificed to the crocodiles, which were kept in a pool. These crocodiles, which were honoured as gods and had sacrifices made to them, were embalmed just like the Pharaohs and were kept in the temple in Kom Ombo.

Prayer at Egypt's centre point

In the day that the Lord restores Egypt, there will be an altar raised to the Lord *'in the midst of the land of Egypt'* (Isaiah 19:19, NKJV). When I asked Egyptian Christians where the centre point of Egypt lies, they answered Heliopolis. If you take the fertile part of Egypt, consisting of the Nile delta and the banks of the river, Heliopolis lies right at the centre. In this place, which is now a suburb of Cairo, there are several prayer groups, and we worked together with them. But Heliopolis is also well-known as a stronghold of the Muslim fundamentalists. Our guide warned us about going into this area, because we had Israelis with us in our group. We began to pray at the same moment that a chorus of Muslim priests, via loud-speakers, called the faithful to prayer in the mosques around us. We prayed that the Egypt of our time would be handed over to the Muslim Brotherhood, the funda-mentalist Muslims.

> '"I will hand the Egyptians over to the power of a cruel master, and a fierce king will rule over them", declares the Lord, the Lord Almighty.' (Isaiah 19:4)

'The Lord will strike Egypt with a plague; he will strike them and heal them. They will turn to the Lord, and he will respond to their pleas and heal them.'

(Isaiah 19:22)

The Muslim Brotherhood qualified for the description 'a cruel master'. Muslim fundamentalism is not only cruel to Christians; it is equally cruel to its own Muslim brothers. When the Egyptians come to see this cruelty on the part of those who exhibit the ultimate consequences of Islam, then they will call out to God because of their oppression; God will give them a deliverer, and they will turn to him.

Several of the obelisks which the Freemasons have transported and set up in the world's great cities came from this place, Heliopolis. One obelisk is still there, and we held a particularly powerful prayer action beside this one remaining obelisk in Heliopolis.

The earthquake in Egypt that struck pyramids and temples

Some months after our prayer journey, on 12 October 1992, Egypt was struck by an earthquake whose centre was at Heliopolis. 140 Pharaonic, Coptic and Muslim monuments and temples were damaged by the earthquake. One of the Pyramids was cracked, and in the great museum in Cairo some Pharaonic statues were broken in two. When the earthquake struck, two blocks of stone, each weighing ten tons, were loosened from the temple of the crocodile-god in Kom Ombo, the same temple where we had been inside and prayed. As a consequence, the authorities closed the temple to tourists. The Lord had reason to judge the gods of Egypt once again, because so much is being done in our own time to revive the worship of the ancient gods. The New Age movement regarded the Pyramids as the centre point for their world-wide meditation, held in the year of our visit. They called the

Pyramids the driving wheel of their occult power system. The Lord was shaking the gods of Egypt in order that Egypt might experience the awakening foretold in Isaiah 19, which will result in the Lord saying, 'Blessed be Egypt my people.'

Report of awakening in Egypt, November 1993

This report about awakening has inspired Christians in England to pray for awakening in their own land. Bob Dunnett, leader of the prayer movement Prayer for Revival, sent me a summary of a report from Egypt, stating that during the eight months following the earthquake, 25,000 people came to faith in Jesus in Egypt.

'God is pouring out his love in a powerful way. It's God because no-one is leading it. It's simply happening, all over the country at the same time in simple village churches. I have seen it.

'In some villages, there is a small Christian church, and usually a few faithful gather every Sunday. They attend a short service and then they go away until the next week. They are persecuted because of their minority religion. The killing of Christian villagers by Muslim fundamentalists is not uncommon. So Christians try to live quiet and uneventful lives in these villages, seeking not to attract attention to themselves. But when a revival comes ... They said it happened spontaneously, and not just in one village, not even in villages close to each other, but in places hundreds of kilometres apart.

'Suddenly the numbers of people attending the churches began to grow. And while they were gathered to worship, the Spirit of God would descend upon the people, and their worship would take on a whole new dimension. They worshipped until late in the night. They started to pray for one another. People were being healed. Muslims were coming to see what was happening. Muslims were being saved. And they came back the next night and the next.

'The churches in the villages began to overflow. Those who couldn't get in, hung around outside, singing and drinking in the atmosphere. The children were the most touching. Young children, 8, 9 and 10 years old with their hands lifted up to God, praising him with all their hearts. Then I knew this was real. Adults can work up a religious fervour but children cannot be fooled by such things.

'It is clear that God is doing something here. This kind of spontaneous revival is the only way it could have happened. A small revival in one church might easily have been squelched by forces of the enemy. But this is God's tactic. You cannot contain something that is erupting all over the country.'[2]

Messianic Jews and Christian Arabs meet in Egypt

Isaiah prophesied that there would be a holy highway between Israel and Egypt (Isaiah 19:23–24) and that these two peoples would enter into a Messianic alliance. During our prayer journey to Egypt, we prayed that this prophecy would be fulfilled. So we took four Messianic Jews with us in our team, who were able to pray together with the Egyptians. After this prophetic prayer journey, we received reports that there had been contacts between Messianic assemblies and Egyptian Christians.

The following is an extract from a newsletter sent out in November 1992 by Reuven Doron, a Messianic Jew who now lives and works in the United States:

'Jewish-Arab Conference in Egypt:
'On August 11, forty-five Messianic Jews from Israel were invited to a conference in Alexandria, Egypt. For the first time on Egyptian soil in modern history, both Jewish and Arab disciples of Jesus gathered

together in one spirit and for one purpose, to glorify the Lord.

'The walls came down on the second day of the gathering as God's Spirit breathed upon this prophetic group with anointed teaching, worship and dancing...

'The conference took place at great risk to both sides, but particularly to the Egyptian brethren. The true church in Egypt is very much under fear of the Muslim terror, to the point of not daring to witness to the masses or bring the message of the Gospel in the open air. These same demonic lies concerning the impossibility of sharing the Gospel were dispelled in Israel in the last few years, thus the Israeli believers were both able to encourage their Egyptian brethren and demonstrate to them the bold liberty we have in Christ. As the Israeli evangelists went to the streets, many Muslims heard the Gospel for the first time during this conference.

'Indeed, the promise of Isaiah 19:23–25 will be fulfilled! And for every opportunity we have to labor and invest toward that end, we give praise, glory and honor to God who can bring Jew and Arab together under the cross of Christ.' [3]

In our prayer conference in Jerusalem in January 1992 we had, for the first time, some Egyptian pastors among us. One was the principal of a pastoral training college, and the Lord had given him light and revelation enabling him to understand the place of the Jews as God's special people. After our prayer conference, a leaders' conference had been arranged to take place in Cairo, with about sixty Egyptian pastors and about thirty leaders of Messianic assemblies in Israel. The most important purpose of this conference was that these two groups should get to know one another. It was the first time that Messianic leaders and Arab pastors had met one another in Egypt. The Messianic assemblies have been going through a stage of pioneering and building-up. Now that they are ready and mature enough to seek contacts outside their national boundaries, it is notable that the first place they turn to is Egypt. But that is exactly what was foreseen by Isaiah in his chapter 19. I am so glad that we were led by the Lord to pray for the fulfilment of the prophecy in Isaiah 19, when we visited Egypt in April 1991.

Notes

1. President Chiluba's speech, made at the State House, Lusaka, on 29th December 1991, was broadcast on Zambia TV. The last part of the speech was also included in a video, *Breaking the Chains*, Christian Vision, West Bromwich, West Midlands (no date).
2. Rev. Bob Dunnett, Birmingham, from 'Quotes and Comment' in *National Call to Quarterly Prayer*, No. 3, November 1993.
3. From Reuven Doron's *Peace of Jerusalem* newsletter, November 1992.

Chapter 3

Restoration of the Individual

I would like to urge you to read this chapter in faith. When I write, I have more faith for your full restoration than you yourself have. During my life in ministry for the Lord, he has allowed me to see examples of people whom I met at their humble beginning, then whom I saw again at the lowest or most humiliating point in their lives, and whom I met again maybe ten or fifteen years later when I marvelled at the way the Lord had brought them into maturity. I am going to teach about being released into our full capacity, and about the tenfold wisdom that the Lord can give to his people in the End Time.

Proclamation of faith

You are created in the image of God. You were appointed as God's heir on earth in order to display the reflection of his glory. God has chosen your life on earth so that you can carry out his will.

There is great grace available for you, even though you have fallen from the lofty position that God gave you when he created you. You can be redeemed through the blood of Jesus and restored by the power of his resurrection, to live to your full capacity and to be anointed with the Omega-anointing, so that you will be able to fulfil the vision of God for your life, and his full purpose for your life's destiny, without hindrance from Satan and his evil tricks.

Created in God's image

God's purpose in the reconciliation of mankind through Jesus Christ is to restore his lost sons and daughters, to welcome them home and to establish them again as his heirs. We are created in the image of God, but we have lost so much of that image that we must be born again and transformed so as to be able to regain his image.

Tage Lindbom has written in his book *The Kingdom of Man* as follows:

'When the Creator commanded *"Let there be light"*, he granted to his image-bearer, mankind, to share in that light, which is a privilege not permitted to any other created being. Therefore mankind possesses a spiritual consciousness, an intellectual knowledge of the divine Truth. Man is not left outside in spiritual darkness, but has the light within him to perceive the revealed omnipotence and to listen to the proclamations of the prophets. The Fall is not merely a dramatic event at mankind's beginning; it is the constant concessions that a person makes in favour of that which earthly existence offers. We are bound hand and foot in this world, and therefore we are constantly subject to temptation to yield to the attractions that the material world has to offer.' [1]

We were created in the image of God as eternal beings. God is eternal, and in him there is no death nor decay, no dissolution nor destruction. The Fall resulted in our losing our eternal life and becoming mortal beings, and therefore the power of death is at work in us to cause our body, soul and morals to decay and dissolve.

We were created in the image of God with a divine

nature. God is holy, he is love, he is righteous, he is peace. We lost the divine nature and therefore lost the fullness of our heavenly Father's divine qualities.

We were created in the image of God, in such a way that we wanted to do good, we were in harmony with his will. Sin was our rebellion which tore us away from God's good and perfect will. Now there is a power in us that seeks to do evil; we are driven by an evil desire.

Peter shows us how our restoration into the image of God takes effect in precisely those areas of our life where that image has been ruined by the Fall. We regain eternal life and the divine nature, and we escape from the corruption that works in us through evil desires:

> *'His divine power has given us everything we need for life and godliness through our knowledge of him who called us by his own glory and goodness. Through these he has given us his very great and precious promises, so that through them you may participate in the divine nature and escape the corruption in the world caused by evil desires.'* (2 Peter 1:3–4)

We were created in the image of God so that we could share in the wisdom of God. Once we are wrenched loose from fellowship and intimacy with him who is truly wisdom, we are left only with the limited wisdom of our own souls and have lost the wisdom that comes from God. The second Fall has left us even more limited. If it had not occurred, we would have been able to gain experience over a thousand years of life, but as it is we are limited to 120 years, only about one-seventh of the original. This in itself means that we are not living to the full capacity for which we were created. When we are deprived of the wisdom of God, there comes a temptation to seek in its place the wisdom of the fallen angels, that is, the demons. Mankind fell into this temptation, and became filled with destructive demonic wisdom that comes from hell:

> *'Such "wisdom" does not come down from heaven but is earthly, unspiritual, of the devil.'* (James 3:15)

Gods, pictures and symbols that form personalities

As people, we have not only lost the image of God in our personality; the likeness to God has been replaced by a likeness to other personalities, so that we are becoming more and more like the false gods that we have taken on in substitution for God himself.

Psalm 115 expresses a spiritual law that affects a person's personality, and even his outward appearance. This concerns idol-worshippers and those who make idols.

> *'Those who make them will be like them, and so will all those who trust in them.'* (Psalm 115:8)

Paul in Romans 1 confirms that people become like the gods they worship:

> *'They became fools and exchanged the glory of the immortal God for images made to look like mortal man and birds and animals and reptiles.'*
> (Romans 1:22–23)

Paul was writing to people living in a culture that honoured the Greek and Roman pantheon of gods. As we read the myths of their family life with their jealousies, intrigues, girl-friends, child murder, homosexuality, and so on, it is hardly surprising that in the same chapter Paul goes on to describe how those who worship such gods have become *'full of envy, murder, strife, deceit and malice'* (Romans 1:29). They have become violent, they invent ways of doing evil, they disobey their parents, they are ruthless. All these traits of man's character (and Paul names others too) can be found among the various Greek and Roman gods and goddesses. People become like their gods and idols, copying their demonic customs and modelling themselves on them.

The Norse Asa-gods are another pantheon with definite family patterns, and where they enter into the culture of a people, personalities and behaviour patterns are formed in the likeness of this family of gods.

Myths and representations of gods are like moulds that form the shape of the man or woman that comes into contact with their castings. In the Philippines the best-known idol is 'Santo Niño', a child-god. You can see it in taxis and buses and in most homes. It was a gift of the Portuguese conquerors as a baptismal gift to a princess who allowed herself to be baptized in Cebu. It is more generally seen than a picture of the Virgin Mary. What effect does it have on the Filipino people that they worship a child-god? They become like him. One Filipino pastor asked me why it is so hard to bring his people into full maturity. 'Our country lacks prophetic voices and mature spiritual leaders,' he said. 'My church members never reach maturity: they are so childlike.'

In one house where I lived in Pakistan, near the Indian frontier, I had a dream-vision. I saw an ape sitting on a wall. I noticed the ape's face. A little later that day, I saw an old woman in the house who looked exactly like the ape I had seen in my vision. The area had at one time belonged to India and during those times the ape-god Hanuman was worshipped there. I have seen pictures of this ape-god Hanuman and the old woman's appearance was the same. She needed freeing from the spirit of the ape-god.

A person who is possessed takes the identity of the spirit possessing him: this applies to character, behaviour and appearance. I have seen someone behaving like a snake, before being delivered from a snake-spirit.

In a Buddhist country where you can often see statues of the Buddha meditating or sleeping, you can also see people meditating or dozing who look just like their example and teacher.

When Derek Prince came to Norway in the 1980s and landed at Fornebu airport near Oslo, he was confronted by the troll spirits. He asked the Lord to show him who was the 'strong man' over Norway, and received a clear word that there was not just one strong man but a whole mass of trolls. I was present when he shared this message, sitting in the home of an elder brother. On the top of his tiled stove there stood a Norwegian troll, and indeed we saw one of these in most of the homes we visited in Norway. Outside a shopping centre stood another troll. When you arrive at Fornebu, you can buy a guide-booklet covering Oslo and Norway. This booklet includes a special feature describing the Norwegian trolls in six different languages, and advertisements for goldsmith's shops where you can buy troll souvenirs of various kinds.

Trolls are not something that God created; they have more in common with the giants that existed before the Flood. In one description of the Norwegian trolls, it says that they have three distinctive characteristics. They are large, the largest creatures existing on earth; they are wicked, and they are stupid. Fear of trolls makes people confused. Trolls represent the evil one in this world, and they are opposed to all that is good. They cannot bear Christian blood; they make war against Christian kings and the Church. The trolls have been part of the Norwegian fantasy, the culture. Well-known artists have had troll motifs in their work. At the opening and closing ceremonies of the Winter Olympics, trolls and forest-spirits poured forth out of the underworld, and black-clad, bat-like figures could be seen moving about with frightened, confused movements.

The troll represents stupidity and confusion. The personality of a nation is influenced by such pictures and symbols, and I maintain that the Norwegian personality is influenced by that of the troll. When attacks come from the powers of darkness in Norway, they cause confusion and dulling of the intellect.

When I have held prayer conferences and meetings in Norway, I have often experienced an attack of confusion. People come with ideas that do not seem to fit in. It is difficult to carry out a plan from God in Norway without being attacked by confusion right in the middle of executing it.

I love Norwegians and would not wish to offend them unnecessarily. Once I prayed to the Lord: If you really want me to make this comment, then you will have to give me a special word from Scripture about the Norwegian trolls. Then I went straight to the Bible and looked up Jeremiah, and my eye fell on a word about idols that are like a bad joke:

> *'Every goldsmith is shamed by his idols. His images are a fraud; they have no breath in them. They are worthless, the objects of mockery* [a joke]. *When their judgment comes, they will perish. He who is the Portion of Jacob is not like these, for he is the Maker of all things, including the tribe of his inheritance – the Lord Almighty is his name.'* (Jeremiah 51:17–19)

> *'For it is a land of idols, idols that will go mad with terror.'* (Jeremiah 50:38)

Trolls and ghosts, monsters and extra-terrestrials all belong to the unknown that both fascinates and frightens children. They are part of an evil plan to create stunted personalities that will take fright and be easily manipulated by those who seek to control the world.

Before the Flood, *'God saw how corrupt the earth had become,for all the people on earth had corrupted their ways'* (Genesis 6:12). God saw how the fallen angels had entered into his creation and given life to beings of a kind that were not part of his original plan. God never included a race of giants in his first scheme for the world, and there were no trolls in his creation plan; they are the product of human minds infected by perverse fantasy. It is these twisted, perverted things that corrupt the original image of mankind, made in the likeness of God, and change us into something like a creation deformed by the fallen angels. I believe too that the artistic gifts will be an outflow of the Holy Spirit's creative activity, and adornment in colours and shapes will glorify the Creator and his handiwork.

> *'If anyone destroys God's temple, God will destroy him; for God's temple is sacred, and you are that temple.'*
>
> (1 Corinthians 3:17)

> *'The nations were angry; and your wrath has come. The time has come ... for destroying those who destroy the earth.'*
>
> (Revelation 11:18)

A restored person is like Jesus

Where God's image in us has been destroyed or corrupted in such a way as to become something quite different, God wants to restore us again and to transform us to become like Jesus.

If we are constantly living with someone and going about with him, we become like that person. My new identity is in Christ and my deepest wish is to learn to know him more, and to be known by him. I have met people who are like Jesus, and what always strikes me about them is how close to Jesus they are. One such was my friend Christy. He and I were walking together in Kabul, capital of Afghanistan. Christy had this closeness to Jesus. As we walked through the bazaar in Kabul, there were moments in our conversation when he felt the need to talk to Jesus. Right in the middle of a group of armed Muslims, Christy stopped. 'Kjell, we must pray about this.' He was not disturbed by all the people around us; he lived in a spontaneous closeness to Jesus, which was why he was so like him.

*'But we all, with unveiled face, beholding as in a mirror
the glory of the Lord, are being transformed into the
same image from glory to glory.'*

(2 Corinthians 3:18, NKJV)

*'But we know that when he appears, we shall be like
him, for we shall see him as he is. Everyone who has
this hope in him purifies himself, just as he is pure.'*

(1 John 3:2–3)

Your lost capacity

You are only a fraction of what God intended you to be
when you were created. You were intended to live for eternity, and your brain was created to assemble and process
information for ever. The first Fall deprived you of the
capacity to function in eternity without ever going to a
funeral or knowing that there was such a word as 'dead'.

The second Fall robbed you of six-sevenths of your
remaining capacity. You could have lived for 900 years
before the Flood, but the Lord took his Spirit away and
limited man's life on earth to 120 years. Fear and unrest
have finally chipped away at your capacity until now you
live about 70 to 80 years. Sin means missing the mark. The
fallen angels know all about the capacity that mankind
once used to enjoy. The occult movements come along
with their alluring invitation to liberate mankind's enormous capacity by means of occult methods; but if we go
by that route, we cannot achieve more than arriving at the
same level of wisdom as the fallen angels possess.

The Lord knows perfectly well what we can become in
our full capacity; therefore he has the right to say:

*'It is too small a thing for you to be my servant to
restore the tribes of Jacob and bring back those of
Israel I have kept. I will also make you a light for the
Gentiles, that you may bring my salvation to the ends of
the earth.'*

(Isaiah 49:6)

That word was spoken to Israel and to their calling; it was also prophetic of Jesus. But Paul and Barnabas received this message as a personal word from the Lord: What you are doing is much too small, too limited; I created you for a higher purpose. When you come into your full capacity, you will become my instrument for reaching a whole people who are in darkness.

> *'He made me into a polished arrow and concealed me in his quiver.'* (Isaiah 49:2b)

The tenfold wisdom

> *'To these four young men God gave knowledge and understanding of all kinds of literature and learning. And Daniel could understand visions and dreams of all kinds.'* (Daniel 1:17)

> *'In every matter of wisdom and understanding about which the king questioned them, he found them ten times better than all the magicians and enchanters in his whole kingdom.'* (Daniel 1:20)

Over a period of three years, Daniel and his three friends Shadrach, Meshach and Abednego had been trained up to give service to the king of a world power. It was expected of them that they should adapt themselves to the Babylonian culture with its worship of false gods, but for Daniel it was important that he should not defile himself with the food provided by the king. On the table there was meat that had been previously offered in sacrifice to the false gods. For ten days their eating discipline, so obviously distinct from the others at the king's table, was tested, and it was then that it became clear that they were ten times wiser than all the magicians and enchanters in the kingdom. Their testing took place in exactly the same area that we are being tested in our own time. There are work-places where everyone is expected to take part in a Transcendental Meditation course, and those who do not take part lose their promotion prospects. There are kings who believe themselves to be reincarnated gods, and this has to be acknowledged in a declaration of loyalty by those who work in their service. God's wisdom can never be given to those who corrupt God's image by compromising with a culture that serves false gods.

The wisdom that Daniel acquired was the same as that originally given to him when he was created. This wisdom comes from God and is given to those who pray for it. It began to function for the first time when Daniel and his friends were tested by the king, and for the second time when they were under the threat of death. When the wise men of Babylon were unable to tell the king what his dream was, the king was so angry that he ordered that the wise men should all be executed. Daniel asked that the executions be postponed, at a moment when the commander of the king's bodyguard had already gone to carry them out, and the postponement was allowed. Daniel's friends prayed through the night, but Daniel himself sought God alone, asking that the secret of the king's dream might be revealed to him. Daniel's prayer was answered and the king's secret was revealed to him: he was given the wisdom he needed in order to save the wise men of Babylon. In his song of praise, he thanked God for answering his prayer and because, he said, *'you have made known to me what we asked of you'* (Daniel 2:23). He knew where his wisdom came from, and the king knew it too, as he showed when he fell prostrate before Daniel and said, *'Surely your God is ... a revealer of mysteries, for you were able to reveal this mystery'* (Daniel 2:47). Daniel's response to God's answering his prayer was a psalm of praise to the Lord, who is wisdom and gives wisdom:

> *'Praise be to the name of God for ever and ever; wisdom and power are his. He changes times and seasons; he*

> *sets up kings and deposes them. He gives wisdom to the*
> *wise and knowledge to the discerning.'*
>
> (Daniel 2:20–21)

He alters dates in history; the Exodus from Egypt should in fact have occurred later. He makes a decision that accelerates the coming of Jesus. God controls history by deposing kings or setting up kings; by allowing one age to succeed another, when one world kingdom is conquered and another takes its place.

Wisdom is to understand God's will and intentions in the world; to know his ways, that is, how God thinks and acts before he comes to decisions.

He gives to the wise their wisdom. They must qualify by being wise already, in order to receive more of the revealed wisdom. Daniel and his friends were wise enough to refuse to be defiled by the Babylonian gods, and wise enough to seek God in prayer; in this way they were qualified to receive God's wisdom which gave them the further ability to advise the king and to save lives.

The true understanding is to receive the revelation in its prophetic setting; this is the insight that God gave to Daniel. Through interpreting the king's dream, he received a revelation of the prophetic development of history right up to the restoration of God's kingdom on earth. This understanding is also a mental capacity to be able to distinguish between evil and good, between wisdom and madness. It does not come about only through purely rational, logical conclusions, but by a thorough knowledge of the rules and regulations that the Creator has laid down for his creation so that the course of history can be guided by them.

Wisdom and understanding are required as foundations for coming to the right conclusions in the development of history and in safeguarding God's creation. We were given this wisdom from God right at the beginning; we lost it through the Fall, but we can be restored and receive it back again.

Daniel received a God-given power to interpret the development of history so that world leaders could hear. This wisdom is an understanding of God's ways, of how he acts in history and of the reasons why he acts as he does. It is to understand God's perfect time-schedules, when the kingdoms of this world are to disappear and when the time has come for new kingdoms to come into being. It is to know when the time has come for the destruction of Sodom and when the restoration of Jerusalem is at hand.

> *'He reveals deep and hidden things; he knows what lies in darkness, and light dwells with him.'*   (Daniel 2:22)

It is only God who can reveal matters that are so deep and complex that they are incomprehensible to the human brain, and mysteries that cannot be fathomed because they are hidden among the secret things of God. There are amongst other things secrets in the creation that are shrouded in secrecy so as to be kept from the eyes of fallen mankind. Noah had a way of communicating with animals. How did he behave? Daniel, who had a tenfold wisdom, could by faith shut the mouths of lions. How did Daniel communicate with the lions in their den in such a way that his visit there became a foretaste of the kingdom of peace? The kingdom of peace operates on God's lines and according to God's wisdom, that same wisdom which we lost when we became limited in our powers following the second Fall.

Paul *'was caught up to paradise and heard inexpressible things, things that man is not permitted to tell'* (2 Corinthians 12:4). Light dwells with God (Daniel 2:22): the Jewish rabbis understood this to mean that the light that was created on the first day was not intended for physical illumination, but for spiritual and intellectual enlightenment. The mind of man was tainted through sin, and we lost the true light, but it has been given back to us through Jesus who said, *'I am the light of the world.'*

'I thank and praise you, O God of my fathers; you have given me wisdom and power, you have made known to me what we asked of you, you have made known to us the dream of the king.' (Daniel 2:23)

Solomon prayed for the wisdom that belongs to the coming kingdom

The Lord gave Solomon the invitation, *'Ask for whatever you want me to give you'* (2 Chronicles 1:7). For Solomon, wisdom took the highest priority, so he prayed, *'Give me wisdom and knowledge, that I may lead this people'* (2 Chronicles 1:10). Then God answered Solomon:

'Since this is your heart's desire and you have not asked for wealth, riches or honour, nor for the death of your enemies, and since you have not asked for a long life but for wisdom and knowledge to govern my people over whom I have made you king, therefore wisdom and knowledge will be given you.' (2 Chronicles 1:11–12)

And so it worked out:

'God gave Solomon wisdom and very great insight, and a breadth of understanding as measureless as the sand on the seashore. Solomon's wisdom was greater than the wisdom of all the men of the East, and greater than all the wisdom of Egypt. He was wiser than any other man ... Men of all nations came to listen to Solomon's wisdom, sent by all the kings of the world, who had heard of his wisdom.' (1 Kings 4:29–34)

Nevertheless, the wisdom of Jesus was superior to Solomon's (Luke 11:31).

Solomon was given his wisdom at the beginning of his reign. The period of his reign is very much like the vision of the reign of Messiah from Jerusalem, when he will settle the strife between nations by his wisdom, and the peoples will come streaming into Jerusalem to see the King's glory. If Solomon had not fallen into sin with all his women and their worship of false gods, his reign might have been the beginning of the reign of peace; as it was, peace reigned for forty years, and his wisdom from God gave him an international influence.

Those who lack wisdom are encouraged to pray for it:

> *'If any of you lacks wisdom, he should ask God, who gives generously to all without finding fault, and it will be given to him. But when he asks, he must believe and not doubt.'*   (James 1:5–6)

We have everything in Christ; we have it as a fruit of his redemption; yet this fruit will never become a reality in our lives without prayer. That which is promised to us must be received in the kind of faith that prays an individual through to restoration into God's original purpose in creating him.

> *'Christ, in whom are hidden all the treasures of wisdom and knowledge.'*   (Colossians 2:2–3)
>
> *'I keep asking that the God of our Lord Jesus Christ, the glorious Father, may give you the Spirit of wisdom and revelation, so that you may know him better.'*
>   (Ephesians 1:17)
>
> *'We have not stopped praying for you and asking God to fill you with the knowledge of his will through all spiritual wisdom and understanding.'*   (Colossians 1:9)

When do we acquire the tenfold wisdom?

In Chapter 6 I shall be saying more about the apocryphal Book of Enoch, the book that is quoted in the letter of Jude. There is a short description of the book at the end of that chapter.

In the Book of Enoch, there is a prediction that seven-fold knowledge will be given to the righteous at the end of a period of time in which an apostate, rebellious generation lives on the earth:

'And after that in the seventh week shall an apostate generation arise, and many shall be its deeds, and all its deeds shall be apostate. And at its close shall be elected the elect righteous of the eternal plant of righteousness, to receive sevenfold instruction concerning all His creation.' (1 Enoch 93:9–10)[2]

Restoration happens step by step. The tenfold wisdom belongs to the era when mankind lived for several hundred years, even up to a thousand years. During a lifetime of that length, a person acquired a vast experience of life, while God's Spirit of life was the source of the heavenly wisdom. The tenfold wisdom was given to Daniel and his friends when they were living in the headquarters of an anti-Christian kingdom.

The extra, supplemental wisdom will be given to the people of God as a step in the restoration process and to equip them for the confrontation with the kingdom of Antichrist that will take place before the return of Jesus.

God is going to give us wisdom in relation to the challenges that we are going to meet in the End Time. At present, an information revolution is taking place; people know twenty times more about you than they ever did before. Computers work more quickly, store larger quantities of information, and can retrieve from other databases by networking. In earlier days, if you wanted a loan for your business, it took two days for the bank to assemble all the information it needed about you and your business on which to base its decision. Nowadays, a bank in Sweden has the capacity to assemble this information in two hours: but the intention is to reduce this time so that sufficient information can be brought on-screen within one minute. The bank employee who makes the decision knows twenty times as much about you as he would have done previously. The deeper problem will then arise in that day when the information system comes to be used by the anti-Christian powers for evil ends. Then, you will need a twentyfold wisdom in order to be an overcomer in the face of Big Brother's information system.

Daniel and his friends were given a tenfold wisdom to demonstrate that God's wisdom exceeded that of the magicians and astrologers who advised the king. Today we have plenty of examples of heads of governments, business leaders and bank directors who consult astrologers, shamans and New Age gurus. The Book of Revelation tells us that:

> '*Your merchants were the world's great men. By your magic spell all the nations were led astray.*'
>
> (Revelation 18:23)

Daniel has become a model for Christians living in countries belonging to the European Union who are aware that the EU is going to be a platform for the Antichrist. Daniel was an overcomer in Babylon, so therefore we can be overcomers in the EU headquarters in Brussels if we have the same spiritual equipment as Daniel had.

The complete restoration of fallen mankind comes through our redemption by the death of Jesus. By the Holy Spirit we share in God's hidden wisdom, prepared for us before the beginning of time:

> '*We speak of God's secret wisdom, a wisdom that has been hidden and that God destined for our glory before time began.*'　(1 Corinthians 2:7)

Through the Church, God will reveal his wisdom before those demonic powers who have conspired to rob mankind of godly wisdom and to replace it by a demonic wisdom:

> *'His intent was that now, through the church, the mani-*
> *fold wisdom of God should be made known to the rulers*
> *and authorities in the heavenly realms.'*
>
> (Ephesians 3:10)

I have a good friend who is an international business-man, who maintains that with the help of the Holy Spirit he arrived at the solution to a technical problem that none of his colleagues had been able to solve, nor has anyone been able to discover his secret since, despite trying to do so. This technical breakthrough has opened the door for him to visit many so-called closed lands. He knows of my longing to travel to closed countries, and he asks me to let him know of any closed land that I particularly want to reach. Then he can find a business opportunity in that country and invite me to go there as an employee of his company. He has a gift of praying for people to be filled with the Holy Spirit, and I have seen him serving people in this way. He believes that it is the same Spirit who helps him to find technical solutions. I believe that my friend has discovered the source of the tenfold wisdom.

I have seen this extraordinary wisdom at work in Christian businessmen, in Spirit-filled designers, constructors and in evangelists. It is part of the Holy Spirit's creativity to solve complicated technical problems and to get into places where no doors seem to be open. Daniel had such millennial wisdom and this was the testimony about him:

> *'This man Daniel . . . was found to have a keen mind and*
> *knowledge and understanding, and also the ability to*
> *interpret dreams, explain riddles and solve difficult*
> *problems.'* (Daniel 5:12)

The humble beginning of the Jesus marches in Brazil

In South Korea recently, I met a number of people that I had worked with five, ten or fifteen years ago during my travels in about seventy different countries. Some of them I had met when they were at the very beginning of their ministry, and now I was meeting them when they were standing at the high point of the work that God had called them to do.

The Jesus marches in Brazil have grown so much that the largest one, in São Paulo, comprised 1.2 million in 1995, the largest in the world, and there are also marches in a hundred different places. The man who started these marches came and asked me, 'Do you remember the night of prayer in São Paulo when you prayed for me at four o'clock in the morning? Something happened then in my life. It was then that it began.' That was six years earlier, when we held a night of prayer in the centre of São Paulo, in the Plaza de Sue where children lie sleeping on the steps of the Catholic cathedral, in the parks and on the pavements. During the previous year 86 children had been killed by retired policemen, who it was believed had been hired by shopkeepers wanting to get rid of the children who stole from their shops. We were there in the city to pray because there was a team from Youth with a Mission working there among the street children.

The Plaza de Sue is right in the heart of São Paulo. Just before the end of our prayer night, a young man came up to me and Pastor Jonathan Santos, and told us that he had been carrying a vision within himself about starting Jesus marches in São Paulo. He knew no pastors or spiritual leaders. He asked us to pray for him that he might be released into bringing his vision into reality. Now he told us that two months after we had prayed together, the Lord had begun to open doors for him and to give him contacts with pastors and other leaders. He had started Jesus marches which proceeded to grow year after year. When we met, he told us that there had been 100,000 in São Paulo, 300,000 in Rio de Janeiro, and Jesus marches taking place at 100 other places in Brazil. Then on 25th June 1994, which was announced as 'A day to change the world', 850,000 Christians danced and sang on the streets of São Paulo in spite of the fact that it was raining and the temperature was at a record low for Brazil. Six years earlier I had met a young, unknown man with a vision. We had prayed that he would be released into his full capacity to fulfil his vision. Now do you understand why I believe that the Lord can multiply your ministry tenfold?

Many such testimonies left me deeply humbled. The leading of the Holy Spirit had arranged for me to be present at the moment of birth of a pioneering work that started with a mere handful of believers. Today this movement has several thousand members. I know pastors whose ministry has multiplied tenfold. In the international prayer movement, I have visited churches and worked together with the prayer leaders. Sometimes, ten years on, the prayer leader of that church I visited has become the national prayer leader, teaching pastors about prayer and leading meetings at which thousands are present.

During my time as a missionary in Lahore, I followed Pastor Yaquub Paul into the slums around Tajpura where we held meetings among the clay-built houses where the sweepers and the poorest people lived. A group of teenage boys were saved there. Of those boys, one is today the principal of a Bible school, while others are pastors of large churches. They are used ten times more greatly by God today.

The Omega anointing – power to complete our task

There is a flow of power available for bringing tasks to completion, and it is this power that you need in the End Time for fulfilling your personal task on earth and, together with all the people of God, for completing the task of mission. I call this power the Omega anointing; it is not so named in the Bible, but one of Jesus' titles is:

> *'I am the Alpha and the Omega, the First and the Last, the Beginning and the End.'* (Revelation 22:13)

Jesus was present at the beginning of the Creation; therefore he can call himself the Alpha, the Beginning. But he will also be present at the end of this age, and can call himself the Omega, the End. I can be absolutely safe in his presence in the End Time; that is where power, encouragement and inspiration are to be found, and it is where you can receive the power to complete your task. So receive the Omega presence, the Omega power-flow.

When we do things in our own strength, there is a great risk that they will be left half-completed. When you redecorate your house, paint the outside or do up one room, can you put your hand on your heart and say you have done the whole job properly, or do you have a tendency to miss out the most difficult parts? In one conference, I was speaking about the power to complete tasks. I asked people to say if they had some half-finished work in a drawer at the office, or a book that lacked the inspiration for writing the final chapter, or a half-completed piece of needlework. Many came forward for prayer, and afterwards those who were prayed for contacted me and told how they were inspired to finish that manuscript, to complete that needlework or to finish redecorating that house. Jesus is not glorified by all the half-finished tasks you leave after you. Our message about the restoration of all things will not be credible if we are in the habit of leaving things behind us half-done.

The *plerophoreo* power

> 'But the Lord stood at my side and gave me strength, so that through me the message might be fully proclaimed and all the Gentiles might hear it. And I was delivered from the lion's mouth. The Lord will rescue me from every evil attack and will bring me safely to his heavenly kingdom.' (2 Timothy 4:17–18)

Paul thanks God for the power that is available to complete his missionary task, to bring it to fulfilment. He uses the Greek verb *plerophoreo* which means to fulfil, to carry out fully.

When Zechariah was urging Zerubbabel to complete the rebuilding of the temple, the word of the Lord came to him:

> *'This is the word of the Lord to Zerubbabel: "Not by might nor by power, but by my Spirit," says the Lord Almighty.'*
> (Zechariah 4:6)

and then again:

> *'The hands of Zerubbabel have laid the foundation of this temple; his hands will also complete it.'*
> (Zechariah 4:9)

Much of what we do remains only half-completed.

> *'Do the work of an evangelist, discharge all the duties of your ministry.'*
> (2 Timothy 4:5)

Here again Paul uses the verb *plerophoreo*. To bring the ministry of an evangelist to fulfilment means fulfilling the evangelist's full capacity in his calling. A person grows into a spiritual ministry. Each spiritual ministry has a beginner stage, followed by a spiritual development, and then it can reach its full capacity at a level of complete restoration. A street evangelist can become a city evangelist. In Argentina they talk of city evangelists, people who set the whole city into motion so that tens of thousands are saved. Then there are national evangelists, people with a message to an entire nation, and world evangelists. He who is trustworthy in a small matter is put in charge of a greater. He who is an elder of a local church can through the Lord's working become an elder in the city or in the nation. I believe in the Omega power that brings your calling into complete fulfilment.

'I have finished the race' (2 Timothy 4:7): here Paul

speaks of the fulfilment of his life's work. God has a redeeming purpose for our life. We can carry out fully everything that God has in his mind for us to do. That is what it means to finish the race.

I will not be hindered by anyone

Paul's testimony was that he had been delivered from the lion's mouth; he then went on to make a proclamation of faith:

> *'The Lord will rescue me from every evil attack and will bring me safely to his heavenly kingdom. To him be glory for ever and ever. Amen.'* (2 Timothy 4:18)

Paul in his letters recounted the hardships he had suffered during his ministry for the Lord, and certainly he was hindered and delayed in his work on many occasions. He wrote to the church in Thessalonica:

> *'We made every effort to see you. For we wanted to come to you – certainly I, Paul, did, again and again – but Satan stopped us.'* (1 Thessalonians 2:17–18)

He also said that he had been prevented several times from travelling to Rome:

> *'I planned many times to come to you (but have been prevented from doing so until now).'* (Romans 1:13)

But we are told too of a period when no-one could hinder him: a time of grace in Rome that lasted for two years. Despite his being chained and under house arrest, no-one could prevent him from spreading the Gospel, because people came streaming to his house:

> *'For two whole years Paul stayed there in his own rented house and welcomed all who came to see him.*

> *Boldly and without hindrance he preached the kingdom*
> *of God and taught about the Lord Jesus Christ.'*
>
> (Acts 28:30–31)

During my time in Pakistan, I myself experienced a period of two years when nothing could hinder me. From 1968 to 1970 I conducted revival campaigns in one town after another. I invited evangelists to take part, and witnessed many miracles of healing. People came by the thousand. We might have four or five thousand gathered in places where there was a church with only 100 members. Once I watched with my own eyes as a Muslim woman, blind in both eyes, was healed and was able to see. The lame walked, the deaf received their hearing, and many people testified of miracles. Each campaign led to our taking a bus-load of candidates for baptism to a river to be baptized. While these campaigns were going on, war between India and Pakistan was coming closer. Mobilization was taking place on both sides of the frontier, and some weeks before war actually broke out, a black-out was ordered. At the time we were in Sialkot near the Indian frontier. The son of the general who was in command of the area came to our meetings, and he persuaded his father to make an exception for us, so that the tent where we held our meetings was blazing with light while all the rest of Sialkot remained in darkness. We continued with our campaign until a few days before the outbreak of war, and our visiting evangelist, Bajhat Batarseh from Jordan, flew out on the last flight that left Lahore airport before the airport was closed and the war started.

Your proclamation of faith

I began this chapter by proclaiming my faith for your restoration. Now it is your turn to receive in faith the restoration that God wants to give you. If you have been reading silently up to now, I want you to speak this proclamation out loud.

'I am created in the image of God. I was made an heir of God on earth in order to shine with the reflection of his glory. God has ordained my life on earth so that I should carry out his will.

'I receive the great grace offered to me through Jesus. I confess my part in the Fall, which caused me to lose the high position that God gave to me in the Creation. I believe that I have been redeemed by the blood of Jesus and restored by the power of his resurrection to live to my full capacity and to experience the Omega-presence, so that I can fulfil God's visions for my life and his full purposes for my life's destination on earth, without any hindrance by Satan or by his evil tricks.'

Notes

1. Tage Lindbom, *Människoriket*, Svensk Pastoraltidskrift, Uppsala, 1978.
2. From R.H. Charles' translation, *The Book of Enoch*, SPCK, London, 1917.

Chapter 4

The Glory of the Lord

It belongs to my calling as an intercessor to pray until the presence of God is manifested. This is what Elijah did also; the fire that fell upon his altar was a manifestation of the glory of the Lord (1 Kings 18:38). It is a part of the restoration process that God should have a resting-place for his glory on the earth.

> *'The city does not need the sun or the moon to shine on it, for the glory of God gives it light, and the Lamb is its lamp.'* (Revelation 21:23)

> *'They ... exchanged the glory of the immortal God for images made to look like mortal man and birds and animals and reptiles.'* (Romans 1:23)

We can also see in Ezekiel 8 how in place of God's glory in the temple, the elders of Israel had set up an abomination, and the glory of God had been taken away.

The radiance of God's glory has always been the same; but he created mankind to radiate his glory. Because we have failed, by reason of sin, to be effective reflecting mirrors for his glory, the extent of the radiance of his glory over the earth has never been as great as God planned it to be.

When everything is restored again, there will also be a

restoration for God, since he is today not fully recognized throughout his creation, in his wisdom, glory and might.

What was it that actually happened after the Fall, when Adam and Eve realized that they were naked? Had they not been just as naked before as they were afterwards? I am not at all sure that they were, in fact. I believe that before the Fall, their earthly bodies were clothed with eternal light and glory. Through their disobedience against God, the radiation of light fell from them, and they stood naked.

> *'Since all have sinned and are falling short of the honour and glory which God bestows and receives.'*
> (Romans 3:23, Amplified Bible)

> *'Meanwhile we groan, longing to be clothed with our heavenly dwelling, because when we are clothed, we will not be found naked.'*   (2 Corinthians 5:2–3)

Adam and Eve were not naked when they were clothed in their heavenly, eternal bodies of glory. Each one of such heavenly bodies differs from another in glory, and all who die in Christ will be raised in glory (1 Corinthians 15:41–43). It will be for us our eternal, indestructible space-suit.

Through the example of certain people, we have been able to see the evidence that mankind will be restored as the bearer of God's glory.

When Moses came down from Mount Sinai where he had been with God for forty days, with the two tablets of the Testimony in his hands, *'he was not aware that his face was radiant because he had spoken with the Lord'* (Exodus 34:29). The people were afraid to come near him because of the radiance, so he hung a veil over his face. Paul quotes this passage and tells us:

> *'But whenever a man turns to the Lord, the veil is taken away ... But we all, with unveiled face beholding as in a*

mirror the glory of the Lord, are being transformed into the same image from glory to glory.'

(2 Corinthians 3:16, 18, NASB)

When the members of the Sanhedrin looked at Stephen, *'they saw that his face was like the face of an angel'* (Acts 6:15).

When Jesus was on the mountain with his chosen disciples:

'He was transfigured before them. His face shone like the sun, and his clothes became as white as the light.'

(Matthew 17:2)

Jesus is God, in the form and appearance of a fully restored man:

'The Son is the radiance of God's glory and the exact representation of his being.' (Hebrews 1:3)

Our natural original state is that we should be radiant Christians and bearers of the glory of God:

'Then the righteous will shine like the sun in the kingdom of their Father.' (Matthew 13:43)

In a strict Muslim country, where Christians are persecuted, I visited a Christian businessman who had fifty employees in his business, most of them Muslims. He told us that among his employees were five Christians. He did not introduce them to us, but after he had shown us round, he asked us whether we knew which of the employees were the Christians. We had noticed five different people whose eyes had life and radiance in them, and we described to the employer which machines they were working at. We had seen correctly; we could distinguish between those who lacked the radiance and those who had the radiance of God's glory in their eyes.

This is just one stage of the process that is visible, but Paul says that we are being transformed into his image and that we are moving from one glory to another. There are stages to be reached that are not yet visible among the saints on earth, but will be revealed when all things are restored.

I once met a man who when he came towards me, had the glory of God shining all over his face. I asked him what had happened to him. He told me that he had just come from a prayer meeting where they had experienced the presence of God and had been given a prophetic message. The Lord had said to them that because darkness reigns over the earth, he is going to reveal more and more of his glory among his saints, the closer we come to the return of Jesus. 'When I come, you will not notice the difference between the glory that you experienced before my coming and the glory you will experience after my coming. You are going to taste my glory before I come, so that you will feel completely at home in my glory when I come.'

This agrees with what Isaiah says:

> *'Arise, shine, for your light has come, and the glory of the Lord rises upon you. See, darkness covers the earth and thick darkness is over the peoples, but the Lord rises upon you and his glory appears over you.'*
>
> (Isaiah 60:1–2)
>
> *'They will be punished ... on the day he comes to be glorified in his holy people and to be marvelled at among all those who have believed.'*
>
> (2 Thessalonians 1:9–10)

This means that his glory will be seen in his saints, in a manner greater and more wonderful than anything we could possibly imagine. When we see it, we shall be overwhelmed like those who dream.

The whole creation *'waits in eager expectation for the*

sons of God to be revealed' (Romans 8:19). Then the creation will be free from the curse under which it has lain ever since the Fall of man. Because of Adam and Eve, the ground was cursed, and that curse has persisted and grown into all the environmental problems that we have today. It was the fault of ourselves, mankind, that the ground was placed under bondage.

So the creation waits for our full restoration. When God at last brings mankind through to full restoration in glory, when Jesus comes back to earth with all the saints, then the creation will finally be free from the curse.

The Gospel is a proclamation to the whole creation. Mark's version of the 'Great Commission' reads:

> *'Go into all the world and preach the good news to all creation.'*   (Mark 16:15)

And Paul says:

> *'This is the gospel that you heard and that has been proclaimed to every creature under heaven, and of which I, Paul, have become a servant.'*
> (Colossians 1:23)

I preach the gospel to sinners, but the freedom and the glory that I have in Christ is something that the whole of creation longs for. As we walk, we represent good news to the whole creation: it can be freed from the curse. Ezekiel proclaimed the word of the Lord in prophecy to the mountains and hills, to the ravines and valleys of Israel (Ezekiel 36:6). Miracles are going to be manifested even now in the creation, as evidence of the kingdom to come.

A farmer who owned land near the town of Örebro in Sweden had a part of his land that was not productive. When he sowed seed on this particular field, the crop came up thin and stunted, and this happened year after year. He went out on the field and prayed to God for fruitfulness before sowing the next crop, and this time it came up normal size and grew properly. When he harvested the crop and took it to the mill, they asked, 'Where did this crop grow? The grain is of the very highest quality.' The Lord healed the unfruitful field and made it produce a top quality yield. When I came to a meeting in the neighbourhood, this farmer came and parked next to my car, and lifted out a 30–kilo sack of wheat flour which I was to take home with me to Lena. When Lena baked with the flour, she said, 'This is the best flour I have ever used for baking. It kneads so easily and makes such good rolls.'

Prophetic answer to prayer for the creation and the environment

The Garden of Eden lay in the region of the rivers Euphrates and Tigris. Where these two rivers in Iraq join together, there stands a dried-up tree known as Adam's tree. There are no green leaves on Adam's tree, and around this monument to the Garden of Eden the ground is untidy and littered. Nearby there is an empty tourist hotel with broken windows overlooking the Euphrates. There, where once the Garden of Eden was situated, today there is only desert and military camps. So far has the Garden fallen that during the Gulf War the area was a place where bombs and shells rained on Saddam Hussein's troops and their weapons and fortifications. This was the place where Adam was placed by the Lord to work the land and look after it.

God assigned tasks to Adam to carry out in relation to his creation: the first one was that he should rule over the fish in the sea, the birds in the air and every living creature moving on the ground (Genesis 1:28). To rule means to put under one's feet.

We are still going on with the process of putting the world under our feet. Our bodies are the temples of the Holy Spirit, and we carry the glory of God in our bodies. Prayer is not merely words; it is bringing the presence of God into places where his presence has not been before.

The Lord spoke to me through a prophetic message: 'I am sending you to the darkest places on earth, to places where the angels do not want to go, so that you can bring my glory into those places.' To walk in faith that we carry with us the glory of God gives us the motivation for prayer journeys, prayer walks and Jesus marches. We capture ground for the kingdom of God, and there is liberation and transformation wherever we go.

Adam's second task was to work the land and to look after the Garden of Eden (Genesis 2:15). The word used for 'look after' is related to the word 'guard' in Genesis 3:24 where it says that God placed cherubim and a flaming sword *'to guard the way to the tree of life.'* It is also related to the word 'watchmen' in Isaiah 62:6 where God says, *'I have posted watchmen on your walls, O Jerusalem.'* This word describes the task of intercessors.

Prophetic watchman's responsibility for the creation

Because Jeremiah had a prophetic calling to be a watchman over his land, he experienced agonies during a terrible drought that afflicted the land. He sought the Lord to know how it could be that people were suffering thirst:

> *'The nobles send their servants for water; they go to the cisterns but find no water. They return with their jars unfilled; dismayed and despairing, they cover their heads. The ground is cracked because there is no rain in the land; the farmers are dismayed and cover their heads.'* (Jeremiah 14:3–4)

Jeremiah received an answer from God when he sought him concerning this natural catastrophe:

> *'Then the Lord said to me, "Do not pray for the well-being of this people."'* (Jeremiah 14:11)

Jeremiah was not to pray for the people, and he understood that this meant that the time of God's judgment had arrived for them. The Lord said to him:

> ' *"I will make them abhorrent to all the kingdoms of the*
> *earth because of what Manasseh son of Hezekiah king*
> *of Judah did in Jerusalem ... You have rejected me",*
> *declares the Lord. "You keep on backsliding." '*
>
> (Jeremiah 15:4, 6)

Many of God's judgments in the End Time will be carried out through natural disasters. His judgments in nature are caused by unconfessed sins that lie waiting for their release through natural and environmental disasters. Sometimes it is our task to warn of approaching judgments; sometimes the Lord wants to show his power in healing the land when his people humble themselves before God and confess their sins and turn from them.

Joel's prophetic ministry was born when he sought God because locusts were destroying all the vegetation.

> *'To you, O Lord, I call, for fire has devoured the open*
> *pastures and flames have burned up all the trees of the*
> *field.'* (Joel 1:19)

After praying in this way, Joel had to bring a prophetic word from the Lord that called the people to repentance, prayer and fasting.

I learn from the example of Jeremiah and of Joel that natural and environmental disasters are my concern: I need to seek the Lord to know the reason for them. Sometimes the Lord says that there is a way for the land to be healed, if the people will confess their sin. At other times the Lord shows us that the sin of the people has grown so great that judgment must fall, and since no signs of repentance can be seen, God allows nature to go out of order.

The prophets were able to interpret the underlying

reasons why the creation was out of order, and to warn the people and their leaders:

> *'There is only cursing, lying and murder, stealing and adultery; they break all bounds, and bloodshed follows bloodshed. Because of this the land mourns* [dries up], *and all who live in it waste away; the beasts of the field and the birds of the air and the fish of the sea are dying.'*
> (Hosea 4:2–3)

Misdeeds of the people can cause weather patterns to be altered:

> *'They do not say to themselves, "Let us fear the Lord our God, who gives autumn and spring rains in season, who assures us of the regular weeks of harvest." Your wrongdoings have kept these away; your sins have deprived you of good.'*
> (Jeremiah 5:24–25)

Prophetic responsibility for the creation and the environment

In 1990 we held a summer 'School of the prophets' course in Bro, my home town in Sweden. The course was entitled 'Prophetic responsibility for the creation and the environment' and I wrote the invitation as follows: 'As we call together the school of the prophets, we are eagerly seeking the Lord for prophetic preaching that leads to repentance, and a prophetic initiative for healing of the environmental destruction of nature. Our common future on earth is threatened.'

Environmental damage is increasing in its extent. The forests and woods are affected by acid pollution; the air that we breathe is poisoned; the earth is plundered and laid under a curse on account of lawlessness. Many more people are dying of hunger, or from natural disasters, or in hurricanes, floods or earthquakes during the 90s than because of war. In the face of many environmental problems, scientists and politicians are helpless. In a time such as this, we need to seek the Lord and to hear his answer. Everything is going to be restored in accordance with God's programme, including that which has to do with nature and the environment.

The time has come when intercessors and prophets need to understand the underlying spiritual connections at the root of natural and environmental disasters, and to call for repentance that will lift the curses and bring in healing miracles into the environment. We can see people today who themselves cause the judgments of God described in Revelation. A prophetic preaching of the need for repentance, addressed to individuals, peoples and nations is a pre-requisite for our being able to see God's healing miracles in nature.

A person who worked with Greenpeace, the environmental activist organization, told me that among the dedicated young people and scientists in the movement there are also magicians and shamans with staring eyes. At a conference about the environment in Moscow, there were Indian gurus present, giving out propaganda to the effect that transcendental meditation would bring healing to nature. Where are the intercessors and prophets, when such threats against our future on earth are being discussed? God's spokesmen will be at work both when God is cleansing, healing and saving his creation and also when God's judgments are pronounced and executed on earth.

Spiritual factors influence nature and the envirnoment

The earth can mourn and languish away. The curse can consume it as it becomes desecrated by its inhabitants, as they stir up rebellion against God's laws and his covenant (Isaiah 24:3–7). The soil of the land has not flourished as the result of seventy years of atheism and godlessness in Russia.

An old Baptist missionary in Pakistan, Ragnar Gustavsson, who has since gone home to be with the Lord, used to say that Allah was a desert god; that all the places where he is worshipped become deserts. The deserts are certainly spreading in most of the Muslim lands. Before Islam came to Afghanistan, the mountains around Kabul were covered with forests. In Spain they have a saying that before the Muslims came to Spain, an ape could swing from tree to tree from one end of the country to the other without touching the ground. The whole of Spain was then covered in forest, but since the coming of Islam the forests have been devastated. In Iraq too it is obvious that where there were once flourishing cities, there is now sterile desert.

In the Muslim land of Sudan, millions of people are threatened with starvation from drought. In those parts of the former Yugoslavia that were conquered by Muslims 500 years ago, there is still a spiritual desert. There are many promises in the Bible which say that the desert will blossom. Abraham's blessing is promised to all the families on earth, including the Muslim families. When the spiritual harvest comes and Jesus Christ is received in Muslim desert lands, the deserts will be transformed into forests, fruitful orchards and fertile arable land.

In 1990, my wife Lena and I visited New Zealand, where we spent some time in the South Island, speaking evening after evening in house-churches among the sheep-farmers. At the time we were there, the burning question among them was what their attitude should be to the Islamic laws of Halal slaughtering. Their Minister of Agriculture had taken part in talks about the export of mutton to Iran. Iran made it a condition that Muslim priests should be present at the slaughter-houses and slaughter the sheep in the name of Allah. The Christian farmers resisted this, and sent their sheep only to those slaughter-houses that refused to admit a Muslim priest. After the slaughter-houses had been made temples of Allah in this way, a two-year drought descended on those areas, and sheep-farming there was struck by one disaster after another. In the areas where they refused to slaughter in the name of Allah, however, it rained.

An unusual May-day bonfire in Helsingborg

On the first of May weekend, an important holiday in Sweden, it is customary to light bonfires. In 1990 I visited the 'House of Joy' church in the southern town of Helsingborg, where Knut Frohm was pastor. We decided to arrange an unusual kind of bonfire on the beach beside Öresund, the strait that separates Denmark from Sweden, outside Helsingborg. Knut Frohm spoke of the destruction of the environment and deterioration of the sea-water along the coast. He had faith that we could influence the sick coastline through prayer. Knut had the environment in his thoughts as he arranged to hold an open-air baptism ceremony on the beach.

Before the day itself we encouraged the members of the church to carry out a spring-cleaning and to burn everything that needed to be burnt from their life, their bookshelves, or their record cabinets, just as the people at Ephesus did with their scrolls, as recorded in Acts 19:18–20.

We had a splendid bonfire on the beach. The people came with bagfuls of things to be burnt, and one after another explained what they were burning and why they were burning it. A newly-saved young man burnt a pornographic video and 130 cassettes of satanic music from Bali in Indonesia. Children burnt comics full of demons, ghosts and wizards. One man burnt his goblin books, which are much in evidence at Christmas time when there is much talk of goblins in Sweden but not many have room for Jesus in their lives.

One lad said that he had plenty of Christian books in his bookshelves, but his flat was a mess. So he had brought with him a bagful of 'disorder' which he wanted to burn in order to clear up his life.

A thick volume of the Social Democratic party's humanistic programme for the 1990s was burnt together with fashion magazines, books on yoga, some mail-order catalogues, health magazines, a large number of records of satanic rock music, pornographic magazines, and theological literature written by unbelievers that had caused many to lose their faith. One woman was parted, by the fire, from her jacket that she had always worn when she took drugs. A man burnt his rucksack that he had carried on his sex-tours to Thailand; another brought a blanket that was a reminder of his former life of degradation. Things were burnt that were associated with bitter memories, for example two bottles of sewing-machine oil that the husband had acquired when the household was divided between him and his wife on divorce. One who had been fascinated by a large number of 'rollspel' games (games in which the players act the parts of monsters, demons and dragons) let them all go into the fire. Novels full of pornography, others full of dragons, and Jehovah's Witnesses tracts, all followed each other into the flames.

Some people who are saved also need to be saved through fire. Every life has its history, and I was very touched to hear one person after another explaining why the fire was needed to burn out uncleanness and bitter memories. We lit the fire as a prophetic act, as we sought the Lord for cleansing of the people and healing of the land.

What follows is an extract from an article printed in a regional newspaper, *Sydsvenskan*, on 12th November 1993:

'ÖRESUND HAS RECOVERED. Öresund is in a better state than it has been for the past five years. The oxygen content has increased. The salt content has increased. And the phosphorus and nitrogen contents in the surface water are relatively low. The Öresund Water Care Association had presented an emergency report about the water in the strait. At that time, Öresund stood on the brink of becoming a lifeless piece of water. Particularly critical was the strip of coastline between Barsebäck and Helsingborg. Now the situation is considerably better.'

When I visited the Faroe Islands, I learnt that fishing and the fishing industry, the principal means of living in the islands, had been hit by a serious downturn in the last few years. The shoals of fish were no longer where they used to be. We prayed that the fish would once again be carried by the ocean currents to the Faroes. As we were on our way to the airport on the Monday morning, I happened to see that a school of whales had swum into a bay and several hundred men stood waist deep in the water, catching and killing them. It was a school of about 200 whales, each weighing about a ton.

Chapter 5

Restoration of the Family

The Fall of mankind brought with it a breaking-up of family relations. Cain was jealous because his brother Abel's sacrifice was more acceptable to God than his own, and his jealousy led to the first fratricide. The break-up of families is a built-in feature of the sinful nature, which continues until now with quarrels between brothers and sisters, who go the way of Cain in their jealousy and their outbreaks of anger towards one another.

The judgment of condemnation for this first murder of one brother by another took the form of a curse upon Cain, the elder brother who had all the rights of the first-born son in the family inheritance of the Garden of Eden. Later, the Passover was instituted in Egypt so that the blood of the slaughtered lamb might protect the firstborn sons from the destroyer. On that night, the firstborn son of every family in Egypt was struck down, except in those households where the blood could be seen on the door-posts. The judgment against Cain's rights as the firstborn appears to be a general condemnation that has continued to affect every individual, but when the Lord restores us through redemption we become a festival assembly, *'the church of the firstborn, whose names are written in heaven'* (Hebrews 12:23). We have once again become heirs in God's family, which gives us the right of inheritance in paradise and in the new, restored earth. We receive back that which Cain previously lost.

> *'Now if we are children, then we are heirs – heirs of God and co-heirs with Christ.'*   (Romans 8:17)

The Fall also caused a whole extended family to be marked for many generations with the same sin. Lamech expected his family to keep the blood-feud going by seeking multiple vengeance:

> *'I have killed a man for wounding me, a young man for injuring me. If Cain is avenged seven times, then Lamech seventy-seven times.'*   (Genesis 4:23–24)

One of the members of my prayer team in Spain was the son of a gipsy king in Barcelona. The son told me that he did not want to succeed his father as king, since it would be his responsibility to maintain the blood-feud for the whole family. In Pakistan, there are families among the Pathan people that carry on such feuds. In this way, a family can become dominated by sin. I have seen an unexplained jealousy being transmitted from generation to generation in one family, while in another family there can be unforgiveness and bitterness, or else pride and a domineering attitude.

The Fall produces its resulting effects with ever-increasing consequences. First it strikes at the individual, then at Adam's family, and then finally a whole line of descendants becomes marked by the destruction of sin. Moses says that a family or a whole tribe can have a bitter root that grows up and poisons the whole (Deuteronomy 29:18).

What sort of sins are the ones that most easily entangle us, that are the easiest to slide into? They are the family sins that are passed on from generation to generation. David fell into adultery, and prayed to God to be forgiven for it. But his sons Absalom and Solomon very easily became entangled in the same areas of sin as their father.

'How many times shall I forgive my brother?' asked Peter. Jesus' answer was an echo of the command given to Lamech's family to continue their blood-feud, but instead of avenging seventy-seven times, Jesus' restoration command to Peter was to forgive one's brother seventy times seven times (Matthew 18:21–22). Restoration happens when a whole family come into redemption and are able to forgive one another.

The year of jubilee – reassembling the family

The year of jubilee, also called by Jesus a year of grace from the Lord, is a message of restoration. The year of jubilee will form part of the constitution of Jesus' kingdom, and will be the basis of his government manifesto when he returns to reign over the earth. The year of jubilee means that God, by his grace, gives to mankind a new start in freedom. When freedom was proclaimed in the land, everyone became free of debt, and received back his family land, where the family could once more gather together. Those who had become slaves were able to return home.

> *'Consecrate the fiftieth year and proclaim liberty throughout the land to all its inhabitants. It shall be a jubilee for you; each one of you is to return to his family property and each to his own clan.'* (Leviticus 25:10)

Just as the year of jubilee began with the gathering of families, so will the kingdom of God begin with family assemblies. Israel is going to become the first nation to receive the Messiah, and they will receive him by families. The Jewish people are very family-conscious; their festivals are celebrated with their families. When Israel comes to be saved, it will happen through a prayer awakening, in which families and clans gather to repent together in prayer (Zechariah 12:10–14). There was no sorrow in the land, except among a few, when the king that God sent to them died on a cross in Jerusalem; but when the Spirit of grace and prayer is poured out, people will undergo sorrow and pain together, family by family, because Jesus, a beloved son and a beloved king, was not recognized. They will grieve as a man grieves for his only son.

The Lord is not concerned with saving organizations, societies, or political parties in his kingdom, but on the other hand he is concerned to save individuals, families, and his church.

Family prayer gatherings

I have explained how the law of sin and death leads to vessels being broken, just as Jeremiah demonstrated God's judgment by breaking a clay pot into a thousand pieces. Families and marriages have been broken up by the law of sin; what a man sows he will also reap. We reap the wages of sin in our children and our families.

The reassembling of those who have been scattered is a key principle of restoration. The diaspora of Israel will regather, and so will families and relatives that were once dispersed.

The kinsman-redeemer – the relative who restores the family

In the law concerning the year of jubilee, there was also a law giving the nearest responsible relative the right to restore a member of his family who had become poor. The kinsman-redeemer had the right to redeem lost family property, and the right to purchase release for a relative who had become a slave. Jesus is for us our kinsman-redeemer who has himself, by his blood, paid the price that purchased our freedom and redeemed the lost family inheritance.

> *'If a fellow countryman of yours becomes so poor he has to sell part of his property, then his nearest kinsman is to come and buy back what his relative has sold.'*
>
> (Leviticus 25:25, NASB)

The kinsman-redeemer – the nearest responsible relative

For saving the family, there is this particular ministry to protect the family, mentioned in the Bible – that of the kinsman-redeemer (*go'el* in Hebrew), translated in some versions as 'nearest responsible relative'. The people of Israel were built up by family and clan relationships. In tribes and nations with strong family cohesion, there is a social security system built into the family relationship. If any relative falls into difficulties, the responsibility for that person is allocated in such a way that everyone knows who is the nearest relative who has the duty to intervene. The kinsman-redeemer has the right and duty to buy back. *Go'el* comes from the verb *ga'al*, meaning to redeem, deliver, free. It is a function contributing to the protection of the family. The kinsman-redeemer, in the law of Moses, had a role in the protection and covering of the national structure and the family's economic interests and existence. His tasks were economic, legal and protective of the family.

The kinsman-redeemer could bring in the year of jubilee in advance

The law of the kinsman-redeemer is linked with that of the year of jubilee in Leviticus 25. The year of jubilee is the basis, in Jesus' kingdom, of its government, its constitution and its economic system. The kinsman-redeemer has a key function in bringing in the year of jubilee, and can even in certain circumstances bring in its effect in advance of its due time, as shown by the provision for the poor relative in Leviticus 25:25 above.

Jesus is himself the kinsman-redeemer who has purchased our freedom from the devil who had power over us. Jesus has stepped in, as our nearest responsible relative, to buy our freedom and give us back our lost family property. He has purchased our release so that the whole family can gather together again after the time of dispersion. As kinsman-redeemer, Jesus has proclaimed a year of grace from the Lord, and that which has been fulfilled in Jesus has its continuation in ourselves as individuals and in the church. Jesus lives in us and carries out his ministries through us, and one of his ministries is that of the kinsman-redeemer.

It is noticeable that God has laid such an emphasis on family responsibility that it has become one of the keys to the bringing-in of the year of jubilee: the kingdom of peace on the earth. But the opposite is also true: Satan's régime on earth can only be brought in through the breaking-up of family responsibility. This is the enemy's plan for preparing a place ready for the Antichrist. Therefore the mission of the kinsman-redeemer includes taking the initiative and hastening the coming of the kingdom of God.

The kinsman-redeemer – bringer of hope for the family's future

Jeremiah was the prophet who most clearly prophesied about the times of restoration to come; but he also, through his life, showed that he took responsibility as kinsman-redeemer for the restoration of his own family, his people (Jeremiah 32). He received the Lord's command to take up his responsibility in this way, at a moment when he himself was in captivity. At the time, Jerusalem was surrounded by hostile armies. The city was already as good as lost, ravaged by famine and plague. The land owned by Jeremiah's family lay within the area that had already fallen to the enemy.

At such a moment, the word of the Lord came to Jeremiah:

> *'Hanamel son of Shallum your uncle is going to come to*
> *you and say, "Buy my field at Anathoth, because as*
> *nearest relative it is your right and duty to buy it."'*
>
> (Jeremiah 32:6)

His relative came with this offer at a moment when no-one in Jerusalem or in Anathoth had any thought of buying houses or land. What awaited them all was seventy years of captivity in Babylon, and no-one knew this better than Jeremiah. It was a time of desperate need, and the people had lost their hope for the future. By his actions, Jeremiah was able to show them that he believed that his family would ultimately return from Babylon, and that there was a future for them in the Land.

Jeremiah took up his role as kinsman-redeemer, and carried out an act of faith that showed he was the bearer of hope for his family's continued existence. He obeyed the Lord's instructions and invested for the future times of restoration, by buying the field and signing the deed of purchase in the presence of witnesses in the courtyard of the guard.

The Lord asked Jeremiah, *'Is anything too hard for me?'* (Jeremiah 32:27). He was enabled to lift his eyes above and beyond the destruction of Jerusalem and the captivity of her people, and to prophesy that the time was coming when the Lord would regather, restore and do good to his people, and then they would buy fields and write and seal the deeds of purchase (Jeremiah 32:36–44). In the description of those who returned to the land from the captivity in Babylon, we find that 128 men from Anathoth returned (Ezra 2:23).

Awakening the kinsman-redeemer's sense of responsibility

The book of Ruth tells us how this can be done. Naomi's family had fallen into poverty: it was exactly the right time for the kinsman-redeemer to intervene. But Boaz' sense of responsibility was not yet awakened. Naomi's family had almost been wiped out; in a time of famine they had abandoned their family land and had emigrated. Naomi's husband and her two sons had all died, and she was left with only her two daughters-in-law. The family was on the point of dying out. The kinsman-redeemer was the only remaining hope for restoring the family into life and giving them a future. Naomi means 'my delight', but she said to the women in Bethlehem, *'Call me Mara* (bitter)*'* (Ruth 1:20).

Naomi's daughter-in-law Ruth went and gleaned the left-over grains of barley in Boaz' fields, behind his team of harvesters. Following her mother's instructions, she went to Boaz at night and lay down at his feet. When he awoke, she challenged him. Would he recognize his relative who was in need? *'I am your servant Ruth', she said, 'Spread the corner of your garment over me, since you are a kinsman-redeemer.'* And Boaz replied saying that he was indeed her near of kin, but *'there is a kinsman-redeemer nearer than I'* (Ruth 3:9, 12).

So Boaz went to the town gate where the elders of the town were assembled, took up his responsibility, redeemed the family inheritance and saved Naomi's family from being wiped out. He took Ruth as his wife, and by that action he revived the name of his dead relative. He also, before the elders, took off his sandal as a sign that he had redeemed Naomi's lost family land.

> *'Now in earlier times in Israel, for the redemption and transfer of property to become final, one party took off his sandal and gave it to the other. This was the means of legalizing transactions in Israel.'*   (Ruth 4:7)

It is believed that this customary action was based on the promise in Deuteronomy 11:24: *'Every place where you set your foot will be yours,'* a promise given when God's people were about to go in and possess the promised land. When a purchase deed was written in the presence of the elders, it was not easy to use the foot as a sign of taking possession of the land from the enemy; so as a token of this taking of possession, one party took off his shoe and placed it on the purchase deed. By this means, the prophetic evidence was given: a lost inheritance was thus given back to the original owning family.

I take responsibility for my family and relatives

I will now speak to you as the nearest responsible relative. You have a calling to take the initiative in saving your family and bringing them into the kingdom of God. You can pray like this:

> 'Father in heaven, you are witness that I take responsibility for my family and all my relatives. Through the blessing promised to Abraham, my family will be restored and will have an inheritance in God's kingdom. Praised be the Lord, who has today ensured that a responsible relative is not lacking in my family. By your power, I can be a bringer of consolation, a supporter, a channel of blessing for my family. In Jesus' name, I now begin a ministry of restoration for families in my nation. Families blessed in this way will lead to the salvation of the people.'

A promise for those who take responsibility for their family

Joel's prophecy about the pouring-out of the Spirit in the last days (Joel 2:28) is addressed to those who take responsibility for the family. It is given to three generations: it is to your sons and daughters, and to your old men; yet it is not given directly to these, but to the responsible ones in the middle generation. Peter explained on the day of Pentecost:

111

> *'The promise is for you and your children and for all who are far off – for all whom the Lord our God will call.'* (Acts 2:39)

Who are the ones who are far off? They are the generations still to come.

I have given you the land: go and take possession of it

> *'See, the Lord your God has given you the land. Go up and take possession of it as the Lord, the God of your fathers, told you. Do not be afraid; do not be discouraged.'* (Deuteronomy 1:21)

The promised land was possessed in six different ways. The family constituted an important part of the strategy for taking possession of the land. The promised land was divided into inheritance portions which were allotted according to tribes and families.

1. *Abraham took possession of the land by faith*

Abraham never took possession of any of the land personally; he wandered about in the land and took possession of it by faith. We follow in the footsteps of Abraham, and walk in faith, when we go on prayer walks, Jesus marches or prayer journeys, all different expressions for taking the land in a journey of faith.

2. *Jacob took possession of the land with his family*

The ups and downs of the family unity or disunity determined whether they kept a foothold in the land, or lost ground.

When Jacob parted from his father-in-law Laban and crossed the border into the land with his family, he set up a heap of stones on the boundary as a witness and marker of the covenant between them, namely that no-one in the family should pass this marker with evil intent. It was also a witness of Jacob's promise that he would not ill-treat Laban's daughters (Genesis 31:45–55).

Jacob's first step on entering the promised land was to be reconciled with his brother Esau, whom he had deceived in taking away his right as firstborn son. Genesis 33 describes their meeting. On the way, as he approached his brother, Jacob bowed down to the ground seven times. Then they embraced and wept, and Jacob saw in his brother the image of God:

> *'For to see your face is like seeing the face of God, now that you have received me favourably.'*
>
> (Genesis 33:10)

Jacob and his family lost their foothold in the land, because the brothers could not maintain their unity in love. Jealousy against Joseph grew among the brothers, until at last they sold him as a slave into Egypt and lied to their father about what had happened to him. The family intrigues led to their losing the promised land and then, because of famine, leaving the land.

God's kingdom is restored in a nation through families that have been healed and blessed, and can hold together in reconciliation with each other. Preparation for the kingdom of Antichrist, on the other hand, is through family conflicts and divorces.

3. *Joshua and his army took possession of the land by military strength*

Joshua conquered the land by military power, but his army marched in family formation. The twelve tribes were divided up by clans and families, and this determined their order of marching. When they set out and lifted up the ark, they proclaimed: *'Rise up, O Lord! May your enemies be scattered; may your foes flee before you.'* And when the ark was set down and they encamped, they proclaimed: *'Return, O Lord, to the countless thousands of Israel'*

(Numbers 10:35–36), meaning, come back with your presence over the clans and families.

Protection in prayer warfare has much to do with unity in families. We battle against a defeated enemy, whose only tactics consist in exploiting weaknesses in our lives or in our families.

> *'Every kingdom divided against itself will be ruined, and every city or household divided against itself will not stand.'* (Matthew 12:25)

4. David and Solomon took possession of the land as rulers

5. Ezra and Nehemiah took possession of the land as part of a process of restoration

They returned from the captivity to a land lying in ruins, and they took possession of it by rebuilding the altar, the temple, the city of Jerusalem and its walls.

6. The heroes who freed the land from occupation

One family of heroes, Mattathias and his sons the Maccabee brothers, refused to compromise their faith during the persecution that was carried on under Antiochus Epiphanes. They defeated a numerically superior enemy army and freed Israel from occupation.

God's purpose is to save individuals and to bless families. Blessing, in God's Word, is closely connected with the family. God promised that through Abraham's descendants, he would bless all the families of the earth. The stream of blessing is dependent on the existence of loving family relationships in which the family can pray together.

> *'"Cursed is the man who dishonours his father or his mother." Then all the people shall say, "Amen!"'* (Deuteronomy 27:16)

One of God's names is 'the God of Abraham, Isaac and Jacob', which implies that God manifests himself as the God of three generations. He is my God, my father's God and my grandfather's God. He is your grandmother's God, your mother's God and your own God. Abraham was given the promise that in his seed, all the families on earth would be blessed. God's blessing is in its highest expression a blessing on the family. Satan knows this very well, so to hinder the blessing he attacks the relationship between the generations and thus tries to prevent the blessing from spreading further.

The blessing flows in channels

The blessing also needs channels to flow in. It flows in families, and becomes deeper and stronger as it is reproduced down the generations. In Satanic sects there are priest-families, who speak of 'gathering the power' or 'building up the power'. This is done by families serving Satan through several generations. It is considered particularly powerful when three successive generations have worshipped Satan, and it is thought a major catastrophe if any of the family comes to faith in Jesus and breaks the continuity of the family power-line. The evil one can never bring about anything other than a counterfeit; it is God who holds the original. The prototype is Abraham, Isaac and Jacob, the three generations who made up an unbroken line of blessing as each father blessed his son and passed on what he himself had received from God.

Your descendants will take possession of the cities of their enemies

Abraham was given a specially strong promise of blessing after he had showed his obedience to God through his willingness to sacrifice his son Isaac:

> *'I will surely bless you and make your descendants as numerous as the stars in the sky and as the sand on the seashore. Your descendants will take possession of the cities of their enemies.'* (Genesis 22:17)

The marching order of the people of Israel was a family formation: they walked tribe by tribe. Using this formation, they would win victories over their enemies. This is the thinking that lies behind Psalm 127:

> *'Like arrows in the hands of a warrior are sons born in one's youth. Blessed is the man whose quiver is full of them. They will not be put to shame when they contend with their enemies in the gate.'* (Psalm 127:4–5)

When Isaiah was going to meet king Ahaz, the Lord told him to take his son with him (Isaiah 7:3). Later on, Isaiah was able to say, *'Here am I, and the children that the Lord has given me. We are signs and symbols in Israel'* (Isaiah 8:18).

The promise given to those who agree together in prayer applies particularly to the family:

> *'If two of you on earth agree about anything you ask for, it will be done for you by my Father in heaven.'* (Matthew 18:19)

Who is the one we are to agree with? If husband and wife agree, if father and son agree, if mother and daughter agree, if brother and sister agree; all these are important. When we are praying about some matter that concerns the family economy, it is most important for husband and wife to agree in prayer, to have faith for the same object. Christian businessmen testify about answers to prayer when husband and wife hear the same things from the Lord and are able to pray together.

In the battle against occult powers that are to be found in a demonized society, it can be of great significance if

116

father and son can battle together. The result can be an open field of action for powers of blessing, which are much stronger than powers of cursing. This is how we can bring our argument into the city gate, where we meet the enemy face to face. Compare this with the promise that Jesus gave to Peter:

> *'On this rock I will build my church, and the gates of Hades will not overcome it.'*   (Matthew 16:18)

We fight against the attack that comes from the gates of the kingdom of darkness. Remember God's promise to Abraham, *'Your descendants will take possession of the cities of their enemies'* (Genesis 22:17). The Lord gives us keys to our overcoming the kingdom of Antichrist and its attempts to usurp power.

Sent with God's message: Return home to your father

When I was on my way out to the Philippines five years ago, I stayed a few days at a prayer conference in Frankfurt. There was a group of intercessors there who prayed for me in connection with my forthcoming journey to the Philippines, and one of the group gave me a prophetic task to carry out. He prophesied: 'The Lord is sending you to bear a message of greeting to a young man in Manila. Say to him that he is to return to his father. His father has sent him a message asking him to come back home. In order that he will know that the message is for him personally, you are to describe the father. The father is a fisherman who lives in a fishing village by the sea. He has a very wrinkled face and has several teeth missing.'

My first meeting in Manila took place one evening when it was raining very heavily, making such a noise on the corrugated iron roof of the church that there were times during the meeting when it was difficult for me to make myself understood. Now Manila is a city of eight million

117

inhabitants, and there was I with a message from God for one of them. So I shared the message of greeting straight away. There was a young man writing on a piece of paper as I spoke: 'This missionary speaks about me': a woman sitting next to him could see what the young man had written. Afterwards he came to the front and told us that his father was a fisherman who lived in a fishing village by the sea; he had a very wrinkled face and had several teeth missing. When the young man was four years old, his father had left home, his parents had split up and for all the years since then, his father had never heard from him. But twenty years later, the father had returned to the mother and become reconciled to her, and they had remarried. Now, the father had written to the son telling him to come home; but the son had refused to go. Because the father had never bothered with the son for all those years, the son was bitter. The young man and I prayed together, and during our conversation the young man reached a decision that he would return to his father; he was willing to be reconciled with him. This incident taught me how important such a message is to the Lord. The Lord was concerned to send me from the other end of the world with a message for a young man that he should return to his father.

Five years later, I again visited Mandaluyong in the Manila area. Ever since my previous visit, the pastors in the area had been meeting regularly to pray for their town. This had resulted in the mayor of the town and his wife being saved, and they too came to the pastors' prayer meetings. After one of these morning prayer meetings, I was invited to breakfast at the home of the mayor, together with a group of pastors. As I sat at breakfast with the mayor, I asked Pastor Jun Ramirez what had happened to the young man to whom I had brought the message of greeting five years earlier, saying that he should be reconciled with his father. Pastor Jun called him. He was one of the pastors, sitting at the other end of the table. He told me how he had returned to the village in obedience to the message, and had been reconciled with his father. He had grown up under the care of his grandfather, and the father had never given him any fatherly care or attention while he was growing up. He told me that his father had recently contracted cancer, but he had travelled to the fishing village and prayed for his father, and his father had been healed. Now he was a pastor, and led worship among the pastors. It was an important grounding for his calling as a pastor and for the joy in his life, that he could forgive his father and that their hearts had been turned to one another.

God has an order, a method, whereby blessing is given to a person. *'Honour your father and your mother, so that you may live long in the land the Lord your God is giving you'* (Exodus 20:12). How do we take possession of the land? By honouring our parents. Those sins that cause a land to spew out its inhabitants are for the most part sins of the family.

When God blesses you, he does it via your parents. You need to have such an attitude that you can receive the blessing through your parents. The highest form of blessing from a parent to his child is that the parent lays his hands on his child and prays a prayer of blessing before he goes home to be with the Lord. To turn the hearts of the fathers to the children and the hearts of the children to the fathers is to create continuing circumstances in which the older generation will be able to bless the younger. When their hearts are locked against one another, they cannot pray together.

Before Jacob died, he called his sons and his grandchildren to him, in order to pass the blessing on to them. When his son Joseph came with his sons to visit his sick father, Jacob said, *'Bring them to me so that I may bless them'* (Genesis 48:9). He laid his hands on his two grandsons' heads, crossing his arms, and prayed:

> *'The Angel who has delivered me from all harm – may he bless these boys. May they be called by my name and*

> *the names of my fathers Abraham and Isaac, and may
> they increase greatly upon the earth.'* (Genesis 48:16)

Then Jacob continued pronouncing blessings upon one
son after another, but there were three of his sons that
he could not bless. He could not bless Reuben, because he
had defiled his father's bed, and he could not bless Simeon
and Levi because of their anger and violence. Instead of
blessing them, he said, *'Cursed be their anger, so fierce,
and their fury, so cruel!'* (Genesis 49:7). It is not enough to
have an old father who is willing to lay his hands on you
and give you a blessing from God. You need to walk in the
light with your father and to have all your sins forgiven
and dealt with, so that those sins will not stand in the way
when you come to receive your spiritual inheritance.

My own father developed cancer when I was seventeen
years old. Following an operation to remove a kidney, he
was told that the cancer had spread all over his body and
he had only two weeks to live. At that time I was not
living for God. I could not pray with my father and I
know that if my father had died then, I would have missed
the spiritual inheritance of blessing that he wanted to pass
on to me. My father prayed, like Hezekiah, to be allowed
fifteen more years to live, and God healed him from the
cancer. 'Give me fifteen more years, and I am willing to
serve you in the darkest places on the earth' was my
father's prayer. He served God in Istanbul, started a
church in Thessaloniki in Greece, and went on to Teheran
where he started another church.

When I was eighteen, I met with Jesus. At that time
there was a revival that touched many churches in
Sweden, a move of God that was characterized by a deep
conviction of sin and caused many to confess their sins.
For two hours I confessed my sins, so that nothing should
stand between God and me. From this experience I came
home and asked my father to forgive me for the pain I had
caused him. Earlier, when he was pastor of a church in
Stockholm, he called all of us children together and

appealed to us, saying, 'If you do not live for God, I cannot continue as pastor. A pastor must be able to manage his own family, and I must have my children living for God.' He wept, but my heart was unmoved. Accordingly he ceased to be in charge of a church. After my saving experience, I became reconciled with my father and had a deep spiritual fellowship with him, which lasted for the rest of his life.

When he was ready to go home to be with the Lord, I was on my way out to Pakistan as a missionary. My father had said to me, 'I know I am going to die, but I don't want you to stay in Sweden waiting for that to happen. You will make me much happier if you go on out to Pakistan and get on with your missionary work.' While my mother was laying the table for our farewell cup of coffee in the kitchen, my father was unable to get up from his bed, but he could see us from his bed, sitting round the table and drinking our coffee. Afterwards, I went in with my wife Lena and we knelt together beside his bed. My father laid his hands on Lena and me, and at the same moment the power of God came upon him. Earlier, he had been unable to rise, but now he stood up and prayed prophetically over our lives. Yes, I was to go out to Pakistan, but he began praying for my ministry in Iran, Sri Lanka, Thailand, Burma, Malaysia and even in Japan. He mentioned nation after nation. Just after he died, I was called to go to Iran for a month, and after that the doors opened into one country after another in the same order in which my father had prayed. The blessing from God that he passed on to me was to continue carrying out his calling to the nations, his calling to go to the places on earth where darkness reigned.

When my father and I were reconciled and our hearts were turned to one another, there arose a deep spiritual communication between us that was not dependent on words. We looked into each other's eyes and understood one another completely. My father was a pastor, a missionary and a Bible teacher who travelled around

Asia, and I was privileged to travel and minister with my father. When we ministered together in a meeting, if the meeting was not developing in the right way, we only needed to look at one another. One glance from Dad, and I knew what I had to do in order to turn things in the right direction. The communication between us was not something that needed many hours of discussion. How are we going to communicate with one another in heaven? We are going to be fully taken up with ministering and worshipping the Lord, day and night. When we meet one another we may have questions to ask. How have you been this last thousand years? Then we can look into one another's eyes, and without saying anything we can read everything that we need to know. We shall have communication with Jesus and with all the saints, face to face, and then we shall come to be fully recognized.

> *'Then we shall see face to face. Now I know in part; then I shall know fully, even as I am fully known.'*
>
> (1 Corinthians 13:12)

The Elijah ministry is to turn our hearts to one another within families, so that a deep communication, without words, can be restored, and so that the blessing can continue to flow on to the next generation.

Preparing for the coming of Jesus

> *'See, I will send you the prophet Elijah before that great and dreadful day of the Lord comes. He will turn the hearts of the fathers to their children, and the hearts of the children to their fathers; or else I will come and strike the land with a curse.'*   (Malachi 4:5–6)

The Lord's great and dreadful day is the period of transition between the two ages of time. It is not just the day of Jesus' coming; it is the period during which God will judge the world. I see it as the time of the Lord's spring-cleaning before the kingdom of God can be restored on the earth.

The Elijah ministry is also to save the land from being cursed. The Lord comes in holiness and wrath against sin. He sees the decline of family life in a nation, a decline so serious that his only course is to wipe out that nation so that it no longer exists on the map of the world. Striking the land with a curse means completely annihilating it. To have an Elijah ministry means understanding that if I can set right that which causes God's wrath over families, then the land can be saved from the curse. The spirit and power of Elijah is used by the Lord to turn our hearts in the right direction when they have long been turned away from one another.

The Hebrew word for restoration is used in the expression 'turning the hearts to the children'. It means bringing back from, for example, captivity. Restoration is returning home to the place where we once were. Family relationships will be restored through lost sons and daughters coming home to their fathers. Fathers who have abandoned their families will return home. It needs the spirit and power of Elijah to bring this about.

Family reawakening and reuniting of families are signs of readiness for the coming of Jesus. John the Baptist was given an Elijah task in preparing the way for the first coming of Jesus; our task in preparing for his second coming is of the same nature.

> '*He will go on before the Lord, in the spirit and power of Elijah, to turn the hearts of the fathers to their children and the disobedient to the wisdom of the righteous – to make ready a people prepared for the Lord.*'
>
> (Luke 1:17)

In the last days, before the coming of Jesus, the pressure is going to increase from every direction. The pressure from the evil one is increasing, but so is the pressure of God's glory. The Lord is going to give us a heightened

123

wisdom and a greater anointing, but the question then is, are we going to manage to live under the harder pressure? Such conditions show up all our weaknesses, and those who do not survive under pressure often have weaknesses in their family relationships.

The family provides a protection for the individual, and a person who is not in a right relationship with his family lacks that protection. When the wrath of God is poured out over the earth, there comes a warning to take shelter.

> *'Go, my people, enter your rooms and shut the doors behind you; hide yourselves for a little while until his wrath has passed by.'* (Isaiah 26:20)

When God's wrath was poured out on Egypt, the families of the Israelites went into their houses. The head of each family slaughtered a lamb and put some of the blood on the door-frame, so that the angel of death passed by that home.

I have often read out those words from Malachi in meetings of young people where the situation today is such that half of those present come from broken homes. Children have suffered much from their parents' broken marriages. They are bitter towards their father who has left and never asked after them, and against their mother who has brought her new boyfriend into the home, so that the home is no longer a protected place for teenage girls, as the mother's boyfriend cannot leave them alone.

When I asked, 'Which of you is unable to pray with your father?' half of the young people put up their hands. It did not depend only on the father not being a Christian. Many had a father who was a believer, but for various reasons they could not pray with him.

I have heard many young people say; I hate my father. I curse my father. I have used black magic against my father. I have not spoken to my mother for ten years. I am never going to marry because I am so disappointed with my parents' marriage break-up. All the intercessors who are present give themselves to ministering to young people such as these, far into the night in counselling, talking and prayer.

Family prayer meetings

I have a good friend who is an American Jew. His mother was the only one in his family who believed in Jesus as Messiah. For thirty years she prayed for her family. Then when the family gathered at her funeral, the Lord began to work among them. Since then, one after another of my friend's relatives have come to the Lord, when the relatives have met at family gatherings such as weddings, celebrations and funerals. Today, about 60 out of 100 relations are believers in Jesus as their Messiah.

When Messianic Jews meet in the towns of Israel, they often meet in homes. Prayer is by families. I met an old Russian Jewish lady there who had been through the Holocaust and had seen most of her family wiped out in Poland. Now she had come to Israel with her sons and their families, and the sons' families had come to faith in Jesus Christ. We prayed together with these families, and as we prayed, I had the prophetic words of Zechariah in my mind:

> *'And I will pour out on the house of David and the inhabitants of Jerusalem a spirit of grace and supplication. They will look on me, the one they have pierced, and they will mourn for him ... On that day the weeping in Jerusalem will be great ... The land will mourn, each clan by itself ... the clan of the house of David and their wives ... and all the rest of the clans and their wives.'*   (Zechariah 12:10–14)

I witnessed the very beginning of a kingdom work of God. If our own people will enter into the kingdom of God and receive Jesus as Messiah and as king, it will happen in the same way. People become well prepared for the coming of Jesus when the hearts of the members of a family are turned towards, and are open to, one another.

Take the initiative in gathering the family together

The kingdom of Antichrist has made itself ready by attacks against the family and against family harmony. In the kingdom of Antichrist a personal number is of greater significance than a family surname. The culture in which unmarried couples live together, marriages break up, and the industrial society causes the population to move about from place to place, has been severely damaging to family harmony; as has pornography, and unbelief.

The family has been badly knocked about and split apart. But when Satan has done his worst to bring about the destruction of God's plans, that is when we shall seek recompense and restoration. I am speaking to you as kinsman-redeemer, as the nearest responsible relative. This is the word of the Lord that comes to you. You are to take the initiative in bringing your family into unity, in gathering your family together. If your brother or sister has fallen into poverty, that is a call to you to take the responsibility for them. The Spirit of God takes pleasure in such initiatives in the present times.

Chapter 6

The Second Fall of Man and the Flood

The second Fall of man is briefly described in the Bible:

> *'When men began to increase in number on the earth
> and daughters were born to them, the sons of God saw
> that the daughters of men were beautiful, and they
> married any of them they chose ... The Nephilim were
> on the earth in those days – and also afterwards – when
> the sons of God went to the daughters of men and had
> children by them. They were the heroes of old, men of
> renown.'* (Genesis 6:1–2, 4)

The fallen angels invaded the earth. Before that time,
evil on earth was only an expression of the evil nature of
fallen man; but it was, until then, not demonized, nor
organized and led by fallen angels. Now, however, the
earth was invaded by organized, demonized evil, which
controlled and exploited through its knowledge of the
weaknesses of mankind.

Sin against the created order

The second Fall of man brought in sin against the order of
things that God had created. The angels abandoned their
natural place in creation. Mankind exchanged natural
sexual relations for unnatural ones. God had created all

things according to their kinds, and within each kind could be found God's own plan for their propagation. It was not within his plan for angels to have sexual relations with mankind. A devilish plan was set in motion to corrupt what God had created.

God was the great designer who passed on some of his own character and personality in everything he created. God wanted to be recognized through his eternal power and divine glory in everything he brought into being. So there is a unique wisdom, devised by God himself, in every combination of colours, in every form, in every movement and purpose in his creation of people, animals, birds, plants, rocks and crystals. In all that he made, he concealed a part of his divine glory and praise, so that anyone sincerely seeking him would be able to praise and thank him. Before the second Fall, every child had been born in the image of God. Now, however, grotesque bastard offspring, half fallen angels and half men, came into the world. These progeny of fallen angels were called Nephilim, a race of giants, and were the first beings who did not have the forms that God had designed. Their designers were Satan and the fallen angels.

A quotation from the book of Enoch about the second Fall of man

The sin of the fallen angels with the daughters of men is described in the book of Enoch, the book that is quoted in the letter of Jude. It is a source that can be called in question. You can read more about the book at the end of this chapter.

'And the angels, the children of the heaven, saw and lusted after them, and said to one another: "Come, let us choose us wives from among the children of men and beget us children." And Semjaza, who was their leader, said unto them: "I fear ye will not indeed agree to do this deed, and I alone shall have to pay the penalty of a great sin." And they all answered him and said: "Let us all swear an oath, and all bind ourselves by mutual imprecations not to abandon this plan but to do this thing." Then sware they all together and bound themselves by mutual imprecations upon it. And they were in all two hundred; who descended in the days of Jared on the summit of Mount Hermon, and they called it Mount Hermon, because they had sworn and bound themselves by mutual imprecations upon it . . .

'And all the others together with them took unto themselves wives . . . and they taught them charms and enchantments, and the cutting of roots, and made them acquainted with plants. And they became pregnant, and they bare great giants . . . who consumed all the acquisitions of men. And when men could no longer sustain them, the giants turned against them and devoured mankind. And they began to sin against birds, and beasts, and reptiles, and fish, and to devour one another's flesh, and drink the blood. Then the earth laid accusation against the lawless ones.

'And Azazel taught men to make swords, and knives, and shields, and breastplates, and made known to them the metals of the earth, and the art of working them . . . And there arose much godlessness, and they committed fornication, and they were led astray, and became corrupt in all their ways. Semjaza taught enchantments, and root-cuttings, Armaros the resolving of enchantments, Baraqijal taught astrology, Kokabel the constellations, Ezeqeel the knowledge of the clouds . . . and Sariel the course of the moon. And as men perished, they cried, and their cry went up to heaven.'   (1 Enoch 6:2–8:4) [1]

The fallen angels' invasion of the earth was begun by their entering into a covenant whereby they agreed to sin and not to abandon one another. We can see, even as early as this, the foundations being laid for the type of covenant that the Freemasons and other secret mystery societies continued through the centuries. Is this the *'secret power of lawlessness'* (2 Thessalonians 2:7) that has been in operation all through history? Such covenants are entered into by the pronouncing of a common curse against those who break them.

An attempt to frustrate God's plan of salvation

This invasion of fallen angels was an attempt by Satan to corrupt the human race and turn it into something quite different from what God had intended. If God had not put a stop to this invasion, it could have frustrated God's entire plan for redeeming mankind. How could Jesus have come to save people if they had no longer been people of the kind that God intended? Perhaps it was also a satanic attempt to anticipate the incarnation, the wonderful act of God in which he became a man. The fallen angels wanted to be incarnated in human bodies.

The second Fall of man had a great influence on all who lived before the Flood.

> *'Now the earth was corrupt in God's sight and was full of violence. God saw how corrupt the earth had become, for all the people on earth had corrupted their ways.'*
> (Genesis 6:11–12)

The earth and all mankind were together corrupted; this means that they were out of God's original created order. They were so corrupted that God was grieved; his heart was full of pain that he had created man, and he decided to put an end to them by sending a great flood.

The time of Jesus' coming will be as it was in the time of Noah. We cannot rule out the possibility that Satan will make further attempts to frustrate God's plan of salvation by, for example, genetic engineering, a new way of corrupting the generations of mankind. In theory, it will be possible to produce a new kind of being, a cross between a man and an animal. There is no salvation for such beings. God will severely judge such interference with the created order, because it frustrates his plan for the salvation of mankind.

False gods that are half animal and half man

In the book of Enoch, it says that the fallen angels had sexual relations with birds and animals. In cultures all over the world where false gods are honoured, it is quite usual to see beings that are half man and half fish, or half lion and half man. African preachers say that these gods that are half animal and half man are always spirits of impurity. We have the mermaid in our Nordic culture, and the Sphinx in Egypt. Where did these fantastic offspring originate? Such demonically inspired fantasies are derived from the prototypes conceived in the second Fall of man. It seems likely that the present-day custom of adorning culture centres and banks with statues or reliefs is derived from the same source. If our eyes are opened to this, we shall be astonished to see what a large number of types of being have been depicted by artists down the ages, whose originals lie in sources other than God's creation. Several of the gods of Babylon were crosses between animals and men, and the Nimrod gates, in all the cities founded by Nimrod, were guarded by formidable creatures carved in stone and representing a combination of animal and man.

Sins against nature

Homosexuality and lesbianism are sins against nature, sins against the order of creation of the same character as the second Fall of man. In the letter of Jude, there is a comparison between the second Fall and homosexuality. Jude first speaks of the fallen angels before the Flood:

> *'The angels who did not keep their positions of author-*
> *ity but abandoned their own home – these he has kept in*
> *darkness, bound with everlasting chains for judgment*
> *on the great Day.'* (Jude 6)

Then he says:

> *'In a similar way, Sodom and Gomorrah and the*
> *surrounding towns gave themselves up to sexual*
> *immorality and perversion. They serve as an example*
> *of those who suffer the punishment of eternal fire.'*
> (Jude 7)

Homosexuality and lesbianism are against God's created order and his plan of salvation. Many of God's promises of salvation are addressed to families and generations of families. The blessing of Abraham was given for all the families of the earth. Homosexual marriage is a family formation that stands outside this promise to Abraham.

God's judgments on the second Fall of man

According to the book of Enoch, the giants, after they died, became demonic powers, spiritual powers of evil – principalities and mighty ones.

> 'As for the spirits of heaven, in heaven shall be their dwelling, but as for the spirits of earth which were born upon the earth, on the earth shall be their dwelling. And the spirits of the giants afflict, oppress, destroy, attack, do battle, and work destruction on the earth, and cause trouble: they take no food, but nevertheless hunger and thirst, and cause offences. And these spirits shall rise up against the children of men and against the women, because they have proceeded from them.

'From the days of the slaughter and destruction and death of the giants, from the souls of whose flesh the spirits, having gone forth, shall destroy without incurring judgment – thus shall they destroy until the day of the consummation, the great judgment in which the age shall be consummated over the Watchers and the godless, yea, shall be wholly consummated ... You have been in heaven, but all the mysteries had not yet been revealed to you, and you knew worthless ones, and these in the hardness of your hearts you have made known to the women, and through these mysteries women and men work much evil on earth.'   (1 Enoch 15:10–16:3)

Restoration in connection with the second Fall of man

Before the Flood, there were two men of God who found grace before the Lord, and stood out as overcomers in an evil age. Both of them are examples for us who live in the age before the return of Jesus. They are Enoch and Noah. Both of them have provided, through their lives, a message for us intercessors.

Enoch lived through the second Fall of man

Enoch experienced the second Fall; he lived during the period before God's punishment was carried out through the Flood. Enoch is mentioned three times in the Bible: he was the seventh from Adam; he was one of the heroes of faith in Hebrews 11; and in Jude's letter, his prophecy is quoted.

Enoch's walk with God ended as God took him away without his needing to die. Enoch and Elijah each went through an experience very like the rapture that will take place when Jesus comes. Enoch is a model for those who live in the period before the coming of Jesus. Walking with

God transformed Enoch, and when God took him into heaven it was the climax of that transformation.

> *'Enoch walked with God 300 years ... Enoch walked with God; then he was no more, because God took him away.'* (Genesis 5:22, 24)

Enoch's long life was summarized in this: that he had walked with God. That means that he had walked conscious of God's presence. It was as if he could see the Invisible by his side. God and Enoch had made an agreement that they should walk together, because two cannot walk the same way unless they have come into agreement. Now, God has made a new agreement with those who want to walk with him. This agreement is built on the grace that is offered in and through Jesus' atonement.

In our own time, when a person's life is being summarized or when a speaker is being introduced, it often appears as a kind of activity report. We hear what the person has achieved, how many books he has written, what countries he has visited. The account of Enoch's life is quite different from this; it is the exact opposite of an activity report. He is remembered as a man who walked with God and was completely taken up with being in fellowship with God, in an evil age.

Enoch's walk with God was a restoration of the fellowship that Adam and Eve had with God in the garden of Eden:

> *'Then the man and his wife heard the sound of the Lord God as he was walking in the garden in the cool of the day, and they hid from the Lord God among the trees of the garden.'* (Genesis 3:8)

The Fall put an end to these evening walks in the garden; but God longed to resume such walks, if there was someone he could have for company. In Enoch he found his response.

Enoch's walking with God transformed him. As we walk with God, we grow to be like him; we are transformed into his image. Enoch became more and more restored into the image of God, the image that God had created for him in the beginning. He walked in preparation for the final transformation, his rapture. When he disappeared, he was missed. They searched for him; he left an emptiness behind him.

Once in a prayer meeting held in our home, I asked the question, 'When you hear the expression "walking with God", what do you associate it with in your own life?' Most of those present told us about their feelings of walking with God directly after their conversion experience.

I remember walking home after my own conversion. I had confessed my sins for some hours in the presence of the one who had led me to Christ. When I had finished, he read out from the Bible, *'If we confess our sins, he is faithful and just and will forgive us our sins and purify us from all unrighteousness'* (1 John 1:9). I had confessed my sins and I knew that I was forgiven. Now I began to walk in the light, as I had fellowship with Jesus. Then God's presence came through to me like a light. On the way home, I was sitting in a tram. I had borrowed a pocket Bible, and I read: *'Blessed are the pure in heart, for they will see God.'* 'Hallelujah!' I shouted out loud in the tram, 'I can feel the presence of God!' And I went home with a wonderful consciousness of God's presence.

The feeling of walking with God has since come to me after I have been together with people of God who live close to the Lord. When I was still young, I spent a week in the company of a man who was being used by God to bring revival. He lived in prayer and in God's presence. For a week after he left, I was surrounded by the presence of God. It was so easy to pray and to have fellowship with him. I remember walking in a wood outside a town in Sweden. It was just as if the Lord was walking beside me on that woodland path. Together, we took delight in his creation. The consciousness of his presence was so strong, although not visible. In my innermost being, I was conversing with him. I asked questions; I received answers and explanations. That walk caused a complete change of course in my life.

There is an unbroken, natural walk with the Lord, conditional only on our walking in the light, enlightened through and through with his holiness. It is walking in a constant humble dependence on his grace.

When a high-jumper has knocked down the crossbar, he has to go back and make a fresh attempt. When the Swedish Parliament decided in 1994 to allow homosexual marriages, it was like knocking down the crossbar. We had fought against it, but we had not succeeded. One of our elders said afterwards, 'Now we have to find our identity in Enoch's close walk with the Lord.' Now I am walking back for a fresh attempt, but this time I am not going to jump; my new approach will be a renewal of walking in fellowship with God. After that vote in the Parliament on 7th June 1994, I feel as if I were a foreigner in Sweden. The empty space that is left will be filled up by the feeling of being at home in God's presence, walking closely with the Lord.

When the Lord walks in a close relationship with his intimate friend, he says to him, 'Come now, Enoch, I'll make it all clear to you. I've got something I want to show you. I'm going to let you know what is going to happen in the future, so that you get a right perspective. I'm going to show you what will happen in the future to the saints, and also what will happen to the ungodly and the rebellious.' Enoch knew that the Lord would come with his saints to judge sinners. According to the book of Enoch, even though he was the seventh from Adam, he knew about Mount Zion, the Mount of Olives and the Valley of Jehoshaphat; and that the Son of Man was going to return. He knew beforehand what people in the End Time would do with their unborn children – that they would abort them and bar themselves from having offspring. All this resulted from Enoch's walking with the Lord.

Once, before a long period of fasting and isolation, I prayed: Lord, please show me what there is in my life that disturbs my intimate, continuous walk with you, and I will confess and repent. What is blocking me from walking in your company, God, as Enoch did? Stress and hurry cause blockages. I look at the clock in the middle of my time of fellowship with God, and I think, Now we have been together for 45 minutes, and that will be enough, because I have other things to do. My Father in heaven never looks at the clock: he lives in eternity. Materialism and worldliness also cause a blockage; activity can disturb my walk with the Lord. I have too little persistence in prayer; suddenly my thoughts turn to how the Lord is going to bless what I shall be doing next month. I want to talk to him about my forthcoming activities, and he wants to communicate with me about himself. I know that I have to change my life-style and to be more particular about only doing those things that allow him to walk with me and share with me.

Enoch was drawn to a deeper walk with God because he experienced a growing sense of being a foreigner in the community that was heading towards the Flood. Walking with God in the last days begins with a decision we are compelled to make. When our community steps outside the boundaries and permits something that God has set a boundary against, then we are taken into the kingdom of Antichrist. We cannot walk with it any longer; we have to distance ourselves from it; we have to decide to depart from it. This departure means that we become more alienated from our community, which we loved but has now become anti-Christian. Then comes the invitation:

> 'Let us, then, go to him outside the camp, bearing the disgrace he bore. For here we do not have an enduring city, but we are looking for the city that is to come.'
>
> (Hebrews 13:13–14)

Enoch was number two in the long series of heroes of

faith who are set out for us as a *'great cloud of witnesses'* and as patterns for us to follow as we fight on with perseverance. He became a hero of faith by walking with God in an evil age.

> *'By faith Enoch was taken from this life, so that he did not experience death; he could not be found, because God had taken him away. For before he was taken, he was commended* [NKJV: *he had this testimony*] *as one who pleased God. And without faith it is impossible to please God, because anyone who comes to him must believe that he exists and that he rewards those who earnestly seek him.'* (Hebrews 11:5–6)

Enoch received a testimony from God, as did some of the other heroes mentioned in this chapter. It was an encouragement, a confirmation and a sign to him that he had found grace with God. Jesus received a testimony of this kind: for him, it was a voice heard from heaven saying, *'You are my Son, whom I love; with you I am well pleased'* (Luke 3:22). Abel was given evidence that his sacrifice had been accepted by God. Those who overcome in the End Time will have a testimony from Jesus, and Jesus' testimony is the spirit of prophecy (Revelation 19:10). Jesus speaks to them and through them, and this helps them to be set in the right direction in the midst of an evil age. We know that Enoch prophesied (Jude 14): God gave him the confidence to hear from him concerning the future. This could have been a testimony that he had found grace in the eyes of God.

Enoch believed that God exists and that he rewards those who seek him; he was rewarded for having walked with God for three hundred years. He was taken up to heaven and did not experience death. To believe that God is a rewarder implies belief in a God who reigns in his creation and makes moral decisions. He rewards the good and punishes the evil. If we believe in a God who judges, then we believe in a God who rewards those who are his.

The atheists believe in a random universe, the Muslims believe in fate, the Hindus believe in Karma; but we believe that it is worth while to seek God and to live in obedience to his Word.

Enoch is known from the Bible as one who prophesied judgment on the ungodly. Here is a quotation from his book:

> 'I understood as I saw, but not for this generation, but for a remote one which is for to come. Concerning the elect I said, and took up my parable concerning them: The Holy Great One will come forth from his dwelling, and the eternal God will tread upon the earth, even on Mount Sinai . . . and appear in the strength of his might from the heaven of heavens. And all shall be smitten with fear, and the Watchers shall quake, and great fear and trembling shall seize them unto the ends of the earth. And the high mountains shall be shaken, and the high hills shall be made low, and shall melt like wax before the flame.
>
> 'And the earth shall be . . . rent in sunder, and all that is upon the earth shall perish, and there shall be a judgment upon all men. But with the righteous he will make peace, and will protect the elect, and mercy shall be upon them. And they shall belong to God, and they shall be prospered, and they shall . . . be blessed . . . And light shall appear unto them . . .
>
> 'And behold! He cometh with ten thousands of his holy ones to execute judgment upon all, and to destroy . . . the ungodly: and to convict all flesh of all the works of their ungodliness which they have ungodly committed . . . against him.'
>
> (1 Enoch 1:2–9)

The next quotation comes from the epilogue to the Book of Enoch:

'For some of them are written and inscribed above in the heaven, in order that the angels may read them and know that which shall befall the sinners, and the spirits of the humble, and of those who have afflicted their bodies, and been recompensed by God; and of those who have been put to shame by wicked men: who love God and loved neither gold nor silver nor any of the good things which are in the world, but gave over their bodies to torture. Who, since they came into being, longed not after earthly food, but regarded eveything as a passing breath, and lived accordingly, and the Lord tried them much, and their spirits were found pure so that they should bless his name. And all the blessings destined for them I have recounted in the books. And he hath assigned them their recompense, because they have been found to be such as loved heaven more than their life in the world, and though they were trodden under foot of wicked men, and experienced abuse and reviling from them and were put to shame, yet they blessed me. And now I will summon the spirits of the good who belong to the generation of light, and I will transform those who were born in darkness, who in the flesh were not recompensed with such honour as their faithfulness deserved. And I will bring forth in shining light those who have loved my holy name, and I will seat each on the throne of his honour. And they shall be resplendent for times without number; for righteousness is the judgment of God; for to the faithful he will give faithfulness in the habitation of upright paths. And they shall see those who were born in darkness led into darkness, while the righteous shall be resplendent. And the sinners shall cry aloud and see them resplendent, and they indeed shall go where days and seasons are prescribed for them.'

(1 Enoch 108:7–15)

Enoch lived in a time very like ours. He is presented to

140

us as one of the heroes of faith, as one who is an example to us. The revelation in which he lived is to be ours also. We need to believe in a God who rewards and punishes. To believe in a God who judges is not popular among today's theologians, and most people do not even want to have a God who rewards those who seek him. But we cannot see restoration happening without God's righteous judgments, those judgments by means of which he teaches the peoples his righteousness.

Enoch was alone in his walk, but today the Lord wants to have a people who will walk with him:

> 'For we are the temple of the living God. As God has said: "I will live with them and walk among them, and I will be their God, and they will be my people."'
>
> (2 Corinthians 6:16)

Noah – the intercessor who comforted God

Noah, together with Job and Daniel, was counted among the intercessors who could save lives, even if he would not have been able to do so in Ezekiel's time (Ezekiel 14:14, 18). None of his prayers can be found written down in the Bible, yet he is an outstanding example for those who keep a close relationship with the Lord. He was one of the few who could comfort God because he existed.

He lived in the time when God was going through his greatest sorrow. God was grieved in his heart, and regretted that he had created mankind on the earth. He was grieving about the fallen angels having sexual relations with the women that he had made. He was grieving at seeing how his creation had become so corrupted that it was almost unrecognizable. In the depth of his grief, he said:

> 'I will wipe mankind, whom I have created, from the face of the earth – men and animals, and creatures that

> *move along the ground, and birds of the air – for I am*
> *grieved that I have made them.'* (Genesis 6:7)

When God is grieved, he needs to be comforted just as much as we do. In his need for comfort, God turned to Noah, and *'Noah found favour in the eyes of the Lord'* (Genesis 6:8). When God looked at Noah, he could begin once more his plans for the future of mankind. Noah was chosen from the beginning to be a comforter: he was given the name Noah by his father Lamech, because, he said, *'He will comfort us in the labour and painful toil of our hands caused by the ground the Lord has cursed'* (Genesis 5:29). Noah means comfort. Lamech needed someone to comfort him in his hard toil on ground that was under a curse. But Noah not only comforted his father; he also comforted God.

When we come to God on the happening of some terrible event, our tendency is to be most concerned with our own shocked feelings. 'Lord, do you realize how upset I am?' That is the immature way of approaching God, and God has to put up with it. But God is himself upset over evil, and he needs someone who understands how to comfort him. When we heard that the police in the town of Norrköping in Sweden had confiscated 2,000 films of child pornography, we were horrified to learn that the youngest child who had been involved in these perverted films was a four-year-old. Yet this was not the worst. It turned out that the youngest of all was a nine-months-old baby who was involved in perverted sexual acts. How did Father in heaven feel, when he had to be a witness to one of the children he had created being debased in this way? In a prayer meeting, it took us an hour before we could overcome our own feelings and identify ourselves with the Father's grief and pain. There was one man who prayed a prayer asking that we might comfort God. As he prayed, I saw in a vision the intercessor, sitting as a child on his father's knee. He stretched his hand up to his father's face and stroked his cheek lovingly to comfort him.

Those people of God who can feel just as God feels are the ones that find favour with God. These are the ones that God makes his friends, the people he wants to keep company with. Phinehas was one who felt exactly the same holy anger against sin as God felt in his heart. God was so surprised that someone could feel just as he felt, that his anger ceased. Phinehas turned God's anger away from Israel, by being zealous as God was zealous. Therefore God rewarded Phinehas by making a covenant of peace with him and with his descendants (Numbers 25:10–13). Prayer is far more than the words we say to God. One of the highest forms of prayer in a time of evil is to have the Father as a starting-point. What do you feel about this situation, Lord? How do you react, you whose eyes are too holy to see what you are seeing now? What can I do so that you can be comforted?

Restoration in relation to the second Fall of man

It was through the fall of Adam and Eve that we lost Paradise. After the garden of Eden there was a millennial kingdom. People lived very long lives, and the power of evil was not so great in the earth, until the fallen angels managed to organize themselves and invade our world. This demonic invasion, and the sin which followed upon it, deprived us of the millennial kingdom. The fall occurred by stages, and restoration will happen by going back the same way: step by step we will recapture the lost territory. By the grace and power of God we shall be restored to the position we once were in.

Prayer strategy for the battle in the End Time

On the same battlefield where we lost the battle against the invasion of the fallen angels, the prayer war for the restoration of the kingdom of peace must take place. Antichrist will look somewhat like one of the Roman emperors, who in turn were incarnations of the Greek gods.

God was grieved as he saw a whole generation taking up a perverted life-style. To comfort him, we must provide a young, holy, dedicated generation that will live all-out for the Lord.

> *'The Lord saw how great man's wickedness on the earth had become, and that every inclination of the thoughts of his heart was only evil all the time. The Lord was grieved that he had made man on the earth, and his heart was filled with pain.'*　　(Genesis 6:5–6)

A corrupt generation and a restored generation

What can persuade God to alter his decision that took away the millennial kingdom from us? God reached that decision with deep regret, grieved that he had created mankind. If God can be comforted at the point where the grief was caused, then he will decide to send Jesus back to the earth.

> *'No-one knows about that day or hour, not even the angels in heaven, nor the Son, but only the Father.'*　　(Matthew 24:36)

> *'It is not for you to know the times or dates the Father has set by his own authority.'*　　(Acts 1:7)

An intercessor has a desire for the Father to come so close that he by his prayers can influence the Father's decision. If you want to, you can pray that God will be comforted by a young, holy, dedicated generation whose highest wish is to serve and obey him. God's sorrow, his regret that he had created mankind, arose when he saw a whole generation perverted and living for sex, violence, magic and astrology, in rebellion against God's order of creation.

Since the Flood, God has seen one generation after another go by in which the majority have lived in rebellion against him. Jesus said of his own contemporaries, *'O unbelieving and perverse generation'* (Luke 9:41), and Peter, preaching on the day of Pentecost, said, *'Save yourselves from this corrupt generation'* (Acts 2:40).

If we want to hasten the coming of Jesus, and the Father's decision to send Jesus back to the earth, then we need to pray for the coming of that new, young, holy generation, more totally surrendered to Jesus than any earlier generation. Pray for that: a young generation who want to live wholly for the Lord.

In Revelation 14:1–5, we can read how John saw a vision of such a generation, when he prayed for the coming of Jesus: an offering of firstfruits to God in the End Time. John saw a crowd of people who were redeemed from the earth and purchased from among men. They were the Father's own special possession, and they were marked with the Father's name written on their foreheads. They sang before the throne, singing a new song that only they knew; no-one else could learn it. No lie was found in their mouths; they were blameless; and they had not defiled themselves with women, but had kept themselves pure.

The generation living before the Flood had defiled themselves through unnatural sex. The generation of those that fall for the propaganda of Antichrist believe his lies and give themselves over to delusions, because they have not allowed room for the truth. Because God has to bear the pain of seeing whole generations ruined and scarred by lies and sex, he will be comforted by seeing a holy generation who can stand the test in these two areas and come through undefiled.

There are no perfect men or women, none who are without temptation and sin. How then will it be possible for God to have this young, holy, dedicated generation? It will have to be through children, in their earliest years, giving their lives to Jesus and being brought up in purity by their parents. That is why I am saying that this chosen generation must begin with the very youngest children.

There are examples in the Bible of parents who were chosen to bring up their children to become God's Nazirites.

We must get rid of our preconceived notions of what God can do among children and young people. Children can, very early in their lives, undergo deep spiritual experiences that affect them for the rest of their lives.

> *'From the lips of children and infants you have ordained praise because of your enemies, to silence the foe and the avenger.'* (Psalm 8:2)

One sign of revival is that God does extraordinary things with children. When the Spirit fell on Azusa Street at the start of the Pentecostal revival, the first two people who were baptized in the Spirit were two children between ten and twelve years old.

Samuel is an example of how God had to pass by a whole generation of older people in order to find someone to whom he could entrust his heart. Eli's sons were priests, but they were wicked men who had no regard for the Lord. They slept with the women who served at the entrance to the Tent of Meeting (1 Samuel 2:12, 22). They taught the people to have contempt for the Lord's sacrifices, because they were corrupt priests.

So God spoke the things that he would normally say to responsible adults, to a young boy. He told the boy that he would judge the house of Eli, whose misdeeds could never be atoned for (1 Samuel 3:12–14).

For a long time, I have followed YWAM's work with 'King's Kids', through which children and young people are brought into praising and worshipping. The children are given a sound teaching that ensures they are brought to maturity, and they learn how to hear from the Lord and to use spiritual gifts. I have listened to children telling of what they have heard from the Lord, and it has impressed on me how God loves to entrust his secrets to children, and to use them, when he cannot communicate with the older people. In Stockholm, the leader of the King's Kids has been holding periodic Praise Parties, which have grown larger each time, when children and young people from different churches have come to worship Jesus, and afterwards have gone out evangelizing on the streets of Stockholm until midnight. David sang about a festival procession on its way into the sanctuary, with the singers in front and after them the musicians. And *'there is little Benjamin, their leader'* (Psalm 68:24–27, NKJV). The older folk from these churches have not yet gone as far as the children in singing, dancing and expressing their festival joy before the face of the Lord. The children have gone in front, showing the way.

In one church, I was teaching one Sunday morning about a young, holy generation. I was told that on the previous Sunday, a twelve-year-old girl had stood in the same pulpit and preached a message from God. The teaching I give these days has often confirmed in remarkable ways how others have heard the same things from the Lord. In prayer meetings, when I have suggested that we pray for a young, holy, consecrated generation, the Holy Spirit has come powerfully upon us. This is clearly an area of prayer that touches the Father's heart.

The last generation created to praise the Lord

'This will be written for the generation to come [this can mean the last generation], *that a people yet to be created may praise the Lord. For he looked down from the height of his sanctuary; from heaven the Lord viewed the earth, to hear the groaning of the prisoner, to loose those appointed to death* [Hebrew 'the sons of death'], *to declare the name of the Lord in Zion, and his praise in Jerusalem, when the peoples are gathered together, and the kingdoms, to serve the Lord.'*

(Psalm 102:18–22, NKJV)

It is believed that this Psalm was a prayer of King

Hezekiah. He was a young king, but he became very ill. He prayed to the Lord and wept before him, and the Lord healed him and added fifteen more years to his life (Isaiah 38:1–5). Hezekiah had been a young man appointed to death, but he prayed:

> *'In the middle of my life I am to enter the gates of Sheol; I am to be deprived of the rest of my years.'*
> (Isaiah 38:10, NASB)

It is said that he was less than forty years old when he prayed that prayer. In this way, the psalm represents a prayer for the young generation.

The last generation will be created to praise the Lord. They will be the generation who will sing the new song. They are called the ones appointed to death, or the sons or children of death; but the Lord will hear their prayers and release them. They may be orphans, parentless children who have survived after massacres or ethnic cleansing. They may be the children of Freemasons or people belonging to other secret orders. When a father makes a covenant with death, his children and family also come under the domination of death. They may be those who have lost hope for the future – they see before them the threat of nuclear war, Aids epidemics, destruction of the environment. But the Lord will release these children of death, and it will be the beginning of a release of all peoples to gather and serve the Lord; and the praise of the Lord will ring out in Jerusalem.

The harvest in the End Time consists of the younger generation. In the countries whose population is increasing the most rapidly, half of the people are under the age of 15, and that is where the harvest will be. When visiting growing churches in South America and in Asia, I have been overwhelmed by seeing so many young people in the churches. I have been in churches with thousands of members of whom 80 per cent are young people; and I have been in church buildings so full of people that many had to stand, and again I was amazed that most of them were young people. Albania and Mongolia are two countries that were for many years closed to mission work, but now they are opened up and new churches are being planted, consisting largely of young people. I have kept in touch with the development of a church in Erdenet in Mongolia, where most of the leaders are about 20 years old.

The task of the older generations is to pray for these people and to nurture them into maturity. God's Word describes several occasions when parents received a revelation from God that they would bear a child who would be a chosen instrument for God. It was a special blessing if the child could be sanctified and dedicated to the Lord while he was still in his mother's womb.

Moses' parents

> *'By faith Moses' parents hid him for three months after he was born, because they saw he was no ordinary child, and they were not afraid of the king's edict.'*
>
> (Hebrews 11:23)

Moses' parents saw that God's calling was resting on their child: they could see the radiance of God's glory upon him: *'he was a fine child'* (Exodus 2:2). So they were given the faith to save him from the ethnic cleansing that Pharaoh had decreed by ordering that all male children born to Jewish mothers should be killed at birth.

Nazirites in the Old Testament were sanctified and dedicated to the Lord for special tasks. They gave such promises to the Lord that they became dedicated to God in a quite exceptional way. The Nazirites that we read about in God's Word could never reach the degree of dedication that the Lord expected of them unless their parents shared in their dedication.

For instance, they were not allowed to drink wine. Therefore, the respective parents of Samson and of John the Baptist knew that their sons would be set apart and sanctified while still in the womb. The nine months from their conception to their birth therefore formed part of their Nazirite service.

> *'You shall conceive and bear a son. Now therefore, please be careful not to drink wine or similar drink, and not to eat any unclean thing. For behold, you shall conceive and bear a son ... the child shall be a Nazirite to God from the womb.'* (Judges 13:3–5, NKJV)

The mother was responsible for the Nazirite status of the son during the time he was a foetus in the womb. If she had drunk any strong drink or polluted herself in any way, the son could not have become a Nazirite.

The holy generation that we are praying forward on to the scene in the End Time will all be Nazirites. They will not reach that position unless we, for several generations, work together in a step-by-step restoration, through each older generation passing on an inheritance to the younger.

Samuel was a Nazirite of God and also a prophet, but it was his mother Hannah who laid the foundation for his dedication, through her intercession, and by dedicating her son to the Lord to be his possession for the whole of his life:

> *'I prayed for this child, and the Lord has granted me what I asked of him. So now I give him to the Lord. For his whole life he shall be given over to the Lord.'* (1 Samuel 1:27–28)

Relay-race: passing the baton between generations

The younger generation needs a blessing from the older, in order to go on further. They can go further with the Lord if they do not repeat the mistakes of the older generation.

Moses and Joshua

> *'Now Joshua son of Nun was filled with the spirit of wisdom because Moses had laid his hands on him.'*
>
> (Deuteronomy 34:9)

Joshua had been Moses' disciple for many years, and had learnt God's wisdom from him, but the explanation of the spirit of wisdom that rested on Joshua was that the two of them had spent a time in prayer together before the face of the Lord, when Moses had laid his hands on Joshua, passing on to him the wisdom from God that rested on his life.

Moses was not allowed to enter the promised land. The reason was that he broke faith with God and did not uphold his holiness among the people of Israel. He lost his temper before the people (Deuteronomy 32:48–52) and therefore was not permitted to go any further.

David and Solomon

David wanted to build a house for the Lord in Jerusalem, but the Lord said to him, through a prophet:

> *'You are not to build a house for my Name, because you are a warrior and have shed blood ... Solomon your son is the one who will build my house.'*
>
> (1 Chronicles 28:3,6)

And David said to Solomon his son:

> *'Be strong and courageous, and do the work. Do not be afraid or discouraged, for the Lord God, my God, is with you. He will not fail you or forsake you until all the work for the service of the temple of the Lord is finished.'* (1 Chronicles 28:20)

The passing of the baton from David to Solomon shows again that David could go no further in the restoration process, because his hands were stained with blood. His son would not repeat that mistake. But David encouraged his son to carry out what David himself was not permitted by God to do, and to be courageous. He prayed for his son:

> *'And give my son Solomon the wholehearted devotion to keep your commands, requirements and decrees and to do everything to build the palatial structure for which I have provided.'* (1 Chronicles 29:19)

These are the stages in restoration. As each generation becomes more fully consecrated to the Lord than the previous one, so holiness increases, and also strength and wisdom. They go from strength to strength, from one degree of glory to another.

The restoration process manifested in the new generation

They will go further than we did, and will carry out what the older generation were unable to do. They will not repeat the mistakes of the earlier generation, but will go on further and reach a new level if they have the blessing of the older generation. They will walk with greater courage than the older generation.

They will console God for all the pain that he has undergone through the fall of man. When God sees the firstfruits of the harvest, he will make the decision to send the Messiah back to earth. Heaven must receive Jesus until the period of restoration of all things: and then Jesus comes and completes the restoration.

The Book of Enoch

The Book of Enoch (1 Enoch) is one of the apocryphal books that were used by the Jews in services and devotions in the time of Jesus, but were never accepted as part of the Bible. It has been disputed by theologians, but was accepted by some of the first Christians. In the Book of Enoch there are trains or patterns of thought that are alluded to in the letter of Jude, in 2 Peter, and in Revelation. The book is generally thought to have been written not earlier than 200 BC, by an author or series of authors who used Enoch's name.

In the letter of Jude there is a direct quotation from the Book of Enoch:

> *'Enoch, the seventh from Adam, prophesied about these men: "See, the Lord is coming with thousands upon thousands of his holy ones to judge everyone, and to convict all the ungodly of all the ungodly acts they have done in the ungodly way, and of all the harsh words ungodly sinners have spoken against him."'*

(Jude 14–15)

Enoch foresaw the abortions of our own time:

> 'And in those days the destitute shall go forth and carry off their children, and they shall abandon them, so that their children shall perish through them: Yea, they shall abandon their children that are still sucklings, and not return to them, and shall have no pity on their beloved ones.' (1 Enoch 99:5)

Reasons for quoting from the Book of Enoch

The Book of Enoch is one of the few books that describes the age before the Flood. It belongs to a group of apocryphal books that began to come into existence about 200–150 BC. They are called 'pseudepigrapha' as the authors wrote under the names of biblical figures such as Abraham, Elijah, Ezra or Enoch. Michael Green describes the Book of Enoch as 'a long apocryphal book probably composed at different periods from the first century BC to the first century AD'.[2]

The Old Testament canon is generally supposed to have been closed in 90 AD at the Jewish synod of Jamnia (Yavne), though many Bible scholars consider that it was well settled much earlier. Two eminent Swedish scholars, Professor Ivar Egnell and a well-known earlier scholar Professor Hugo Odeberg of the University of Lund, believed that the Jewish rabbis who were deciding which were the Jewish holy books also hesitated to exclude certain writings because they could with advantage be used by the Christians in their differing interpretation of the Bible.

In the part of the Book of Enoch known as the Similitudes, written before the time of Jesus, there is a description of the coming of the Son of Man in the End Time. He is depicted as suffering, just as he is described in Isaiah 53.

> 'And one portion of them shall look on the other, and they shall be terrified, and they shall be downcast of countenance, and pain shall seize them, when they see that Son of Man sitting on the throne of his glory ... For from the beginning the Son of Man was hidden, and the Most High preserved him in the presence of his might, and revealed him to the elect. And the congregation of the elect and holy shall be sown, and all the elect shall stand before him on that day. And all the kings and the mighty and the exalted and those who rule the earth shall fall before him on their faces, and worship and set their hope upon that Son of Man, and petition him and supplicate for mercy at his hands.'   (1 Enoch 62:5, 7–9)

It is known that the Book of Enoch was considered in certain Jewish circles at the time of Jesus to have canonical standing. Likewise, it was accepted by some of the Church Fathers during the early Christian era.

The fact that the Book of Enoch is quoted in the letter of Jude, an accepted part of Scripture, gives it extra authority.

Notes

1. This and all other quotations in this chapter from the Book of Enoch are taken from R.H. Charles' translation, *The Book of Enoch*, SPCK, London, 1917.
2. Tyndale New Testament Commentaries: *2 Peter and Jude*, by Michael Green. Tyndale Press, Leicester, 1968, p. 48.

Chapter 7

Restoring the Church

Every time that a new church has been started, or a new movement has begun, we have believed in our enthusiasm that it was a new, fresh planting of wheat, containing no weeds. But after a while, we saw that the enemy had been there from the very beginning, sowing weeds among the wheat. The good seed was sprouting and growing up, but the weeds were growing up too. So we must always pray, 'Lord, restore us again, take us back to the place we once were in.'

Sin, and the law of death, have been active in breaking down the Church of God. The movement that began with the pouring-out of the Spirit of God on the day of Pentecost, and continued with the apostles and the Christians of the first few centuries who came to give their lives as martyrs for Jesus, ended in the Babylonian captivity of the Church which lasted from the fourth century until the time of the Reformation. When the imperial power found that it could not conquer the Church by persecution, the Emperors nevertheless managed to turn the Church into their obedient instrument, which they could control, by making it into a state religion. By forsaking its Jewish roots, the Church opened itself up to the influence of Greek philosophy and the infiltration of all kinds of pagan influences. The Church lost the gifts of the Spirit and the spiritual ministries, and acquired instead an organization and a hierarchy. God's Word then became no longer the decisive authority; it was replaced by the tradition of the Church. The Church lost the power it formerly had in the name of Jesus, and instead became rich with gold and silver.

The course of restoration in the history of the Church of God

Since Martin Luther and the Reformers, one movement after another has come along and restored to the Church forgotten truths, with the pace of this restoration quickening after the beginning of the twentieth century. A restoration movement often takes a particular Bible truth and pursues it to its ultimate outworking, so that the movement is at first controversial, causing conflict and division within the Church, and then as it matures, it becomes so balanced that it can be accepted by everyone.

In the sixteenth century, through Martin Luther, John Calvin and the other Reformers, there occurred a movement restoring faith in God's Word and scriptural doctrine. Through the Protestant movement, the restoration of the Church was set in motion after the long centuries of darkness.

In the eighteenth century, through John Wesley and the Methodists, there was a restoring of the sanctified life.

In the early 1900s, through the Pentecostal movement, there was a restoring of the experience of the power of God.

In the 1940s, through William Branham, William Freeman, A.A. Allan, Oral Roberts and Tommy Hicks there was a restoration of the healing ministries.

In the 1950s, the Latter Rain movement took part, among other things, in the restoration of the practice of laying-on of hands together with a word of prophecy. Before this, the Pentecostals were praising God with hallelujahs, but it was through the Latter Rain movement that the practice arose of using songs in praise and worship, with greater spontaneity and freedom in meetings, raised hands, clapping and dancing.

In the 1960s came the charismatic movement, with the baptism in the Spirit spreading across all church and denominational barriers. Through this came restoration of the charismatic gifts, and a new unity between the members of the Body of Christ.

In the 1970s, Kenneth Hagin and the faith movement brought an emphasis on the Word of God and its reliability, the importance of meditating on it, practising it, speaking in accordance with the Word and in faith, and confessing it. They accordingly restored a new level of faith; they believed in confessing this faith freely and openly; and they restored faith in success for the Church of God.

In the 1980s came the prophetic movement, with prophets appearing in groups. This movement is restoring the whole prophetic dimension to the Body of Christ: the ministry of prophecy, prophetic speaking, prophetic singing and prophetic acts. The sign of the pouring-out of God's Spirit will be that *'your sons and your daughters will prophesy,'* that is, that the gift of prophecy will become the most widely used of all the spiritual gifts. Up to the time of writing these words, speaking in tongues has been the most obvious outward sign of the pouring-out of the Spirit.

In the 1990s, Peter Wagner and a group of successful evangelists from Argentina began to emphasize prayer warfare as a key to church growth. This teaching is spreading among churches and intercessors throughout the world, resulting in increased prayer for unreached peoples, prayer teams travelling to closed lands, and the realization of the need for pastors, evangelists and mission workers to have personal prayer backing by intercessors. The teaching on prayer warfare is restoring the Church to a state of preparation for battle in the day of the Lord against the evil one before the return of Jesus.

Restoration of the five spiritual ministries in the Body of Christ

For a long time in the history of the Church, it was considered that the ministry of apostles and of prophets belonged only to the early days of the Christian era, but in the last part of the twentieth century, we have come to realize that one after another of the spiritual ministries has come into focus in each decade.

The 1950s was the decade in which the Lord raised up the ministry of the evangelist, through people such as Billy Graham, Oral Roberts, T.L. Osborn and others, who were equipped to reach the masses by means of tent meetings. Some of them became known for praying for the sick at the same time as they were preaching the Gospel.

The 1960s was the decade in which the ministry of the pastor was emphasized, through the charismatic movement.

In the 1970s, the faith movement in particular contributed to the restoration of the ministry of the teacher; through faith teaching, a renewed platform was provided for the Word of God, and thousands attended Bible schools where they could listen to the teaching, while many others listened to it through the use of cassettes and video tapes.

The 1980s was the decade when the Lord began raising up prophets among the nations and bringing them together. The prophetic movement arose in Kansas City and like many such movements of restoration became controversial, but it contributed to the prophetic ministry being set in focus.

In the 1990s, the ministry of the apostle is primarily an equipping for pioneering work and for laying the foundations of new churches, but it is also coming to imply the restoration of the apostolic authority with its accompanying signs and wonders, the spiritual gift of faith and the gift of performing miracles. The restoration of the ministry of the apostle is bringing a new unity in the Body of Christ.

Restoration in the local church

I believe both in the planting of new churches and in the restoration of old ones. Every one of us can play a part in the process of restoring our own local church. It needs leaders with vision, who seek God to know what their next step is, and give true direction to the Church through Bible teaching and leadership.

The praying church

In former times in the north of Sweden, the place where a free church used to meet was called the prayer-house. It was a place where people came to pray. Jesus came to the Temple area in Jerusalem and drove out those who were buying and selling there, quoting from Isaiah and Jeremiah:

> '"My house will be called a house of prayer", but you are making it a "den of robbers".'   (Matthew 21:13)

How long does it take for a a house of prayer to become a den of robbers? It does not need more than a couple of weeks. In a church where regular prayer takes place, for example every morning, it is sufficient to stop the regular prayer; then the weeds begin to grow at once in the spirit world, problems grow in the church, and it soon becomes a den of robbers. I had first-hand experience of this in one church, where we had prayer between 6 and 7 in the morning every day for several years. During all this time the church grew and there was a continuous movement of restoration. But every year at Christmas time, the Christmas rush and the materialistic life-style took the upper hand, and for two weeks the morning prayer gatherings did not take place. During those two weeks the problems within families increased. I had to sort these out and to arrange spiritual counselling to save marriages that were threatening to break up. Conflict and disunity grew when there was a lack of prayer in the church. I learnt gradually that I needed to have a week of prayer and fasting just before Christmas, so as to stand in the gap for the church when it was failing in prayer. How has it become possible for such a decline to happen in the church? It is because churches have become activity-houses instead of prayer-houses; everything possible happens except prayer.

The growing church

The promise about the growing church goes right back to the moment when, before the Fall, God blessed Adam and Eve and said to them:

> *'Be fruitful and increase in number; fill the earth and subdue it.'* (Genesis 1:28)

God wanted Adam and Eve to be fruitful and increase in number so as to fill the earth with God-fearing people. This promise can only be fulfilled today through a church that has God's blessing upon it.

Jesus wanted his disciples to bear rich fruit, and he associated such fruitfulness with their prayer life.

> *'I chose you and appointed you to go and bear fruit – fruit that will last. Then the Father will give you whatever you ask in my name.'* (John 15:16)

> *'This is to my Father's glory, that you bear much fruit, showing yourselves to be my disciples.'* (John 15:8)

Ephraim was blessed by Jacob with a blessing of fruitfulness.

> *'"His descendants shall become a multitude of nations." And he blessed them that day, saying, "By*

you Israel shall pronounce blessing, saying, May God
make you like Ephraim and Manasseh!'' '
(Genesis 48:19–20, NASB)

Joseph gave his second son the name Ephraim, because
he said,

'It is because God has made me fruitful in the land of
my suffering.'　　　　　　　　　　　(Genesis 41:52)

Ephraim means 'fruitfulness' or 'twice fruitful'; the
picture is of a storehouse filled many times over.

The task of an intercessor is to break curses and causes
of stagnation, so that a church can be blessed into growth.
Growth is a blessing and stagnation is a curse. There are
always reasons why a church ceases to grow, but we can
do something about these causes of stagnation through
prayer. One indication that a church is being restored is
that it becomes a growing church and a mother church
that gives life to daughter churches.

When Rebekah was ready to leave her own family in
order to be Isaac's bride, her family blessed her with
one of the fullest expressions of fruitfulness in all the
Bible:

'Our sister, may you increase to thousands upon thou-
sands; may your offspring possess the gates of their
enemies.'　　　　　　　　　　　　　(Genesis 24:60)

That blessing amounts to a very large number of
descendants, but in spite of the promise of fruitfulness
spoken over her, Rebekah remained childless and Isaac
had to pray that his wife might bear children:

'Isaac prayed to the Lord on behalf of his wife, because
she was barren. The Lord answered his prayer, and his
wife Rebekah became pregnant.'　　　(Genesis 25:21)

In the same way, there are churches that already hold God's rich promises of fruitfulness, but we are so totally dependent on God, that the intercessors need to pray for the release of the promised fruitfulness.

In 1977, when I was pastor of a church in Järfälla, an outer suburb of Stockholm, we spoke out a faith goal, to the effect that the church would grow by 100 new members within one year. After six months had passed, we still had not had many new members joining. One Sunday morning, I was so filled with birth pains for the unfulfilled faith goal that I was unable to go up into the pulpit to begin preaching, when the one who was leading the meeting announced 'Now our pastor will preach.' He asked me to explain to the congregation why I had such difficulty in going up to speak, and I told them how I wanted to live in faith and to speak in faith about church growth. I did not want the faith message to be taken away from me. If it was not going to be fulfilled in my own church, I would not have the boldness to speak in faith to other churches. Then the leader, Lennart, came forward to me and said to the congregation, 'We are going to untie this knot now, by prayer.' He prayed a prayer that reached to heaven. My birth pains ceased, and a heavy weight was lifted from my heart. That same Sunday evening, a number came to faith in Jesus, and were baptized and welcomed into the church. From that day on, it was as if the ice was broken, and our church experienced a steady growth right up to New Year's Eve, when we counted up and found that we had received 104 new members during that year.

For ten years, during which the church grew from 80 members to 650, I was given faith through a promise of God that was part of Jeremiah's message to Israel about restoration:

> *'From them will come songs of thanksgiving and the sound of rejoicing. I will add to their numbers, and they will not be decreased. I will bring them honour, and they will not be disdained.'* (Jeremiah 30:19)

Prayer for spiritual breakthrough to a new level

The church is growing, step by step, to new levels of maturity. The leadership of the church needs to seek God for direction on what teaching is needed to lead to restoration. We need also to ensure that the church benefits from the renewal that is going on in the Body of Christ and the truths that the Holy Spirit is emphasizing in our time. Whenever new Bible truths are rediscovered that open up the way for new phases of the restoration process, there is usually confrontation and opposition. Our denominational loyalty should not lead to our conforming rigidly with all the other churches in our denomination. Instead, we should follow the path of those churches that are living in renewal and restoration, which is quite different from following a standard denominational pattern within, say, the Pentecostal tradition. When I was leading a church to a new level of restoration, it was done by concentrating the teaching for a long period on a single topic such as faith. In the next stage, I taught on discovering our gifts and knowing our calling, with the ultimate purpose that every member of the Body should function in his or her calling and gifts. I need to lead the church into becoming a praising church, a prophetic church, a church that takes its responsibility in the community and in the nation, a church with a missionary vision, a church that understands prayer warfare, and a church that has a right relationship with Israel and the Messianic fellowships in Israel.

Every stage in a spiritual restoration requires a spiritual breakthrough and a widening of the spiritual horizon. Immediately before the church breaks through to a new level, there is strife and agony. God is the God of breakthrough, but an effective spiritual breakthrough needs to be prepared for by persistent prayer.

The church's isolation is broken

The restored church reigns with Christ. It is situated in the very centre of events, and it has a key function in the community. It is filled with the one who fills everything in every way. The evil one can only advance his kingdom if he can persuade the church to serve his purposes. He knows that in the end the church is going to reign with Christ, so he has to work together with backsliders, or with a church that is failing Christ. Every advance made by the kingdom of darkness has been achieved by the enemy exploiting the Church's weaknesses or compromises. Antichrist is going to co-operate with the apostates, those who at one time were among us but have since deserted us. Every step in the process of falling away from Christ has taken place in co-operation with an apostate church.

During the first week of August in each year, the homosexuals in Sweden hold a propaganda week, filled with activities and demonstrations. Then during the following week, the 'water festival' takes place. This festival has grown to become the biggest event in the country, with half a million people pouring into Stockholm's inner city. The water festival began with the Carnival in Rio de Janeiro as its prototype. These two weeks in August are the time of the year when the Stockholm churches are least active; it is the middle of the holiday period, and most of the church members are scattered. Everything is at a low ebb, and the deputy's deputy is in charge. Our enemy has been able to exploit this empty space that the churches have abandoned, in order to advance the cause of his kingdom.

> *'One who breaks open the way will go up before them; they will break through the gate and go out. Their king will pass through before them, the Lord at their head.'*
>
> (Micah 2:13)

Under some régimes, Christians are only permitted to hold services inside church buildings. They are not allowed to build new churches, nor to hold meetings in homes. By such means the régime can control the Christians, so that they become hemmed in between the four walls of their building and cannot carry out their function of filling everything in every way. But there does not have to be a Muslim or a communist régime for the Church to remain in isolation within four walls. Such isolation has happened in the Western world through secularization of the Church.

The enemy's tactics are to push the church into a corner, to confine it in an out-of-the-way spot; but Paul could say to Festus:

> *'The king is familiar with these things, and I can speak freely to him. I am convinced that none of this has escaped his notice, because it was not done in a corner.'*
> (Acts 26:26)

An angel of the Lord freed the apostles from prison and said to them:

> *'Go, stand in the temple courts ... and tell the people the full message of this new life.'*   (Acts 5:20)

Prayer that breaks the Church's isolation

In my calling as an intercessor and leader of prayer in Stockholm, I have given the highest priority to supporting those who preach the Gospel on the streets and in the public squares. I keep myself informed about where they are working, and I always let them know that we intercessors are serving them. The intercessors and the street evangelists together form a spearhead to break the Church's isolation inside the walls of its buildings.

In Stockholm there is a street preacher named Charles. When he was teaching young people at a 'Go Festival' about the nine spiritual gifts, he illustrated each one of the gifts in action by stories of things that had happened on the streets of Stockholm. Charles believes in power

167

evangelism. He prays for the sick on the streets; he receives words of knowledge and prophetic messages. We intercessors had prayed that the isolation of the Church should be broken, because we have become too accustomed to seeing the spiritual gifts in action only within church buildings or house church meetings.

We are preparing the way for the final invitation to the wedding feast, which is being given out on the highways and byways, on the streets and in the market-places. Jesus healed the sick in public in the open air, and Peter healed the sick in the name of Jesus on the city streets, when his shadow fell on them.

During the last ten years, I have travelled from town to town, gathering the Christian believers to intercede for their town. We held our prayer meetings within church buildings, but there was always a longing to go out on the streets to pray. We did prayer walks on the streets, and it felt as if there was something missing if we failed to go into the town centre to pray in the main square, late at night or early in the morning. It has been the Spirit of God who has led us to prepare the way for the Church to break out of its isolation, to go out on to the streets and to invite the wedding guests to come to the feast.

A further step in the restoration process is that the spiritual ministries burst out of their isolation within church buildings and reach out into all sections of the community: into business life, the world of commercial enterprise, the working place, the offices, and all parts of the life of the community.

Among the prophets, Daniel is the example of the complete community prophet. Jeremiah, Isaiah, Ezekiel and Zechariah can be called Temple prophets. Some of these were sons of priests, and much of their ministry was related to the Temple which was their frame of reference, even when, like Jeremiah, they stood outside the Temple gate prophesying to those going in. Daniel, on the other hand, was a prophet in the service of the king of Babylon. He was not one to come forward and prophesy to the religious leaders. We in modern times have had church prophets, but the restoration is going to bring in community prophets and business prophets, so that we shall have the five spiritual ministries in action within all sections of the community. When this happens, we shall have broken the Church's isolation.

Lewi Pethrus, the apostle of the Swedish Pentecostal movement, did not only lay the foundations of new churches. Later on in his life, he used his apostolic ministry to start a daily newspaper and a bank. He started a radio station, and a ministry of rehabilitation centres for alcoholics. It needed an apostle to lay the foundation for a Christian daily newspaper in Sweden. This man was both a church apostle and a community apostle.

For those who have a spiritual ministry, there is always a 'next step' to take. For many years, I worked in the planting of new churches; the first time I planted a new church was when I was 23 years old. During my time as a missionary in Pakistan, I planted churches in Rawalpindi, Islamabad and Lahore. Later in my life, I worked in laying the foundations of national prayer movements, which is just as much an apostolic ministry as planting churches. As we seek the Kingdom of God in the world of education or of business, we need the apostolic ministry in order to lay a proper foundation, so that others may build on it.

The Full Gospel Businessmen's Fellowship International ('FGB') was started by Demos Shakarian in order to restore the evangelistic ministry in the world of business. Through this movement, businessmen acquired a forum in which they could witness for Christ to their colleagues. The FGB magazine *Voice* always contains clear evangelistic testimonies written by businessmen whose lives have been transformed by Christ.

The International Christian Chamber of Commerce ('ICCC') takes businessmen one stage further on. They seek the Kingdom of God in the world of business enterprise, and their aim is to see not only the ministry of the evangelist, but all five of the spiritual ministries mentioned in Ephesians 4:11, established in the commercial world. They are fully aware that Mammon has traditionally held power over the world of finance, but they have learnt to practise prayer warfare in order to see the strongholds of Mammon broken down and the way prepared for the establishing of the economy of God's Kingdom. These are the kind of businessmen who believe in co-operating with those who pray. In their prayer fellowship, I come upon the beginnings of all the five ministries. There is the lawyer who is a Bible scholar, the professor with a prophetic ministry of making prophetic analytical forecasts. There is the director of a business with many employees, who has a shepherd's heart for them. I have listened to experienced shepherds in business giving advice on how to handle problems with employees. The manager with a shepherd's heart tries to find ways of solving the problems of co-operation, instead of taking the easy way out by dismissing people. I know businessmen who have a special ministry as shepherds for colleagues who are about to become bankrupt. Also, when a new business is being started, there is a need for someone with an apostolic calling to lay a proper foundation that can be built on by others; and there is an apostolic pioneering spirit for going ahead and serving the Lord in new markets.

I used to know a man who managed a woodworking factory, who was a shepherd for his 200 employees. He prayed every morning for their protection. For many years, there were no accidents at his factory. The safety inspector was very surprised that this woodworking factory never had any accidents, and asked, 'What is your secret, that you have never had any accidents at your factory?' He told the inspector how he prayed for protection for all his employees every morning. I remember that factory manager as a shepherd and a father-figure. Then in one church where I was pastor, one of the elders was a bank employee. In the church, he had a ministry as an elder and a spiritual counsellor, but at his place of work he functioned in a similar ministry. Eventually his superiors in the bank moved him out of the foreign exchange dealing department into a new position as a personnel manager for the bank.

I believe that Jesus, through his Body, must have an influence on the community. The spiritual ministries that are being restored in the church are also coming into being in the wider community. We are living near the time of Jesus' return; we must therefore work with the ambition of building that which will withstand fire and shaking in the End Time. That will happen as long as we plant and build by using the spiritual ministries.

The five ministries: apostles, prophets, evangelists, pastors and teachers, work best when they work together as a team. I have seen such teams develop, for example out of the pastors and elders in a church; but I have also seen the same thing happening when a group of businessmen in a town come together regularly to pray and to support one another in seeking the Kingdom of God in the business world.

I have had the privilege of following what happens when businessmen have discovered that they need the help of intercessors in order to serve the Lord in their business life. At certain important times we have asked businessmen to gather together with their intercessors; anyone with a spiritual ministry is dependent on having intercessors praying for him. Pastors, evangelists and missionaries all need intercessors. When businessmen are seeking to serve God in a spiritual ministry in the world of commerce, they challenge the strongholds of Mammon, the area over which Satan has hitherto regarded himself as having a monopoly. They become completely dependent on God and on the help and leading of the Holy Spirit throughout the working day, and to be able to move forwards they need to have a word from God. For this reason, they need to have the support of intercessors: for their protection, and so as to be able to reach the right decisions, and so as to overcome all the obstacles that stand in the way of the accomplishment of God's will. It is where this co-operation between intercessors and businessmen is in working order, that we see people whose spiritual ministries grow and become fruitful.

A common task for world-wide intercessors

Prayer for the '10/40 Window' is becoming the greatest concentration of prayer ever known, as most of the world's prayer movements are united in this common task. The 19th-century praying missionary John Hyde had a vision before he died in 1912; he had prayed for the Punjab district in India, but the Lord showed him in his vision that the prayer battle he was involved in was much greater, taking in also China, Japan and Africa. The Lord showed him that Christians had generally been thinking in terms of restricted areas: for the area of their own mission, or for their own denomination; but that a day would come when the Lord would gather the intercessors from all the various nations and denominations, joining one prayer army with another until a force was assembled for a single mighty prayer battle. Praying people would be united in prayer for the whole world, and this would lead to a great victory in preparation for the coming of Jesus.

In our own time, an international prayer network of this kind is now taking shape. During the last few years there have been a number of such concentrated international prayer assaults, for example, intercession for the Muslim world during the Muslims' fasting month of Ramadan.

Two parallel streams of restoration flowing together

Since the end of the nineteenth century, we can discern two parallel restoration movements. As the Lord restores the Jewish people by bringing them back to the Promised Land, so at the same time there is a restoration taking place in the Church. As Israel has been given back the land that belongs to her according to God's promises, so at the same time the Church has advanced into new areas in its mission work. As the immigration of Jewish people into Israel has increased, so at the same time there has been a harvesting and awakening in the Church. As the Jews resurrected their ancient mother tongue, Hebrew, as a modern spoken language, so at the same time the Pentecostal movement arose, bringing in Spirit baptism and speaking in tongues, and the Church received back its original prayer language. Today we can see these two streams of restoration flowing in parallel, but one day we shall see them united and flowing together in a saved Israel and a restored Church.

The Church rediscovers its Jewish roots

The Church was born on the day of Pentecost in Jerusalem among Jewish people, and its first leaders were all Jewish; but not long afterwards, the Jerusalem roots were cut off. The early church had to undergo persecution from the religious Jews. So instead of Jerusalem, the capital city of the Church became Rome, which was a spiritual extension of Athens with its Hellenistic culture, patterns of thought and rationalism. Now, the Church stands at the parting of the ways between Athens and Jerusalem, between humanism and the revelation of God. God himself has chosen Jerusalem and has established his name there for all eternity. It is to Jerusalem that Jesus will return, and it is Jerusalem that will become the world capital when Jesus gathers all the peoples into his world kingdom. Our future is all bound up with the day when Jerusalem will become an object of praise in the earth, when all the prophecies concerning Israel and Jerusalem will be fulfilled.

Having a Jewish heart

The process of restoring the dried-up Jewish roots of the

Christian faith involves much more than learning about Jewish values, history and culture in the abstract. It involves the restoring of relationships. In his book *Our Father Abraham*, Marvin R. Wilson has written:

'If one approaches this subject in a purely academic manner, it will not take hold. One cannot be involved in this discipline in an impersonal or detached way. There must be something deeper at work on the subjective or personal level. Perhaps we might call this orientation "having a Jewish heart". One must acquire a personal, living feel for the world of Judaism. A fire must be burning within. This feeling cannot be imparted in a solely objective or programmed manner. In brief, it must be caught; it cannot be taught.

'A profound and abiding Christian appreciation for Jewish culture and the Jewish people comes from sensing inwardly that one's deepest spiritual identity is with a Jewish Lord, and that *"salvation comes from the Jews"* (John 4:22). It is being cognizant that one has received a spiritual heart transplant, of being changed from the inside out. It is the existential realization that spiritually one is "grafted into Israel", a Jewish people. It is to recognize that through father Abraham one enters a new family and a new world of relationships (Galatians 3:29). This personal perception is particularly fed by a consciousness that one owes an enormous debt of appreciation to the Jewish people. One of the most gratifying, self-imposed responsibilities is not merely to acknowledge that debt, but also to seek meaningful and constructive ways to repay it.'[1]

Christians must send out a new message to the world. To attack the Jews is the same thing as attacking the Christians, so when the Jews are attacked we can never again be mere passive spectators. When the Jews are in need, we must show that we are on their side. When it really becomes costly to stand up for Israel, then we must be tried in the fire.

Restoration of the Messianic firstfruits in the Body of Christ

In the early days of the Church, many Jews believed in Jesus as their Messiah and Saviour. Paul could speak of *'one new man'*, the result of Jews and pagans being reconciled and becoming one through the cross of Christ, whereby the *'dividing wall of hostility'* was destroyed (Ephesians 2:14–15). But there came a time when the Church forsook its Jewish roots and no longer maintained any Jewish representation in Jerusalem. In our own time, a new harvest has begun among the Jewish people. More Jews are coming to faith in Jesus than has ever happened before. There are Messianic fellowships in every major town in Israel; in Jerusalem there are eight of them.

I believe in a house of prayer for all nations, with Jerusalem as its centre. Therefore, in working with an international prayer team as a global intercessor, I have for many years felt it important to keep in touch with the intercessors in Jerusalem and in Israel. In forming a team of intercessors from various nations, I am concerned that there should always be a representative of the Messianic Jews. I believe that this releases a power and an authority that comes with believing Jews being once more together with us in the Body of Christ.

Many Christians come to Israel as tourists on pilgrimage journeys. Some of these concentrate their visit solely on the 'holy places', a procedure that tends to create a species of romantic Christians, out of touch with reality. The believing Jews have a low opinion of such visitors. But also, many Christian tourists and pilgrims make no contacts with the Messianic Jews, and therefore miss sharing in a most important part of the restoration process. The Jews who believe in Jesus form a vital link between the Church and Israel. I have met Christians who are fascinated with the plans being made for the construction of the Third Temple, and apply to go on study visits to see all the various objects being collected in preparation for the services to be held in the new temple to be built on the Temple Mount. Christians collect money for this new temple, which is the place where one day Antichrist will take his place to be worshipped by the world. There are romantic charismatic Christians who speak in tongues, clap their hands and sing in the Spirit, but lack the power of discerning the Body of Christ – the temple that is built of living stones and is also to be found in Jerusalem. They are too much taken up with the stone-built temple and miss seeing the living one that the Lord is building in our time through our Messianic brothers and sisters in Jerusalem. I am writing this in order that you should not be led astray.

The restoration of the Jews will be resurrection life for us

'For if their rejection is the reconciliation of the world, what will their acceptance be but life from the dead?'
(Romans 11:15)

Israel's salvation and restoration is going to be such a life-giving event for the Church that it is compared by Paul with resurrection from the dead. Already, a 'firstfruits' of saved Jews has been added to the Church, and wherever Messianic Jews and Gentile Christians are brought together, new life comes into the Church. I believe this is a very important factor in the restoration of the Church.

God's Word takes on new life when we have representatives of the people of the Book with us. There is a great enrichment for us Christians in going about with a Jewish sabra who believes in Jesus as his Messiah and speaks Hebrew as his mother tongue. It is like being alongside a living dictionary, and enables us to draw out entirely new nuances of meaning from the original text. In the team's Bible studies, rich new insights into the Word are given out to us. I am always glad to obtain commentaries by Jewish writers on the Old Testament books. When orthodox Jews come to faith in Jesus, they bring with them such a wealth of Bible knowledge that they provide the Church with whole new dimensions in Bible teaching and in our understanding of the prophetic word.

The Jewish feasts

Celebrating the Lord's Supper becomes a far richer experience for a Christian who has shared with a Jewish family in starting the Sabbath on a Friday evening, by breaking bread and drinking wine. The Jewish/Christian festivals of Passover (Easter), Pentecost and Tabernacles acquire a much deeper meaning when we can celebrate them with Messianic Jews who can explain their prophetic significance in the light of Jewish tradition. There is something lacking in our appreciation of Easter unless there is a Jew present to tell us the full meaning of the Jewish Passover ceremony. It is the Church that celebrates the feasts that will be able to invite people to the wedding feast. We need to experience the festival spirit of the Jewish feasts before the true festival spirit can be restored in the Church. One contribution to this restoration is that thousands of Christians from all over the world travel each year to Jerusalem to celebrate the Feast of Tabernacles. Lately, too, Christians have begun coming to Jerusalem to take part in Passover and Pentecost. In the light of the Jewish feasts, we are beginning to discover how pagan our Western Christmas has become with its tree, tinsel, turkey and plum pudding, and all the attributes of our materialistic life-style.

Hebrew songs of praise

The Jewish folk-songs take their texts from the Bible. Messianic Jews sing many of David's psalms in the manner they are sung in the Jewish tradition. In every spiritual awakening or renewal, new songs are born and spread all over the world. So the Church of God throughout the world has already started to be enriched by songs of praise that come out of Israel.

Samson – a prophetic type of the restoration of the Church

Samson was a man with many flaws and defects, but there was an overruling grace in his life that led to restoration at critical moments. He ended his life by praying for restoration, and the Lord strengthened him for one great final effort so that the victory achieved by his death was greater than all those he had won in his lifetime.

The Lord restores weary heroes

After one of his greatest victories, Samson was overcome with thirst. He had been betrayed by his own people, who had tied him up with ropes and handed him over to the Philistines. Then, when the Philistines came towards him shouting, the Spirit of the Lord had come upon him in power and the ropes had dropped from his hands. Samson had taken the jaw-bone of a donkey and had struck down a thousand men. But after this victory:

> *'Because he was very thirsty, he cried out to the Lord, "You have given your servant this great victory. Must I now die of thirst and fall into the hands of the uncircumcised?" Then God opened up the hollow place in Lehi, and water came out of it. When Samson drank, his strength returned and he revived.'* (Judges 15:18–19)

Once when I prayed, 'Lord, raise up your heroes and send them in to fight on the battlefield of the End Time,' I asked at the same time, 'Where will the heroes and heroines come from?' The answer I received from the

Lord was, 'I am going to gather them from the place you least expect. I will fetch them from the battlefield where the heroes have fallen. Many of them are weary and burnt-out. They have been deserted by their own people and left to stand alone on the battlefield against the enemy. Some have been struck down and lie wounded on the battlefield.'

The lament that David sang, when he heard the news that Saul and Jonathan had fallen, has touched me deeply, because I myself have seen heroes and heroines fall and give up the fight.

> *'Your glory, O Israel, lies slain on your heights. How the mighty have fallen!'* (2 Samuel 1:19)

The Lord showed me that he is the shepherd who goes around the battlefield, binding up the wounds of the fallen heroes and raising them up.

> *'He gives strength to the weary and increases the power of the weak.'* (Isaiah 40:29)

The same applies to churches that are tired and have given up. Like the weary Samson, the Church will in the end shake off the binding ropes and the dust, and will be restored to life and rise up in heroic power.

Restoration of the Nazirite vow – total dedication

Samson was God's Nazirite, and the secret of the extraordinary power over his life was the vow that his parents had made on his behalf, from the time when he was still in his mother's womb.

In evil times, God needs instruments who will live under a voluntary discipline of remaining completely at his disposal. In the Old Testament they are called God's Nazirites: Samson and John the Baptist are two examples.

179

A Nazirite was one who of his own free will made a vow that he was separated to the Lord. So long as he remained under the vow, he was consecrated to the Lord: he had to abstain from wine or other strong drink, no razor might be used on his head, and he could not go near a dead body (Numbers 6:1–8). In the End Time, too, there will be a select group of Nazirites. The signs of their separation will be that no lie will be found in their mouths, nor will they have defiled themselves sexually (Revelation 14:4–5).

I do not believe that the New Testament Nazirites will refrain from cutting their hair, as Samson did. The Lord can test the genuineness of a person's dedication in other ways. When David Wilkerson came to New York (see *The Cross and the Switchblade*), [2] he was called to be a kind of Nazirite. For him, it was a matter of abstaining from watching TV. This is not something that can be laid down as a universal law for all Christians, but the Lord can test a person's separation and obedience by means of such a concentration on the Lord.

When I returned from my time as a missionary in Pakistan in order to become a pastor in Sweden, I sought the Lord as to how I might be his servant without becoming stressed or burnt-out. His answer was: 'Refuse to go on any committees, and use the time in going to prayer meetings instead.' So, because I could not go to meetings of committees or councils, I could not join any organization. At that time of my life, when I was between 40 and 50, I received a number of invitations to sit on various boards, and I said 'no' to them all. This was my Nazirite vow. Instead, I went to morning prayer meetings, pastors' prayer gatherings, and so on.

Samson's status as a Nazirite was the secret of his extraordinary strength throughout his life. The Philistines and the woman Delilah tried to discover this secret. They could not understand it, but they tried every way to find it out. It was only when Delilah persuaded him to tell her his secret that the enemy obtained power over him.

Paul in his vision (2 Corinthians 12:1–4) heard

'inexpressible things, things that man is not permitted to tell.' The Lord can test us by entrusting us with prophetic secrets that we are not permitted to share with anyone at all. Before we entrust God's secrets to any person, we must first have evidence that that person is living in prophetic revelation; otherwise we shall be throwing our pearls to pigs. We cause loss if we share spiritual things with those who trample them underfoot.

Samson's humiliation and disgrace

The Philistines captured Samson, gouged out his eyes, bound him with bronze fetters and set him to grinding in the prison. Then they called a great assembly to celebrate their victory, and they called Samson in to entertain them. Here Samson is a picture of the humiliated church that has forsaken its dedication to the Lord and has thereby lost its power. Such a church, that has lost the prophetic revelation, is blind and has to grind the heavy mill of tradition in its own prison. The powerless church becomes an object of ridicule as it plays the clown before the world, knowing what it has to say and do in order to keep the world applauding, now that it no longer has God's approval.

Samson was brought into the temple of the Philistines' god Dagon where all the rulers were assembled, worshipping their false god, praising him and offering a great sacrifice to him, because they had defeated the one who served the true God and had rendered him harmless. When they saw Samson:

> *'They praised their god, saying, "Our god has delivered our enemy into our hands, the one who laid waste our land and multiplied our slain."'* (Judges 16:24)

Samson's prayer and restoration

> *'Then Samson prayed to the Lord, "O Sovereign Lord, remember me. O God, please strengthen me just once*

181

> *more, and let me with one blow get revenge on the*
> *Philistines for my two eyes."'*   (Judges 16:28)

In the last days, the Church will be renewed in its separation to the Lord, and as it experiences the powers of lawlessness and darkness, it will pray: 'Lord, restore us again, do not let the enemy triumph over us; bring us back into the power that we once enjoyed, use us in the final battle so that we can see all Satan's power-structure fall with one blow.'

It was a young servant, a boy, who led the blinded Samson out into the middle of the temple of Dagon, to the exact position where God would restore his strength for his last task on earth. In the same way, I believe that a young, holy, dedicated generation will lead the Church to its proper position in the End Time. Many awakenings have started with God doing extraordinary things through children and young people.

From a strategic position, Samson grasped the power-structure of darkness

Dagon was a fertility god, worshipped by the Philistines as their national god. He was worshipped by fishermen around the Mediterranean, and was represented as half man and half fish. He was the 'strong man' of Gaza. It was between the centre pillars of the temple that the people entered into covenants with the god.

When Samson could feel both the centre pillars that held up the roof of Dagon's temple, he was in a strategic position where he could topple the whole of Dagon's power-structure over Gaza. It was a direct hit, worth dying for. Samson pushed with all his might, and the temple came crashing down. In the Old Testament, the greatness of a victory is measured by the number killed. In the New Testament, we do not measure victories in that way; rather, we count up the number of those freed from the power of darkness.

Samson, in his last moments on earth, did exactly what God wants to do in the Church's last moments of this present age. When Jesus returns, he will come as a man of war. He will come at the head of the heavenly hosts, to judge men and to do battle in righteousness. A church that is prepared for Jesus' return must have the same kind of fighting spirit. The warrior church, like Samson, will take a strategic grasp of the structures of darkness that are laid as a covering over the nations.

Notes

1. Marvin R. Wilson, *Our Father Abraham*, William B. Eerdmans Publishing Company, Grand Rapids, Michigan, 1989, p. 321.
2. David Wilkerson, *The Cross and the Switchblade*, 1964.

Chapter 8

The Third Fall of Man and the Restoration of Society

For about twenty years I have been involved in intercession for cities and nations. It has often been in connection with a number of churches in a locality coming together, so that there has been preparation for our praying: the city's origins and history have been studied. I have travelled with international prayer teams to mission lands, and to places in the Middle East; we have visited the ruins of Babylon, Nineveh and Ur, towns that Nimrod built; and the ruined temple cities and Pyramids of Egypt.

When we compare places in the cradle of civilization with modern cities, we find many links. Despite the buildings and the town planning being much more modern and advanced, there are many similarities between the planning of today's cities and designing the external appearance of their public buildings, and their equivalent in ancient Babylon, Egypt or Athens. Brasilia, the new capital of Brazil, is like an Egyptian city. In the world's financial centres, you can see banks that look like Greek temples. In the United States, cities have been named after those in Egypt and Greece such as Memphis or Athens. The artist who designed the Statue of Liberty in New York harbour derived his inspiration both from a

Babylonian goddess and from the ancient monuments of Egypt.

Is there a spiritual affinity between our modern society and Babylon, Egypt and Greece? Is it the case that the nature of man has remained basically unaltered? The Fall of man created certain patterns of society that have continued to reproduce themselves in our own time.

Lucifer was created with wisdom from the beginning: he was wiser than Daniel. But that wisdom left him, and the evil one is no longer creative. When the serpent's head was crushed through Jesus' victory at Golgotha, he became brain-damaged. He lost his creative capacity, and since then has been unable to summon up any new ideas or strategies. His old patterns of action from the time before he was beaten survive as reflex movements or death-throes. In the occult movements, presented today in New Age format, there is nothing new, but only a repetition of very old religious patterns and traditions from Babylon, Egypt, Greece, and the Canaanite peoples.

In John's vision on the island of Patmos, time after time he heard proclamations from heaven: *'Fallen! Fallen is Babylon the great!'* (Revelation 18:2). Now it collapses and falls, so that nothing is left of it but a heap of ruins. It disappears like a large millstone being thrown into the sea:

> *'With such violence the great city of Babylon will be thrown down, never to be found again.'*
>
> (Revelation 18:21)

The end product of the kingdom of Antichrist will be a society that is a mixture of Egypt, Sodom, Babylon and Jerusalem. This mixture will provide a stage for the beast.

All these different types of society are mentioned in the description of the End Time in Revelation:

> *'Now when they have finished their testimony, the beast that comes up from the Abyss will attack them, and overpower and kill them. Their bodies will lie in the*

> *street of the great city, which is figuratively called*
> *Sodom and Egypt, where also their Lord was crucified.'*
> (Revelation 11:7–8)

Four different types of society are named here: *'the great city'* was an expression used in the Bible for Babylon; the city where Jesus was crucified was the old religious Jerusalem, which bears children who are to be slaves, and is known for killing the prophets and messengers of God. In his letter to the Galatians, Paul writes of the old Jerusalem, characterized by slavery, in contrast to the new Jerusalem which comes from above and bears her children into freedom.

Some time ago, five churches in Copenhagen combined to hold a whole day's prayer gathering, interceding for their city and sending out prayer teams to pray in the streets. At the start of the day, I described to the gathering the various types of society mentioned in Revelation 11:7–8 above, and asked them: Where in Copenhagen can you find Sodom localized? What reminds you of Babylon? Where is the headquarters for dead religion? What reminds you of the beast? Is there anything in Copenhagen that represents Egypt? There were no difficulties in finding the links. Sodom was there in the pornography industry, one of the largest in the world. Babylon was present in the New Age centres; the beast was situated in the headquarters of the mass media. The Masonic temple was built like an Egyptian temple. We prayed that Copenhagen might be, in the End Time, a city where the Lord's messengers would be able to carry their message from God without being hindered or killed, that it might be a free city. We prayed that it might be a city that would welcome Jesus back to the earth.

In order that we may have faith to pray for the restoration of society, we must study the third Fall of man and the influence of the Fall on society. We shall see that the Fall has created certain patterns or models of decay and ruin that are still apparent in our modern society.

Through understanding the direction in which the Fall has led society, we shall be able to discern the vision for society when it is restored.

The third Fall of man – the building of Babylon

Babylon, both as a city and as a type of society, has had a growing influence on society right through the millennia. The history of Babylon carries on all the way through the Bible. It has had its own recent history through Saddam Hussein, who is so fascinated with Babylon that he has allowed the ancient city to be rebuilt, he has had Baghdad's airport renamed 'Babel', and he is a worshipper of Ishtar, Babylon's favourite goddess. Babylon follows us until the End Time; before the society of the Kingdom of God can be restored on earth, Babylon the great must collapse.

Babylon originated in an organized rebellion against God, led by Nimrod. It was the beginning of the rebellion described in Psalm 2, which will reach its climax in the coming of Antichrist. Men affected by the Fall came together in unity and for the first time rebelled against the Lord and his anointed one, and said to one another, 'Let us break their chains and throw off their fetters.'

Nimrod, the mighty hunter – conqueror of the leopard

At the time when Nimrod came to the fore, after the Flood, the wild animals in the forests had increased in numbers more quickly than the humans, and had been causing bloodshed and havoc among the scattered small communities of men and women, bringing great fear into their lives. The great achievements of Nimrod, through his successful hunting and defeat of the wild animals, led to his becoming in the eyes of men the great benefactor of mankind. In this way he became the first of the mighty men on earth; and thus he acquired political power to build the first great cities after the Flood. As he gathered people inside the secure city walls, he achieved still more: he allowed people to live their days in safety. They were now free from the dangers that had beset them in their former scattered existence, where no-one knew whether he might at any moment be involved in some deadly conflict with wild animals, defending his life and everything that was precious to him.

Because they had found safety inside their high city walls, everyone realized what a great debt of gratitude they owed to Nimrod, so much so that various legends say that people actually began to worship him. Then by making himself king, he became the first person to be a community leader, without being one of the patriarchal leadership that grew out of the family line. He used his position of power to be the first person to gather people together in official ceremonies of sacrifice to the false gods.

Nimrod led the building of Babylon, but was also known as a leopard-tamer. He clothed himself in a leopard skin and so made an impression on people, setting their fantasies in motion. When they saw him, they called him 'the conqueror of the spotted one' because the leopard's skin was spotted. From this he derived his name, Nimrod, from *nimr* a leopard.

Duraya Simba, who is a banker and leader of intercessors in Zimbabwe, has made a study of the way that African leaders and medicine-men identify themselves with the leopard as a power animal. The Inkatha warriors among the Zulu people in South Africa dress in leopard skins, as does their chief Buthelezi. President Mobutu of Zaire puts on a leopard skin and a leopard head when he meets a new government. They swear their oath of allegiance as Mobutu looks them in the eye one after another, wearing his leopard head. Simba counted up a long list of African presidents, tribal chiefs and prime ministers who identify themselves with the leopard as a power animal, and he maintains that to be identified with Nimrod and his leopard-figure is to be identified with the demonic principality over the whole continent of Africa.

The traditions from earliest times bear witness to Nimrod's apostasy and his success in leading mankind away from the faith of the patriarchs who lived before the Flood, and away from their influence which still persisted after Noah and his sons. He freed men's minds from the fear of God and the judgments of heaven, a fear that had remained over them while the memory of the Flood was still fresh in their minds. He led mankind into being no longer dependent on God, and it is in that spirit of independence that the Bible describes the building of the tower of Babel (Babylon):

> 'Then they said, "Come, let us build ourselves a city, with a tower that reaches to the heavens, so that we may make a name for ourselves and not be scattered over the face of the whole earth."'   (Genesis 11:4)

The tower of Babylon was built in accordance with occult power principles, so as to concentrate the magic power in a manner similar to the Pyramids. Each platform of the tower was dedicated to one of the seven planet-gods, with Saturn at the bottom, then Venus, Jupiter, Mercury, Mars, the moon-god and the sun-god. At the top of the tower the sun-god was worshipped.

The tower was an occult power-point and place of cult worship. At the top of this and other similar ziggurat towers was a room containing a single piece of furniture – a bed. The king, who was at the same time the high priest, used this bed to receive a visitor from heaven. In this bed, the king of Babylon had to sleep once a year, in order to be one flesh with his god, in a kind of symbolic intercourse. The same kind of ceremony was enacted in Japan in 1990 when the Emperor had to sleep with the sun-goddess Amaterasu so as to become an incarnate god.

Ishtar was the goddess with whom the rulers of Babylon made themselves united as one.

According to the programme in Japan, a seat suitable for a goddess had been set in place for Amaterasu, and her bed on which the Emperor had to lie for three hours was called her resting-throne. The Shintoists describe the Emperor's relation to the sun-goddess in the following terms:

> 'The emperor is heir to the long lineage of Shinto priests, he is the present manifestation of that lineage. He is successor to the primal ancestral spirit of the chief priest in whom dwells the spirit of the highest spirit of all Shrine Shinto, the spirit of Amaterasu Amikami, he is the chief master of Shinto ceremonies.' [1]

We could see precisely the affinity between this Daijosai ceremony and Babylon. The ceremony was secret, but the researchers into Shintoism maintained that the Emperor simulated sex with the sun-goddess, and this corresponds with other historic examples of kings going through ceremonies so as to become incarnate gods. The kings of earth have committed adultery with the prostitute of Babylon (Revelation 17:3, 18:3).

Nimrod built a number of cities, all after the same pattern as Babylon. Each had a ziggurat tower right in the heart of the city, and gates like those of Babylon, guarded by a pair of gigantic winged oxen with human heads. In the centre was the temple to the gods of the city. In all cities built on occult principles, the false gods and their power points require to have the heart of the city reserved as the place from which they can influence all the people who live in it. Each of the gates of Babylon, and of the other cities that Nimrod built, was dedicated to its own particular god. The Ishtar gate of Babylon was the most important, leading directly into the main processional street. Another gate was dedicated to Marduk.

Babylon – a gathering-place and haunt of all evil spirits

Hammurabi, one of the kings of Babylon, caused a selection of his legal judgments (generally called the 'Code of Hammurabi') to be written on a stele (stone slab) which was found at Susa early in the present century. The king introduced his judgments by setting out a long list of gods and goddesses to whom he owed a debt of gratitude that he was able to reign. Then after the judgments themselves, there follows an ending in which he again lists his gods and asks them to bring curses on those who do not keep the laws. He calls on Enlil, he is obedient to the god Shamash, his helper, and after he has gone through all the long list, he closes by saying that he is the favourite of the goddess Ishtar. Seeing that the king of Babylon welcomed such a large number of gods with whom he co-operated, it is not surprising that Babylon became a dumping-ground, a rubbish-tip for all evil spirits.

> *'Fallen! Fallen is Babylon the Great! She has become a home for demons and a haunt for every evil spirit, a haunt for every unclean and detestable bird.'*
>
> (Revelation 18:2)

The society where man seeks to make a name for himself

The driving force in the building of Babylon was the people who wanted to make a name for themselves. The ruler of Babylon made sure that his name was carved on every brick that was made, so that he would be remembered. The spirit of Babylon was one that wanted to be 'the great city', greatest, best and most widely known in the world. It was in the spirit of Babylon that Nebuchadnezzar cried out:

192

> *'Is not this the great Babylon I have built as the royal residence, by my mighty power and for the glory of my majesty?'*
> (Daniel 4:30)

Even as these words were on his lips, God's judgment was pronounced over his pride. The kings of Babylon wanted to be worshipped during their lives and remembered after they were dead; hence statues and memorials were put up in their honour. Those who were worshipped as gods in their lifetime are worshipped as gods after they are dead, through their graves and memorials. Well-known people nowadays are honoured by having streets or squares named after them.

During the New Year holiday in 1986, Steve Lightle and I led a prayer team to Moscow. One of our tasks was to pray inside the Lenin mausoleum. It was necessary to queue for several hours in order to get into this chamber of the dead. Classes of school-children were brought in to pay homage to the dead Communist leader. Our international prayer team of fifteen people came into the mausoleum and started to sing in the Spirit. The guards, surprised, tried to quieten us. We pronounced a proclamation in unison together over the name and memory of Lenin, using the words the Jesus used to curse the fig-tree: *'May no-one ever eat fruit from you again'* (Mark 11:14). It was not long after that day that the statues of Lenin were lifted away by great cranes, and streets and squares bearing his name had their names changed, while the city of Leningrad reverted to its old name St Petersburg.

The restoration-vision for Babylon is Jerusalem, the city where the Lord himself places his name and is honoured; just the opposite of Babylon's pride.

> *'I did not see a temple in the city, because the Lord God Almighty and the Lamb are its temple.'*
> (Revelation 21:22)

There is not going to be any need for a temple. Often,

when a temple or a church is built, it is done so that the builder can be remembered. A temple is often called after a king, a queen, a saint, or the person who built it. How many people take the honour that rightly belongs to God, through what we can find manifested in our cities? Men, and false gods, have placed their names in places where in fact:

> *'The throne of God and of the Lamb will be in the city, and his servants will serve him. They will see his face, and his name will be on their foreheads.'*
>
> (Revelation 22:3–4)

The people are trapped with the help of occult networks

Babylon was the first city to be built with the use of occult town planning, and it has become a model for many cities built in later times. By means of occult town planning, a net or covering is laid over the inhabitants of the town, so as to control them and to steer them in whatever direction the occult leader may require.

There is an occult net that is laid over peoples and nations to imprison and manipulate them. The prophet Habakkuk described this occult net which the Chaldeans used to entrap people.

> *'The wicked foe pulls all of them up with hooks, he catches them in his net, he gathers them up in his drag-net; and so he rejoices and is glad. Therefore he sacrifices to his net and burns incense to his drag-net, for by his net he lives in luxury and enjoys the choicest food. Is he to keep on emptying his net, destroying nations without mercy?'* (Habakkuk 1:15–17)

The Chaldeans burnt sacrifices to their net in order to make a good catch. It was no ordinary fishing-net; it was a net for catching peoples and nations.

Hammurabi, the ruler of Babylon from 1792 to 1750 BC, laid down a set of laws once considered the oldest promulgation of laws in human history. In his introduction to his code of laws, he praises his gods and describes how each of them has served him. One of the gods who helped him to fight his enemies was the god Enlil, whom he called, amongst other titles, 'the net ensnaring the enemy'. [2]

When the Bible says that the whole world is under the control of the evil one (1 John 5:19), it is describing a system of exercising power. Satan has a plan for keeping the earth occupied. That plan will be completely exposed and frustrated by the army of the Lamb during the prayer warfare that will be carried out in the End Time before Jesus comes. We shall be praying for a much greater understanding of the enemy's strategy and the structure of evil, so that we can strike down and annihilate these structures.

> *'On this mountain* [the Lord] *will destroy the shroud that enfolds all peoples, the sheet that covers all nations; he will swallow up death for ever.'*
>
> (Isaiah 25:7–8)

Isaiah's word points forward to Jesus' victory on Golgotha and his resurrection. Life has triumphed over death. The covering of death will be lifted off, on the ground of Jesus' victory. The shroud holds people in darkness. I suggest that the shroud that blinds people and keeps them in ignorance of Jesus' victory is an occult manipulation originating in ancient paganism, kept alive today through the secret societies. Half the victory lies in exposing what the enemy is doing. As long as he can keep his secrets in the dark, he can retain a measure of security. Occult secrets cannot bear the light of God shining and revealing them.

As we proclaim Jesus' victory, so the covering is removed. Occult manipulation always has many vulnerable points that are within our reach as we pray. Secret societies work together with demonic spiritual powers, but Jesus who lives in us is stronger than those powers.

Canberra was built to a secret occult plan

Canberra, the Australian capital, was built in accordance with principles of sacred geometry. The central point of the city was placed where two ley-lines (lines of power) crossed one another. The city architects and designers, Walter Burley Griffin and his wife Marion, derived their knowledge of occult town planning from such sources as Freemasons, Swedenborgians, Rosicrucians and Theosophists.

When I was there in 1987, I was told that the land on which the city was built belonged to a high-ranking Freemason who owned a sheep-farm. My informant was a relative of this man who had become a Christian and took part in our prayer conference.

The designers started their planning from three ancient high places of sacrifice, holy to the aboriginal people. The parliament building in the centre of Canberra was built in accordance with the occult lines of power, and contains many pyramid patterns. Christian students told us that they had seen occult ceremonies being carried out, in the utmost secrecy, when the foundations of the building were being laid.

Professor Peter Proudfoot of the University of New South Wales has said of the designers of Canberra that they had tried to incorporate esoteric forces into Canberra by their city planning:

'Their design sought to channel the best cosmic forces into the capital and place a spiritual emphasis on the decisions made there.

'Among their influences were geomancy, an ancient science placing man in harmony with the earth, which is reflected in the sacred geometry of monuments such as Stonehenge and the Egyptian pyramids: *feng shui*, a Chinese philosophy of landscape design that stresses the importance of mountains and the "dragon lines" that link them as sacred landforms; and in the belief in the crystal as a potent symbol.'[3]

How Hitler and Himmler relied on ley-lines

Hitler was inspired by the occult and by secret societies. He was influenced by Rudolf Steiner and the anthroposophists, who today are a part of the New Age movement.

Himmler often spoke of 'earth magic' and ley-lines, and he loved to talk about Wewelsburg as an occult centre of power that would be of equal importance with Stonehenge, as he imagined. In the official periodical *Ahnenerbe* in which the SS research office published its material, a number of articles were published on this subject. Wewelsburg, which the Nazis built as an occult headquarters, lay near Paderborn in Westphalia. It was never completed. It was described by Himmler as the centre-point of the world. In the northern tower of Himmler's fortress was the cult-centre where a sacred flame was kept burning in the exact centre of the whole building.

The Nazis built their Third Reich using occult knowledge in order to control men's minds. In the stadium in Nuremberg where Hitler spoke to the assembled masses, he had a Pergamon temple built, into which he used to go to obtain power, before going out on to the podium to speak to the masses. Pergamon was the place where Satan had his throne (Revelation 2:13). Ley-lines are part of a satanic system of mind-control designed to steer mankind into the paths desired by the occult powers.

In the book of Revelation, a great city is described which *'is figuratively called Sodom and Egypt'* (Revelation 11:8). Brasilia is not the only city which is inspired by Egyptian mythology. Babylon and Egypt are the two great sources of inspiration for the occultism that has spread world-wide.

Town planning – occult or heavenly

When Abraham was called to go out from his city of Ur, he was leaving a city built on occult principles. There is a ziggurat there which is an intersection point in an occult network. He had faith that God was building cities of a different kind, which would not have an altar to the sun or the moon-god in the centre:

> *'For he was looking forward to the city with founda-tions, whose architect and builder is God.'*
>
> (Hebrews 11:10)

God is certainly the architect of the new Jerusalem, which he planned long before the architects of Babylon planned to build a city in rebellion against God.

When we pray for the freeing of a town or community, we need to have a deeper understanding of what they are to be freed from. In Babylon we looked for the roots of the city-building that still continues.

How it began, as the Freemasons themselves describe it

How did we come to have occult monuments, associated with Greek gods or Greek temples? We have traced their origins, time after time, to the people of the secret orders such as the Freemasons.

In the city of Nashville, Tennessee, there stands an exact copy of the Parthenon, the great temple that still stands on the Acropolis in Athens. In the temple at Nash-ville there is an enormous statue of the goddess Athena. This temple was built by Freemasons, and the foundation stone was laid with all due ceremony in accordance with Masonic ritual. The State Capitol, which stands on the highest eminence in the city, was designed by a Masonic architect, and its foundation stone too was laid with Masonic rites, accompanied by a procession of Masons.

Stephen Mansfield has carried out a spiritual mapping of Nashville, and has concluded that the Egyptian and Greek architecture of the city has come about through the influence of the Freemasons. Mansfield says:

> 'The rule of thumb in American cities is that the more Masonic a town has been, the more Greek, Egyptian, and Babylonian its architecture will be.' [4]

The Masons stand for religious syncretism – they are found within all religions, and they preach tolerance. They behave as if they were the owners of the cities, and adorn them with their mixture of religions.

Through prayer, we must deal with all that the Freemasons have built up in their efforts to maintain their occult influence over lands and peoples. What is it that these Masons are building? Is it only symbolic language? Their symbols and building tools are, for example, compasses, square, trowel and plumbline. Their initiation ceremonies are built around the legends concerning Hiram of Tyre who built Solomon's temple. They call their god the great architect and the great master builder. What are they trying to build? Is it just a spiritual temple, or is it something that is visible and shows itself in our cities and our society? Are they building visible structures, and what is their purpose in building? They regard themselves as the trustees of an ancient secret craft of building, once lost but now recovered and administered by their secret orders. Is there an occult craft of building of which they are the guardians? Is the purpose of that craft a kind of occult manipulation, which favours the initiated and helps them to control the world?

The Freemasons and earth magic

In ancient pagan times, places of sacrifice, whether or not they were placed on high points, were linked by lines of power that formed a network. Between these high places of sacrifice, various stone memorials, for example standing stones or stone circles, were set up.

With a divining rod, the ley-lines (lines of power) can be traced from one place of sacrifice to another, and today groups of diviners make excursions to places of sacrifice and pagan cultic sites in order to make detailed maps showing where the ley-lines run.

The Chinese, in their view of ley-lines, saw them as having both negative and positive effects. Through their knowledge of earth magic, it was possible to manipulate the powers, so that by putting up stones or arrangements of stones, one could direct the positive powers to the places where the rulers or the rich people lived, and the negative powers towards the abodes of the poor.

As we examine, today, how our towns were originally planned, we often find that they were built in accordance with the same ancient occult principles. How does it happen that towns built up in the last century follow the same patterns as those built up in pre-Christian times? Where lies the link between ancient paganism and its modern outworking? I suggest that the link lies in the Freemasons, the Knights Templars and a leadership that is influenced by various secret societies that keep the ancient building craft active and carry on bringing to us their pagan message, their blending together of various religions through a language of symbols.

The Freemasons say that they are the present-day heirs of the ancient fraternity of masons who had charge of the traditional secrets of the art of building. Masons built churches and cathedrals in accordance with secret principles, and this secret wisdom was based on the occult science of earth magic.

This means that the same knowledge that was used in the building of a pagan temple or an altar of sacrifice was also used by those who built churches and cathedrals. This connection is shown in Guy Underwood's book *The Pattern of the Past* [5] which describes the connection in detail. The same matter is also dealt with by Francis Hitching in his book *Earth Magic*[6].

A study of these matters in the literature about earth magic leaves the reader astonished to realize that the pagan system used to join up high places of sacrifice still continues to be used in modern town planning. The architects of today still use the old occult science, and modern towns are planned using earth magic. Where the lines of energy cross, that is the position where a city centre will be located or a monument erected.

David Tidy of England has shown in a video presentation[7] that a modern town centre has been located at the point where energy lines cross one another in a hexagram pattern. The old occult network is still being connected to today's building.

How the foundations of Sydney were laid

A few years ago, I was invited by Intercessors for Australia to a prayer conference in Sydney that was being held in co-operation with seven churches in the city. In preparation for the conference, a group had studied the history of the city, with special emphasis on finding out how its foundation was laid.

There were Freemasons on board the first immigrant ship in 1788, which carried the first convicts to Australia. Some of the Freemasons were officers in the ship's crew. This meant that Freemasons took part in the original founding of the city.

One of the group that studied Sydney's history went to the Masonic headquarters and asked to be allowed to study their archives concerning the early history of Sydney. She found that they had carefully documented evidence that Freemasons had laid the foundation stones of most of the churches and public buildings, obelisks and monuments in central Sydney. 'It is of the utmost importance to them that the foundation stones have been laid by Masons. Great spiritual significance is attached to this apparently unimportant act,' she wrote in her report. In their tradition they go back to Nimrod, the first empire-builder, who laid the foundations of Babylon and Nineveh.

Isaiah prophesied to those who made a covenant with death:

> *'See, I lay a stone in Zion, a tested stone, a precious cornerstone for a sure foundation; the one who trusts will never be dismayed.'* (Isaiah 28:16)

We know that that cornerstone is Jesus, he whom the builders rejected. By laying a foundation stone in the name of another god, the city is made ready for Antichrist instead of Jesus. The god of the Freemasons is not the God and Father of Jesus Christ. In God's Kingdom everything is consecrated and set apart for the Lord. It is our task to welcome Jesus first and foremost by being sanctified ourselves, but also by consecrating buildings, streets and squares.

Since our cities are built in honour of Lucifer instead of Jesus, the intercessors must act accordingly so that the cities may not be overthrown and wiped out when the kingdom of God is restored.

> *'The cities of the nations collapsed. God remembered Babylon the Great and gave her the cup filled with the wine of the fury of his wrath.'* (Revelation 16:19)

The meaning of this scripture becomes clear as we gain insight into the way that our cities have been founded in the spirit of Nimrod, who built Babylon and Nineveh.

Judgments of condemnation after the third Fall of man

> *'The Lord said, "If as one people speaking the same language they have begun to do this, then nothing they plan to do will be impossible for them. Come, let us go*

*down and confuse their language so they will not under-
stand each other." So the Lord scattered them from
there over all the earth, and they stopped building the
city. That is why it was called Babel [Babylon] –
because there the Lord confused the language of the
whole world. From there the Lord scattered them over
the face of the whole earth.'* (Genesis 11:6–9)

Confusion of languages as a barrier against unity in rebellion

The Lord confused men's languages so that they might be
prevented from forming the kind of unity that is generated
when men join in rebellion against God. The inability to
understand one another is one of the judgments that
comes to an end in Christ. Even people who speak the
same language can be subject to this judgment. Their
words flow past one another; they have lost the ability to
listen to one another, and it becomes impossible for them
to come into unity. The God who laid the barriers so that
men would not understand each other's languages is the
same God who, through the cross of Jesus, can break
down the dividing walls so that men can once again
understand each other and achieve unity together. By
understanding the extent of the Fall, we can better
appreciate how God has reconciled and restored us.

The outpouring of the Holy Spirit was God's act of
restoration in direct relation to the judgment on Babylon
that caused men not to understand one another's speech.

In the restoration process, people from different
language groups become filled with the Holy Spirit and
understand one another through the Spirit. In the Spirit,
there is fellowship between different peoples and races.

Confusion and dispersion

The Lord judged Babylon, and the punishment for its
people was to be scattered over all the earth (Genesis

11:8). This is the same punishment that he gives to communities that rebel like Babylon. *'He who scatters has come up before your face'* (Nahum 2:1, NKJV). Because Israel slid into the worship of false gods and occultism, they were scattered among the peoples; but it is not only Israel that has been condemned in this way.

> *'I will disperse the Egyptians among the nations and scatter them through the countries.'*   (Ezekiel 30:23)

One nation after another has been struck down by this judgment, when the people have gone after false gods.

There are particular sins that cause the land to vomit out its inhabitants (Leviticus 18:28). It is a part of the birth-pains in the End Time that the streams of refugees increase on the earth.

> *'See, the Lord is going to lay waste the earth ... and scatter its inhabitants.'*   (Isaiah 24:1)

Tibetans, Iranians, Lebanese, Bosnians, Haitians, Somalis and Rwandans flee from their lands. A society steeped in the worship of false gods and occultism is not a safe society. God judges nations for the sins of Babylon, and when he does so, he scatters them. Then, when he restores them, he gathers them together again and lets them live in safety. The vision of the kingdom of peace is:

> *'They will build houses and dwell in them; they will plant vineyards and eat their fruit. No longer will they build houses and and others live in them, or plant and others eat.'*   (Isaiah 65:21–22)

Restoration is the Lord coming as a shepherd and gathering the nations into his church.

In God's Word, the vision of restoration for the Babylon society is always Jerusalem.

'Hear the word of the Lord, O nations; proclaim it in distant coastlands: "He who scattered Israel will gather them and will watch over his flock like a shepherd."' (Jeremiah 31:10)

'The Sovereign Lord declares – he who gathers the exiles of Israel: "I will gather still others to them besides those already gathered."' (Isaiah 56:8)

'Lift up your eyes and look about you: all assemble and come to you; your sons come from afar, and your daughters are carried on the arm. Then you will look and be radiant, your heart will throb and swell with joy; the wealth on the seas will be brought to you, to you the riches of the nations will come.' (Isaiah 60:4–5)

Sodom – the society where sin becomes full-grown, ready for judgment

Sin goes on developing all the time until it becomes full-grown and reaches its ultimate consequence. God has set ethical boundaries that society must observe; when society oversteps these, then judgment follows.

'Then the Lord said, "The outcry against Sodom and Gomorrah is so great and their sin so grievous that I will go down and see if what they have done is as bad as the outcry that has reached me."' (Genesis 18:20–21)

So the Lord sent two angels to Sodom, and they were invited into Lot's house as guests. But:

'Before they had gone to bed, all the men from every part of the city of Sodom – both young and old – surrounded the house.' (Genesis 19:4)

These angels, staying overnight in Lot's house, were on their way to exposing themselves to homosexual rape by the men of Sodom. Sin becomes full-grown when homosexual rape takes place and there is no moral standard in the community to prevent it. The righteous were frightened into passivity and silence, and no-one dared to intervene. The men of Sodom were lawless, and did not accept the authority of anyone sitting over them as judge. Homosexuality was the accepted norm in their community and everyone was compelled to fall in with it. There have been examples of the same thing occurring in closed prison conditions, where newly arrived prisoners have been forced to take part in homosexual or lesbian acts.

All generations took part, all the men of the town; the older men did not try to stop the younger ones. They could not all take part in the rape personally, but they came to watch. When the men of Sodom lived out their lusts, it was regarded as a popular amusement or entertainment. The full-grown sin consisted in people doing these things without any feeling of shame, openly in front of the whole community. Sodom was a community that had no barriers, nothing to hold back the tide of evil. If there had been ten righteous men to stand up and protest, to try to stop the evil one, the town could have been saved. The homosexual life-style had so taken over that no-one dared to protest. The men of Sodom would not allow Lot, a single man and a stranger, to exalt himself over them as a judge. They kept bringing pressure on Lot and moved forward to break down the door; then God's first judgment hit them and they all, young and old, were struck blind by the angels.

Sodom was the community that was under God's sentence of destruction. The angels had been sent out to destroy Sodom, and the same angels urged Lot, *'Hurry and get out of this place ... Flee for your lives!'* (Genesis 19:14, 17). The Lord wants to save his children out of a community that is ripe for God's judgment. He does not want to destroy the righteous together with the ungodly. In the End Time there will be two kinds of communities: one that we have to flee from, and the other that is a free city to which we flee for refuge. The vision of restoration for society is that it should become a place of refuge, a place where there is shelter for its own people and also a place where those who flee to it from areas of trouble and disturbance can find safety.

> *'If he condemned the cities of Sodom and Gomorrah by burning them to ashes, and made them an example of what is going to happen to the ungodly; and if he rescued Lot, a righteous man, who was distressed by the filthy lives of lawless men (for that righteous man, living among them day after day, was tormented in his righteous soul by the lawless deeds he saw and heard) – if this is so, then the Lord knows how to rescue godly men from trials and to hold the unrighteous for the day of judgment, while continuing their punishment. This is especially true of those who follow the corrupt desire of the sinful nature and despise authority.'*
>
> (2 Peter 2:6–10)

For every community there is a restoration vision. Sodom was the community laid in ruins by a natural catastrophe, but God's word promises that the ruined cities will be rebuilt. I have a friend whom God called to Dubrovnik to help in rebuilding its ruins. We have seen the towns and villages of the former Yugoslavia shattered to pieces, but there are those who have heard the Lord speaking to them and saying, 'You are to take part in rebuilding the ruined cities.'

> *'Your people will rebuild the ancient ruins and will raise up the age-old foundations; you will be called Repairer of Broken Walls, Restorer of Streets with Dwellings.'*
>
> (Isaiah 58:12)

> *'They will rebuild the ancient ruins and restore the places long devastated; they will renew the ruined cities that have been devastated for generations.'*
>
> (Isaiah 61:4)

Egypt, a culture identified with the kingdom of death

Ancient Egypt was a society that was very much concerned with death. The Pharaohs and the rich used to work all their lives to build themselves suitable graves. The Pyramids were after all only lavish graves. Beside the Nile there is a town called Necropolis (city of the dead), where the rich built their graves in the form of palaces or hewn-out burial chambers in the rock. They spent their lives building such places, and their rich possessions and their gold was buried with them. They worshipped the sun-god in various names and forms; they perceived every sunset as the sun dying, to be reborn at sunrise the next day. The obelisk is a death symbol used in decorating graves. The best-known book about Egyptian religion is called the *Book of the Dead*. The Jewish scribes saw Egypt as a synonym for the kingdom of death. To 'go down to Egypt' was an expression meaning to enter the kingdom of the dead.

Egypt is a symbol of a society identified with the culture of the kingdom of the dead. Nineveh had among its gates one that was called the Gate of Death. The reliefs adorning the walls of the palace in Nineveh are divided in the middle by a horizontal line. The upper part of the relief shows the daily life of the city; the lower part shows the kingdom of death which influences the city's life. We seek and derive our inspiration from that which is above, where Jesus sits at the right hand of the Father. But there are societies that seek their inspiration from the underworld, and declare that their roots are in the kingdom of death.

The culture of the kingdom of death imposes its influence on art, adornment, literature, poetry and music. On the other hand, I would call the culture of the kingdom of God a Hosanna culture. As subjects of God's kingdom we are concerned with welcoming the King back, and that concern influences everything that we do. Once you have been awakened to this dimension, you will be surprised to see how much in our society is influenced by the culture of the kingdom of death. I once went into an art gallery, where I found one hall in which every single work of art showed the characteristics of death. That this is so frequent in our society is the result of many leaders in all fields of our culture entering into covenants with death in secret rituals in which they use coffins, skulls, bones, gallows and nooses round the neck.

Egypt is the end of the line, the terminus, for a society identified with the Fall. We fell from Paradise and ended in a house of slavery. Sin puts God's creation into slavery. We who are born into freedom as the children and heirs of God end up as slaves of a tyrant.

During the famine in Egypt, people came to Joseph crying for bread.

> *'Since our money is gone and our livestock belongs to you, there is nothing left for our lord except our bodies and our land. Why should we perish before your eyes – we and our land as well? Buy us and our land in exchange for food, and we with our land will be in bondage to Pharaoh.'* (Genesis 47:18–19)

The lowest level in the course of the Fall of man is reached when we become slaves under a tyrant who owns us, our land and our homes and we are obliged to obey him in order to be given our daily bread. The Bible describes the society of Antichrist in just such terms. The Fall leads us into the grip of a despot, a tyrant who makes us his slaves and thinks that he owns us. The society of Antichrist is a consequence of the Fall. When we have fallen to our lowest point, we become a sacrifice to the tyrant: we have a dictator. *'I will hand the Egyptians over to the power of a cruel master'* (Isaiah 19:4). Israel was handed over to the power of a cruel Pharaoh, and Egypt became for them a land of slavery; but then, *'With a mighty hand the Lord brought us out of Egypt, out of the land of slavery'* (Exodus 13:14).

Is modern Brasilia an Egyptian city?

In Brasilia, the capital city of Brazil, I was invited to participate in a conference for about 700 charismatic leaders
and pastors from all the states of Brazil.

The President who founded Brasilia, Rafael
Kubitschek, was a spiritist who believed in reincarnation.
He thought that he was a reincarnation of the Egyptian
Pharaoh Akhnaton, who himself built a new capital,
Aton. Several important buildings in Brasilia are in
pyramid form or look like Egyptian temples. The great
buildings in the centre of the city are laid out in a
geometric pattern in the form of a hexagram.

In Brasilia there are a number of sets of stone steps, and
pillars, planned in accordance with Egyptian Tarot
numerology and Jewish kabbala. The layout of the city is
like an Egyptian ibis, and along the line of the bird's spine
lie the Parliament building, the main processional street, a
pyramid monument, and the mausoleum of the founder
containing his coffin. In a tourist brochure, all the similarities between Brasilia and an Egyptian city are described. I
was given this by a pastor after I had led the group in
prayer warfare and proclaimed freedom for the city from
the spirits of death and of Pharaoh.

Exposing Masonic symbolism in La Plata, Argentina

Victor Lorenzo, himself a native of Argentina, has
described this strategy:

> 'My research confirmed that all of those who partici-
> pated in the founding of the city a little more than
> one hundred years ago were Masons. Dardo Rocha,
> known as the father of the city, was a high-ranking
> Mason.'[8]

He goes on to describe the city layout in some detail,

with a map. The city is planned with an overall geometric design using basic Masonic symbolic forms. Two diagonal boulevards cross each other to form an almost perfect pyramid, and the design also features the Masonic compass, square and inverted cross. Dardo Rocha, the founder, travelled to Egypt and brought back with him 16 mummies,

> 'presumably with the intention of helping to secure the city permanently under the power of dark angels. Today 4 of them are housed in the Natural Science Museum. No one I have contacted knows where the other 12 are, but some historians suspect that they lie buried in strategic points of the city where their potential occult power could influence the greatest number of inhabitants.' [9]

In the central Plaza Moreno are four large bronze statues of attractive women, each representing a curse over the city. These statues were ordered from a foundry in Paris owned and operated by Freemasons. The only statue in the centre of the plaza is a muscular archer with an arrow in his bow ready to shoot. The arrow points directly towards where the cross should be on the top of the cathedral; but the cathedral has no cross. The evil archer clearly symbolizes that the crucified Jesus has been shot away from the city's Christian centre.

On a straight line from the cathedral lies the 'historic axis of the city', which runs through all the power centres such as the Provincial Government headquarters, the city hall, the Argentine theatre, the Ministry of Health and the Army headquarters. This axis runs along where 52nd street should be, but there is no surface street. Instead, there is a tunnel running under all these buildings.

> 'Some say that the Masons conducted secret rituals under the centres of power in the city, thus

211

exercising, to the extent possible, spiritual control over the people.'[10]

The figure 6, prominent in the occult, features in the city layout plan, and the number 666 is displayed on many of the public buildings. Grotesque demonic faces also, beautifully painted and gilded, form a striking decoration on many buildings.

How Egyptian obelisks have ended up in New York, London and Paris

In Central Park in Manhattan, New York, stands an obelisk taken by the Freemasons from Heliopolis in Egypt. In Heliopolis itself, which is now a part of Cairo not far from the international airport, today only one obelisk is left. The others have been placed all around the world by the Freemasons; one is Cleopatra's Needle by the Thames in London. I have led prayer teams, praying and doing prayer warfare at these obelisks. We have used the words of judgment that the prophet Jeremiah pronounced over these same obelisks in ancient Heliopolis;

> *'And I shall set fire to the temples of the gods of Egypt, and he will burn them and take them captive. So he will wrap himself with the land of Egypt as a shepherd wraps himself with his garment, and he will depart from there safely. He will also shatter the obelisks of Heliopolis, which is in the land of Egypt, and the temples of the gods of Egypt he will burn with fire.'*
> (Jeremiah 43:12–13 NASB)

So Jeremiah pronounced the judgment of God over those obelisks that the Freemasons have taken and set up in different parts of the world.

Even the Statue of Liberty at the entrance to New York harbour stands as a monument to Babylonian and Egyptian influence. Freemasons in Paris presented it to

New York by way of confirming the freedom ideals of the French Revolution. The artist who created the statue took his inspiration from Egypt where he had been studying the Pharaonic monuments. The Pharos of Alexandria was the model for the plinth. We bought a card showing a Babylonian goddess from a museum in Baghdad; she had a torch and a diadem just like the Statue of Liberty.

Freemasons have, through the centuries, shown great interest in obelisks. They have succeeded in placing them in prominent places in great cities such as London, Paris, New York and Washington. I want to follow this track in order to prove the Freemasons' interest in occult town planning; and also to show that they have had such positions of power that they have managed to place the obelisks where they are without disclosing their true occult purposes.

In ancient Egypt, an obelisk was a sacred form dedicated to the sun-god Re or Ra, the creator of mankind, the source of heat and light, the being that all mankind is dependent on. The sun-god was worshipped in On (Heliopolis, city of the sun) where the first obelisks were erected.

> 'The spirit of the Sun-god was supposed to enter the stones at certain periods, and on these occasions human sacrifices were offered to it. The victims were probably prisoners of war who had been captured alive, and foreigners, and when these failed, the priests must have drawn upon the native population.'[11]

In later Egyptian history, it became customary to erect obelisks connected with Osiris, the god who is supposed to give life to the earth, vegetation and the Nile flood. Osiris is the god that the Freemasons are most interested in.

Osiris was a king of Egypt who married his sister Isis. According to the version of the story accepted by

Freemasons, Osiris was murdered and his body was torn into fourteen pieces. Isis recovered all but one of the pieces and gave Osiris a proper burial, but she never recovered his penis, which had been thrown into the Nile and eaten by fish. So she made an artificial organ and with its help she became pregnant and bore a son. The Egyptians established a cult and festival around the phallus of Osiris, and the obelisk became a fertility symbol standing for fatherhood: 'the rock that begot'.

Martin Short, in his book *Inside the Brotherhood*, quoted above, devotes a whole chapter to the Freemasons' interest in 'Obelisks and Egypt'. In it he shows how in the 19th century, Freemasons in England, France and the United States arranged for Egyptian obelisks to be transported and erected in Paris, London and New York, and for a much larger new one, of marble, to be erected in Washington, DC: the Washington Monument.

The people who arranged for the erection of the obelisk in Central Park in New York in 1880–81 were an editor, William Hulbert; a financier, William J. Vanderbilt, who provided the funds; and a sailor-cum-engineer, Lt-Cmdr Henry Gorringe, who was responsible for carrying the obelisk across the Atlantic. All three were Freemasons. Nine thousand Freemasons marched with bands through the streets to the park where Jesse Anthony, the Grand Master of New York Masons, laid the cornerstone. He said in his speech to those present:

> 'There can be no question but that in the secret societies of Egypt are to be found some elements now embraced in the principles or symbolism of Masonry.' [12]

The Washington Monument, 555 feet high, centrepiece of the grand vista facing the Capitol in Washington, took many years to complete, but was finally dedicated on 21 February 1885, birthday of America's founding President, George Washington. In the dedication cermony,

'...one prominent brother spoke of Masons now as builders of human society. Their stones were living men, "their minds enlightened with divine love, their hearts radiant with discovering the joy of pure love, their souls cherishing – like the ancient Egyptian worshippers of Osiris – the hope of immortality."' [13]

A forest of obelisks have been put up around the world by Freemasons. Some were erected as war memorials, some as memorials to Indian chiefs or statesmen, some to commemorate historical events. For example, at the place where the first boat-load of immigrants landed in Sydney, the Freemasons put up an obelisk; distances in Australia are reckoned from it. What people fail to realize is that these phallic symbols give an entry-point for demonic fertility thinking. People think they will achieve success and fruitfulness by means of a consecrated sex-organ of an Egyptian god. What actually happens is the exact opposite: the setting-up of a sex-organ in the name of the sun-god leads to unfruitfulness. Crime, violence, prostitution, sex clubs, drug peddling: these are the usual things to be found in connection with obelisks.

Obelisks are also incorporated in the occult town planning that the Freemasons use to control people, and to ensure that they themselves achieve success in the name of their gods. Obelisks are tied in with ley-lines – the occult lines of power.

Obelisks also have a function similar to American Indian totem-poles. These are likewise phallic symbols, bearing carved images of Indian gods. The pole marks the god's territory, and in the same way the Freemasons have set up their monuments, their gods and their obelisks to mark their territory. By these, they lay claim to the centre of the city and the most important centres of power.

The obelisk erected in Central Park in New York is dated 1600 BC. It bears an inscription that proclaims that the power of the sun-god On will be extended over all the world. The ancient Egyptian obelisks often carry inscriptions that are proclamations in the name of the gods. These proclamations are the exact opposite of the claims made by Jesus. Jesus is the Lord of lords and the King of kings. When we call on Jesus as Lord, we break all other territorial claims.

An obelisk is a stone pillar symbolizing an erect phallus, the male sex organ. The fact that so many came to be put up is proof of the enormous power that the Freemasons had in the nineteenth century, and their love-affair with the most provocative symbol in Egyptian religion – the obelisk.

Judgment over Egypt

Sin, when it is full-grown, gives birth to death. In a society where the power of death rules, judgment comes in the form of death. Note the differences carefully: Babylon was condemned to confusion, differences of languages, and scattering; Sodom was condemned to annihilation; but Egypt was condemned to be a house of sorrow, with one person dead in every household as the Destroyer went out among the people. Death will be the last among all his enemies to be robbed of its power. Death is expressed in the Bible as a personality, one of Jesus' enemies; and there is an angel of death.

> *'When the Lord goes through the land to strike down the Egyptians, he will see the blood on the top and sides of the door-frame and will pass over that doorway, and he will not permit the destroyer to enter your houses and strike you down.'* (Exodus 12:23)

> *'At midnight the Lord struck down all the firstborn in Egypt, from the firstborn of Pharaoh, who sat on the throne, to the firstborn of the prisoner, who was in the dungeon, and the firstborn of all the livestock as well. Pharaoh and all his officials and all the Egyptians got*

> *up during the night, and there was loud wailing in Egypt, for there was not a house without someone dead.'* (Exodus 12:29–30)

When the fourth seal is broken (Revelation 6:7), death will ride out over the world, followed by the kingdom of death. They will be given power over a fourth of the earth, to kill. I do not believe that death will acquire this power by mere chance. It is clear that he will take power everywhere that mankind has made a covenant with him by making use of symbols of death or the culture of the kingdom of death, such as requiems or black masses; and everywhere that places are adorned with death symbols, pyramids, obelisks and death monuments. In such places, death is welcomed in, the Destroyer can feel at home, and can harvest his fruit for eternity.

Vision of restoration for the society of the kingdom of death

The new Jerusalem is built in such a way that down the middle of the wide main street of the city there flows the river of life.

> *'Then the angel showed me the river of the water of life, as clear as crystal, flowing from the throne of God and of the Lamb down the middle of the great street of the city. On each side of the river stood the tree of life, bearing twelve crops of fruit, yielding its fruit every month. And the leaves of the tree are for the healing of the nations.'* (Revelation 22:1–2)

> *'There is a river whose streams make glad the city of God, the holy place where the Most High dwells.'* (Psalm 46:4)

This is not just a vision of a heavenly kingdom. We

pray, 'Let your kingdom come.' We want God's will to be done on earth as it is in heaven. We want to see a foretaste of the heavenly kingdom in the society we live in. Live churches are life-giving churches in the places where they are. In a town where there are a lot of Christians, an initiative is taken in the matter of life-giving. On each side of the main street of the city there are living churches, and along that main street there are Christian shops and businesses. I walked down a pedestrian shopping street in one town in Brazil, where my host took me into one shop after another where we met believers, people we could pray with. Right in the heart of the town is a place of prayer, where people can gather to pray at any time of the day or night.

Is there a river of life flowing through your city centre, or a river of death? If we lay out on the map an occult town planning pattern designed by Freemasons or anthroposophists, we often find that a line of death can be traced running straight down the main street.

In one town in the United States, on a single straight line beside the town's main street lie a Masonic temple, an Oddfellows lodge, a war memorial, obelisks, lifeless churches whose foundation stones were laid by leading Freemasons, a cemetery and a high place of sacrifice where the Indians in pre-Christian times sacrificed human beings to the sun-god. All these places I have mentioned have something to do with death. This has invited a spirit of death to come over the people of the town – the straight main street is like a spinal column of death running through the centre of the community. The town centre is known as a place with a high rate of suicides, violent crime, broken homes and depression.

The city that welcomes Jesus

The goal of restoration is a society preparing to welcome Jesus back as king over all the earth. Jesus is expecting to be welcomed in Jerusalem when he returns.

'For I tell you, you will not see me again until you say, "Blessed is he who comes in the name of the Lord."'

(Matthew 23:39)

Jesus will not come back until Jerusalem has learnt the lesson of 'Hosanna'. When Jesus rode into Jerusalem on a donkey, the welcome given to him was not complete. The children, Jesus' own disciples, and the ordinary people welcomed him, but the leaders of the people interrupted the cries of homage. So Jesus waits for Jerusalem to be ready to receive him as king. What festivities there will be when the king comes home to his capital city! The Father is not going to send the Son to be humiliated once more on the earth; when he comes, the people will have learnt to honour the Son. We are working now to make our community ready to welcome Jesus when he comes back. In more and more towns an annual march for Jesus is being held; they are taking place in most of the world's capitals.

At the same time, we must be aware that many cities have an annual pagan festival, in which the city's god or patron saint is honoured. The number of carnivals, too, is on the increase. A town or city must either prepare itself to welcome Jesus or, if it does not, then it is preparing to welcome Antichrist. A large proportion of the world's population will worship the beast, and are making themselves ready to do so.

'The whole world was astonished and followed the beast. Men worshipped the dragon because he had given authority to the beast, and they also worshipped the beast and asked, "Who is like the beast? Who can make war against him?"' (Revelation 13:3b–4)

Occult annual festivals

George Otis Jr has been working for three years on the task of spiritual mapping of the countries where unreached peoples live. He has travelled in over 100 different countries seeking to find out what it is that keeps people bound. He believes that people have made pacts with demonic powers. Every year the pact is renewed with the false god of the city, the tribe or the people, through a festival held in honour of the god. The dragon-god or the snake-god is brought out, or it may be the relics of the local saint, or as in Kandy in Sri Lanka the Buddha's tooth, and they are carried in a procession like a carnival. Religious festivals, ceremonials and pilgrimages take place somewhere in the world every week of the year to the honour of one or another god. Some of these are visited by a million people. In Spain they hold a fiesta in honour of the saint who protects the town, as for example, Pamplona. George Otis Jr has mapped 3,000 such festivals: Shinto festivals in Japan, festivals like Kumbha Mela in India, Inti Raymi in Peru, and Halloween in the US.

Festivals where Satan renews his lease with the people

George Otis Jr says that through such demonic festivals, Satan renews his lease with the people so that his fallen angels can carry on in occupation for one more year. Festivals are conscious transactions in the spirit world. They are opportunities for the younger generation to renew the covenants that their forefathers concluded in the spirit world. To hold a festival is like putting out a welcome mat for Satan's angels. During carnivals and feasts in honour of false gods, the Christians in the area have an overwhelming sense of darkness. That is the time when demonic attacks and persecution generally come upon missionaries and churches, and demonic signs and wonders generally take place.

Stockholm's Water Festival and the Water-god

The Water Festival in Stockholm, held in the second week of August, has become the biggest folk-festival in

Sweden. A high point in the Water Festival is the carnival in which people dance the samba and dress up, naked women are painted grey and homosexual couples walk about arm in arm. Carnival means giving free rein to the lusts of the flesh. New Age folk have been working for ten years to import carnivals of the kind held in Rio, and now their work has borne fruit. The carnival in Rio has its own goddess who is worshipped during the carnival. She is called Aparicida (she who comes out of the sea). So who is the god of the Stockholm festival? There is a monument that stands on a well-known quay in the Old Town of Stockholm, called the Water-god. The central part of the city is closed to traffic during the festival, and on one evening 300,000 people were gathered there.

God's plan for Stockholm is that the song of praise to Jesus should be heard in the streets, in the squares and in the city centre. Satan's plan is to use the Water Festival to build up a platform so that he can rely on annual renewals of his lease with the people of Stockholm. If Satan takes control, the people will allow the lusts of the flesh to rule unchecked; but we want to see the Jesus marches increasing in numbers from year to year until the return of Jesus. We want Jesus marches instead of carnivals. Jesus is worthy of festivals in his honour in the same format as the Water Festival.

The society of Antichrist

According to the book of Revelation, the society of Antichrist will be a collected mobilization of all the various patterns of society that have grown to maturity in history since the third Fall of man. Babylon, the occult city; Sodom, the city where sin grew to its fullest extent; Egypt, where the culture of the kingdom of death found its fullest expression and slavery kept people captive under a despotic ruler; and the religious Jerusalem, where in the name of religion the prophets sent by God were persecuted and killed; all these together will become the society of the beast.

It will become the battlefield of the End Time; there will be both martyrs and overcomers. That is where we shall bear our testimony and go on doing so until Jesus comes. It is on that battlefield that we shall bring in the final harvest and complete our missionary task. The intercessors will be there preparing for the coming of Jesus.

> '*Now when they have finished their testimony, the beast that comes up from the Abyss will attack them, and overpower and kill them. Their bodies will lie in the street of the great city* [a term for Babylon], *which is figuratively called Sodom and Egypt, where also their Lord was crucified.*' (Revelation 11:7–8)

John speaks of Jerusalem, which does not receive those whom God has sent, and stones the prophets.

When we pray for our own area, we need to ask:

– In what way is Sodom expressed in our town? Porn-clubs, homosexual clubs, the pornography industry; places where we can say that sin has reached its fullest extent and flaunts itself.

– In what way is Egypt expressed in our town? Pyramids, obelisks, Masonic temples are all Egyptian temples where the culture of death predominates.

– In what way is Babylon represented? Occult centres, occult town layout and planning, a centre of pride, expressions (such as statues) of man making a name for himself, grandiose buildings. A society resembling Babylon will be condemned in the same way as Babylon.

> '*The cities of the nations collapsed. God remembered Babylon the Great and gave her the cup filled with the wine of the fury of his wrath.*' (Revelation 16:19)

– In what way is the old Jerusalem represented? Religious headquarters; a ministry of religions; religious centres that generate persecution against those who love Jesus and believe the Bible.

– Is there any expression of the society of the beast? TV channels or newspapers that publish scandal about Christians. A great mouth, a dragon with many heads.

– In what ways are we preparing to welcome the Antichrist into our community? We pray instead for expressions of welcome to Jesus, such as Jesus marches.

– What witnesses does Jesus have in our area? We are to protect the harvest field so that our town does not become a high-risk area for those who witness boldly for Jesus.

Notes

1. From Shomoto 1969:172, quoted in a magazine article.
2. The Code of Hammurabi is written in cuneiform script around a black diorite shaft, now in the Louvre Museum in Paris. The translation into English appears in G.R. Driver and John C. Miles, *The Babylonian Laws*, Oxford, 1955, Vol. IX pp. 7–107.
3. Professor Peter Proudfoot, *The Secret Plan of Canberra*, University of New South Wales, 1994, quoted in an article by John Huxley in the *Sydney Morning Herald*, 22 January 1994.
4. Stephen Mansfield, *Releasing Destiny*, Nashville, Tennessee, (1993), p. 36.
5. Guy Underwood, *The Pattern of the Past*, London, 1972.
6. Francis Hitching, *Earth Magic*, London, 1976.
7. David Tidy, video presentation, *The Root and Fruit of the Spirit of Freemasonry*, City Vision, Hemel Hempstead, Herts, 1994.
8. Victor Lorenzo, 'Evangelizing a city dedicated to darkness', Chapter 7 of *Breaking Strongholds in Your City*, ed. C. Peter Wagner, Monarch Publications, Tunbridge Wells, England, 1993, p. 183.
9. Victor Lorenzo, ibid. p. 184.
10. Victor Lorenzo, ibid. p. 187.

11. From E.A. Wallis-Budge's notes on Ra/Re, included in the Medici Society reprint of *The Book of the Dead*, University Books, Secaucus, New Jersey, 1960; quoted in Martin Short, *Inside the Brotherhood*, Harper Collins, London, paperback edition 1993, pp. 115–6.
12. Martin Short, ibid. p. 121.
13. Martin Short, ibid. p. 122.

Chapter 9

The Battle for Restoration

Humanism and the Greek gods

Prayer movements have sprung up in nation after nation, and the network linking them has become a world-wide prayer movement. It has been in connection with the unreached peoples and the unreached within the 10/40 window that the national movements have found a common purpose and sense of belonging together. Prayer for Israel has also become an important area of common concern for intercessors from many nations. Each year, intercessors from different countries assemble in Jerusalem to pray with Messianic Jews from congregations in Israel. There are some intercessors today who say that God has called them into a world-wide intercessory ministry. The world-wide network of intercessors has also been established with a calling to prophetic prayer before the closing of the present age. This calling is to prophetic prayer for the restoration of all things before Jesus comes.

Whenever I am leading a group in preparation for prayer warfare, I am concerned to define exactly the battlefield we are entering on, to declare what are the spiritual principalities operating on that battlefield, and to give the group motivation for the battle and what it is about. There is a prayer battle to be fought, in which the giants are to be defeated and all things are to be restored again.

Who are the last giants who have to be defeated before the kingdom of God can be established in victory and Christ can come back? George Otis Jr in his book *The Last of the Giants* [1] reckons that the last enemies to be conquered will be the spirits governing Islam, Hinduism and Buddhism, and the principality over Persia who is behind both Iraq and Iran. These powers must be defeated and laid under the feet of Jesus, and the missionary task must be completed, before Jesus comes in his kingdom. But my own view is that the last giants that we have to conquer in the final battle on the day of the Lord are not Islam, Hinduism and Buddhism; they are the powers governing humanism and the Greek gods, and they have their stronghold in the secularized Western world, for example in Europe and the United States.

Before the prayer conference in Jerusalem in January 1994, the Israeli leadership had met in advance of the conference and defined the power operating in many of the immediately urgent areas for prayer in Israel as being humanism. It is identified in the Bible as 'the sons of Greece' (Zechariah 9:13) in a passage which points forward to the battle in the End Time, in which we are already engaged.

> *'I will bend Judah as I bend my bow and fill it with Ephraim. I will rouse your sons, O Zion, against your sons, O Greece, and make you like a warrior's sword. Then the Lord will appear over them; his arrow will flash like lightning. The Sovereign Lord will sound the trumpet; he will march in the storms of the south, and the Lord Almighty will shield them. They will destroy and overcome with slingstones.'* (Zechariah 9:13–15)

The Lord is going to use the sons of Zion as living projectiles against the sons of Greece. We interpret the 'sons of Zion' in this scripture as meaning those Jews and

Christians who fully accept God's revelation in his written Word and all those who live their lives according to the Spirit. The 'sons of Greece' are the wise men and philosophers of Greece and their gods, and all who live their lives according to the flesh and the wisdom of man. The sons of Greece can mean Plato, Pythagoras, Socrates and Aristotle, but it can also mean those who identify themselves with the Greek gods. The final battle that takes place in the End Time will be between these two groups. The Lord himself will fight, and the sons of Zion will emerge victorious.

The Humanist Manifestos

Greek thought has given us humanism, which received its own confessions of faith in the form of the Humanist Manifestos which were signed in 1933 and 1973. These manifestos have, among other things, formed the foundation for education in the schools of the United States.

Here are some extracts from the 1973 Manifesto:

> '*First:* In the best sense, religion may inspire dedication to the highest ethical ideals ... We believe, however, that traditional dogmatic or authoritarian religions that place revelation, God, ritual or creed above human needs and experience do a disservice to the human species. Any account of nature should pass the tests of scientific evidence; in our judgment, the dogmas and myths of traditional religions do not do so ... We find insufficient evidence for belief in the existence of a supernatural ... We begin with humans not God, nature not deity ... No deity will save us; we must save ourselves.
>
> '*Second:* Promises of immortal salvation or fear of eternal damnation are both illusory and harmful. They distract humans from present concerns, from self-actualization, and from rectifying social injustices ...

227

'*Sixth:* In the area of sexuality, we believe that intolerant attitudes, often cultivated by orthodox religions and puritanical cultures, unduly repress sexual conduct. The right to birth control, abortion, and divorce should be recognized ... neither do we wish to prohibit, by law or social sanction, sexual behaviour between consenting adults. The many varieties of sexual exploration should not in themselves be considered 'evil' ...

'*Seventh:* ... a full range of **civil liberties** ... includes a recognition of an individual's right to die with dignity, euthanasia, and the right to suicide ...

'*Twelfth:* We deplore the division of humankind on nationalistic grounds. We have reached a turning point in human history where the best option is to **transcend the limits of national sovereignty** and to move toward the building of a world community in which all sectors of the human family can participate. Thus we look to the development of a system of world law and a world order based upon transnational federal government ...'[2]

Christian ethics and Western humanism

Western humanism originates in Greek thought, and is carried through as the basis of action and purpose today, according to the manifestos. In Sweden, the political parties all have humanism as a common denominator in their programmes. When the Swedish Christian Democratic movement wanted to have Christian ethics written into the national aims for education, they had to add Western humanism as well in order to receive any backing from the other political parties. Christian ethics and Western humanism may be the moral principles that win majorities, but in fact they form an impossible compromise, if we read what the manifestos actually say. The two simply cannot be made one.

The conflict between Greek wisdom and the wisdom of God

Paul knew when he came to Corinth that the Greeks desire wisdom, and he saw the conflict between human wisdom and the wisdom of God. So he resolved that he would not come to the people of Corinth with eloquence or superior wisdom. He chose to know nothing while he was with them, except Jesus Christ and him crucified (1 Corinthians 2:1–2). He did not want to bring them wise and persuasive words, since their faith might then rest on men's wisdom; his aim was that their faith should be based on God's power.

> *'We do, however, speak a message of wisdom among the mature, but not the wisdom of this age or of the rulers of this age, who are coming to nothing. No, we speak of God's secret wisdom, a wisdom that has been hidden and that God destined for our glory before time began. None of the rulers of this age understood it, for if they had, they would not have crucified the Lord of glory.'* (1 Corinthians 2:6–8)

Who are *'the rulers of this age'* (KJV *'the princes of this world'*)? Perhaps in Jerusalem they were Pontius Pilate, Herod and the high priest; but can we really call those men the rulers of their age? They were only political and religious leaders on the local plane who decided to crucify Jesus. They did not have the authority to affect the whole of their age. It is much more likely that Paul meant the spiritual rulers – the powers standing behind Greek wisdom. He describes them as having considerable power as rulers or princes, as powerful, it seems to me, as the Greek gods, or the spiritual powers standing behind the Greek gods. They have taken control and are the world rulers.

Hugo Odeberg says of this expression in his commentary on 1 Corinthians that in his view *'the princes of this age'* are the invisible powers that represent the birth, growth, flowering and decline of the world kingdom and world culture.[3]

In Daniel's interpretation of Nebuchadnezzar's vision of the four world kingdoms, it is only the third one, the Greek kingdom, that he describes as ruling over the whole world:

> *'Next, a third kingdom, one of bronze, will rule over the whole earth.'*
> (Daniel 2:39b)

The Greek kingdom still rules over the whole earth through Greek culture and what we call Western humanism.

The abomination of desolation in the holy place

When Jesus was instructing his disciples about the time before his coming, he gave them a sign:

> *'So when you see standing in the holy place "the abomination that causes desolation", spoken of through the prophet Daniel – let the reader understand...'*
> (Matthew 24:15)

This is a warning about the coming of Antichrist. Antiochus Epiphanes was an anti-Christian personality who did exactly that which Daniel prophesied. We can read the history in the books of Maccabees in the Apocrypha.

Antiochus Epiphanes decided to get rid of every trace of orthodox Jewish faith. He identified the God of Israel with Jupiter, and he set up an altar to Jupiter in the temple in Jerusalem. Pigs were sacrificed on this altar. This altar to Jupiter was the *'abomination that causes desolation'*. The Jews were forbidden, on pain of death, to practise circumcision, or to celebrate the sabbath or the Jewish feasts. If any scrolls of the Law were found, they were torn up and burnt, and anyone in whose house the scrolls were found was put to death (1 Maccabees 1:41–64).

The representative of Antiochus came to Modin, a village 15 miles from Jerusalem, where he set up an altar to Jupiter, gathered the village people and demanded of the priest Mattathias that he should make a sacrifice on the altar. Mattathias refused, but another Jew came forward to make the sacrifice. Mattathias, inflamed with zeal, rushed out and killed the Jew and also the king's commissioner. Then he fled into the desert with his five sons, and a rebellion against Antiochus began (1 Maccabees 2:1–30).

There were many Jews in the time of Antiochus who had adapted themselves to the Greek culture and its gods. They had become Hellenistic Jews, and this tendency has at various times in history been a temptation for Jewish people, as also in our own time. Influenced by world leaders who speak about the New World Order, it is easy for Jewish leaders to compromise with God's word. Are they to believe in the prophets and in revelation, or are they to seek man's own logical solutions in the new humanistic world order? In the New World Order there is no place for Israel as a chosen, separate people, living in a land and in a city that the Lord calls 'my land' and 'my city'.

The Christians of the first century lived through a time of persecution by the Roman Emperors. The Emperors demanded to be worshipped as gods, and as a sign of their loyalty to the empire, it was expected that the people should make sacrifices to Jupiter. The Christians could avoid being thrown to the lions in the Colosseum if they would renounce their faith. The conditions were that they should deny Christ and sacrifice to Jupiter.

The final Antichrist is going to be very like the earlier anti-Christians, such as Antiochus Epiphanes and the Roman Emperors such as Nero. This implies that our confrontation is going to be with Zeus, or Jupiter as the Romans called him.

The Greek influence over the church

The early church proclaimed Jesus as the only way to God and defied all other gods. This was a threat to the craftsmen and worshippers of the Greek gods, as in Ephesus (Acts 19).

But the church broke away from its Jewish roots and consequently could not continue to withstand the pressure from its surroundings. It became more and more influenced by and rooted in the Greek culture. A most important step in the restoration of the church will be a return to its Jewish roots, which will necessitate a new relationship, free from all compromise, with the Greek influence.

Ralph Stob, a Christian philosopher, has written:

> 'This element of the Greek spirit had a great influence on ... the Christian movement in the first three centuries. At the same time it was the factor lying at the bottom of many of the delusions that arose.'[4]

Marvin R. Wilson comments that 'the Church became vulnerable to these heresies by cutting itself off from the very root that nourished its beginnings.'[5]

Our tutors who led us to Christ were Moses and the prophets, not Plato and Aristotle, and that applies both to Jews and to Christians, to the people of the Old Testament as well as the New Testament.

John Spong says, 'When Christianity cut away the bands that bound it to Judaism, the Christian faith itself became distorted.'[6]

The church cannot be fully restored until it again discovers its Jewish roots and at the same time lays an axe to the root of the Greek humanistic influence.

Norman Snaith has written:

> 'The object and aim of the Hebrew system is *da'ath elohim* (knowledge of God). The object and aim of

the Greek system is *gnothi seauton* (know thyself). Between these two there is the widest possible difference. There is no compromise between the two on anything like equal terms. They are poles apart in attitude and method. The Hebrew system starts with God. The only true wisdom is knowledge of God. "The fear of God is the beginning of wisdom" ... The Greek system, on the contrary, starts from the knowledge of man, and seeks to rise to an understanding of the ways and nature of God through the knowledge of what is called "man's higher nature". According to the Bible, man has no higher nature except he be born of the Spirit.' [7]

There are some denominations and Christian groups that seldom preach from the Old Testament, and are therefore ignorant of it. They never manage to read Jewish books. They are typical of Christians who have cut themselves off from their Jewish roots, and instead open themselves up to humanist influence.

The Emperor Constantine was a man who did much to bring about the blending of Christianity with paganism. During the period 323–327 he built a large number of church buildings for Christians at the expense of the state. During the first three centuries, Christians had met together in homes; it was the Roman state that had churches built. In his Roman thinking, Constantine had each church building dedicated to some well-known Christian, because he was used to temples dedicated to Greek or Roman gods. So the churches were called St Joseph's or St Mary's or St Peter's, in the same way as the temples had been called after Apollo or Zeus. In one of the great churches he had thirteen statues put up, one of each of the thirteen apostles. Constantine himself became the thirteenth apostle, and his statue was larger than all the others.

John Chrysostom ('golden-mouthed') had a great influence on Christian preaching. He studied rhetoric and was himself much influenced by Aristotle, the Greek father of the art of public speaking. Preaching, homiletics and oratory as taught in theological colleges have been influenced more by Greek oratory than by the Jewish prophets. Prophetic preaching was stifled when Greek speaking came into the church and replaced it. Human wisdom shone out of the pulpit rather than revelation from God.

During the first 300 years of the Christian church, no titles such as bishop, priest or pastor were used when addressing Christian leaders. Only the Christian name was used. 25,000 fragments of letters or engravings attributed to Christians of those first centuries have been found, and not one of them uses a title in addressing a leader. As only Christian names were used, it was not possible to tell what class of society a person came from, whether from slavery or from a rich family. Putting pulpits in churches and drawing up a formal order of service are traditions arising from the Emperor Constantine's time and from Greek influence.

The church must be freed from Greek humanist domination and be restored again to find its Jewish roots. Greek thinking must be defeated all over the world before the Jews, the people of revelation, can stand as the key people that God intended them to be. By being a separated people and by holding fast to the revelation that God has given them, the Jews are going to be the only alternative to the humanistic world order.

Greek Humanism today in the architecture of our cities

If we carry out spiritual mapping of our cities, we see in certain cities a strong Greek influence in the architecture and form of some of the buildings. Sometimes a whole building is a copy of a Greek temple; or else we may see statues or ornamentation in the form of Greek gods or goddesses. Often these trends can be seen in banks or stock exchanges in the world's financial centres. The

Greek god Hermes (Roman Mercury) is usually found as protector of a financial centre, because he is the god of businessmen and thieves. In the centre of Gothenburg, Sweden's western port city, there is a statue of Poseidon, the Greek sea-god (Roman Neptune).

When investigation has been made as to how these temples and statues came to be where they are in the cities, their history often takes us back to the Freemasons. Either the city architect was a Mason, or else the money for the ornamentation of the building was given by a group of Masons. In the United States, the Greek influence over architecture and ornaments is particularly marked. The different Masonic lodges have varying traditions in their links with the ancient cultures: some follow the Greek tradition and others the Egyptian, and this difference shows in the whole spirit of the city. Huntsville, Alabama, is one of the centres of NASA's space programme; the Apollo rockets were built there. It is interesting that they were called Apollo, which is the name of the city's first Masonic lodge, while the second lodge is called Helios (sun). (Apollo is the sun-god.)

Nashville – 'Athens of the South'

Stephen Mansfield writes about Nashville, Tennessee:

'There is a connection between the Greek and Egyptian architecture of Nashville and Freemasonry. The Masons even use Greek architectural terms to identify divisions of their organization. For example Doric, Ionic and Corinthian are the names of three of the five divisions of the "Ancient and Accepted Scottish Rite". They are also terms of classification for Greek architecture. The symbolism of Freemasonry centers around architecture and its history, tools and terminology. The rule of thumb in American cities is that the more Masonic a town has been, the more

Greek, Egyptian and Babylonian its architecture will be.'[8]

In Nashville the Freemasons have built a Parthenon in Centennial Park which is an exact copy of the Parthenon on the Acropolis in Athens. Inside the temple stands an enormous statue of the goddess Athena. The foundation stone of the Nashville Parthenon was laid by Freemasons to the accompaniment of their traditional rites. There is a great deal of Greek architecture in Nashville, which Stephen Mansfield in his mapping has been able to attribute to the strong Masonic influence in the city. He also writes of the Greek thinking which restricts people's minds throughout the city:

'The phrase "Athens of the South" is more than a nickname for Nashville. It also defines what the city has yearned to become during its history. Nashville has chosen for her model the chief city of the ancient Greeks, as clearly evidenced by her architecture and street names, as well as her world view.

'We should not be surprised, then, that Greek philosophy pervades so much of the city's religious and cultural life. The problem, though, is that Greek philosophy is humanistic and rationalistic and to the extent that Nashville is shaped by such thinking she is being moulded by a force at odds with the Gospel of Jesus Christ...

'Consider how this would affect Nashville. In matters of religion, a Greek orientation would produce an arid intellectualism. Churches would become lecture halls rather than spirit-filled places of celebration and biblical teaching. People would be content to hear for the sake of hearing something new, but not hear for the sake of "doing the Word". We would expect leaders to be academically qualified people with little spiritual power and their congregations to be like them. We might also expect a strong emphasis on books, seminars, teaching and information as solutions to spiritual problems rather than prayer, Bible reading, godly counsel from spiritual authorities, fasting, and worship. And since Greek philosophy emphasizes a social hierarchy based on knowledge rather than spiritual calling or gifting, we might also expect the people of such a world view to be rebellious and independent. If this sounds like Nashville today, then the Greek way of thinking is already bearing fruit.

'Since knowledge leads to salvation in the Greek perspective, a city strongly influenced by Greek philosophy will have an excessively high regard for the value of schools and learning. Nashville has 16 colleges and universities...

'Pride follows close on the heels of a society which sees its salvation in knowledge, its deliverance in education, and its truth in science.

'Some would call what we are describing an "intellectual spirit" ... [Others] would probably see it as a fruit of the Greek rationalism which pervades Western civilization ... It is a force which opposes biblical Christianity and which serves as a barrier to the purposes of God for Nashville.'[9]

Greek architecture in Edinburgh

Tony Walker, of Edinburgh, wrote as follows in some notes made in preparation for a prayer conference:

'Calton Hill, which has an impressive overview of Edinburgh, contains many buildings which were inspired by Greek architecture. For example there is the National Monument which was erected in 1816 as a memorial to those who died in the Napoleonic wars. There is also a reproduction of the Parthenon, which was dedicated to Athene...

'Opposite Calton Hill [is] the Royal High School. The building was inspired by the Temple of Theos in Athens...

'Along the Water of Leith, between Dean Bridge and Stockbridge is the pump room, located near St Bernard's Well. The architectural style of this edifice is that of a Doric temple. At the centre of this temple is a statue of Hygeia, the Greek goddess of health...'[10]

The influence of humanism over sectors of society

It is easy to see the influence of humanism within all sectors of society: schools and teaching, art and culture, the mass media, politics, sociology, philosophy and theology. I will give some examples.

Schools and teaching

We tend to think that humanism teaches children to be human, kind, friendly and civilized in their relationships with one another. In reality, however, to teach children humanism is to teach them something very like a religion, by instructing them in the principles of what lies in humanist doctrines and creeds.

Humanism is propagated in schools; it is not something abstract or inaccessible, but is very real and easily identified, as long as you know what you are looking for.

Harry Conn in his book *Four Trojan Horses of Humanism* writes as follows:

'Specifically, what are some of the principles or articles of faith of Humanist belief that find their way into public and even private education? Above all, Humanists do not believe in God and, of course, they do not believe in salvation and damnation. They believe in the theory of evolution, a theory that is often presented as fact in many schools and textbooks. Humanists believe that everyone has the right to full sexual freedom, the right to express their individual sexual preference as they desire. They believe that everyone, regardless of age and condition has the right to determine the values and goals that affect their lives. They believe in the right to suicide, abortion and euthanasia. They adhere to situation ethics morality, meaning they do not live by or believe in absolute standards of morality. They recognize no immutable rights or wrongs as revealed in the Ten Commandments. They believe everyone has a right to maximum individual autonomy, meaning the right of each to do his own thing, whatever it may be. Humanists do not believe in national sovereignty, but in a world government.' [11]

Psychology

According to Jungian psychology, the Greek gods are within us as myths, in the form of archetypes deep down in our collective conscience from former times. A paper issued by the Centre for Jungian Psychology in 1993 states that the god-myths are a feature of mankind's personality. Some examples: Poseidon lives his secret life in many people through outbursts of feeling; he is the ebullient man of passions, partly anger and lust for revenge, partly mercy: for example, Saddam Hussein. Zeus lives in a personality through will-power, coolness and lust for power: the example given is Margaret Thatcher. The Hades personality is recognizable by coolness and introspectiveness: the example is Greta Garbo. [12]

Sociology

Humanism is a belief that man has within himself the resources to solve all his problems without the help of any supernatural power or personality.

Theology

Peter Beyerhaus, formerly Professor of Missions at the University of Tübingen, Germany, has written as follows:

> 'The misery of modernist theology is that it has participated in the original sin of the Enlightenment, the idolization of man's reason. In a hidden way, idolization of our unilluminated reason is still influencing all our theological work, even the work of many conservative scholars. The healing of our theology and our churches in Europe and America can only take place if we penitently subject our intellect in faith to the guidance of the Holy Spirit.' [13]

The Olympic Games and the Greek gods

It is customary for YWAM to have large groups of young people evangelizing at every Olympiad. When the Winter Olympics were held at Lillehammer in Norway in February 1994, I was asked to lead the intercession for this evangelistic offensive. In the course of two visits to Lillehammer, before and after the Olympics, I came to see how strong was the influence of the Greek gods over the Olympic movement. Before the opening ceremony, which was watched on TV all over the world, 400 schoolchildren were to sing a hymn of praise to Zeus. Ragnhild, a 13-year-old girl, and her friend did not want to take part or to praise Zeus because of their Christian faith. 'I don't want to break the first commandment, "You shall have no other gods before me",' Ragnhild told me.

When we look at the words of the Olympic Hymn to Zeus, it becomes clear that Zeus is a spiritual power with ambitions of becoming a world ruler.

The Olympic Hymn
Immortal spirit of antiquity,
Father of the true, beautiful and good,
Descend, appear, shed over us thy light
Upon this ground and under this sky
Which has first witnessed thy imperishable fame.

Give life and animation to those noble games!
Throw wreaths of fadeless flowers to the victors
In the race and in the strife!
Create in our breasts, hearts of steel!

In thy light, plains, mountains and seas
Shine in a roseate hue and form a vast temple
To which all nations throng to adore thee,
Oh immortal spirit of antiquity! [14]

The Olympic Games and the Greek 'lighting the flame' ceremony

The Norwegian press reported, with pictures, the lighting of the Olympic torch at an altar on the Greek mountain of the gods, Mount Olympus. Twenty Greek priestesses, dressed in robes like Iris (goddess of the rainbow), kindled the flame with the aid of the sun's rays while they worshipped Apollo and Zeus. Bearing the newly-lit torch, they turned in worship towards an olive-tree symbolizing peace. Afterwards the torch was taken to the original stadium in Athens where the heart of the founder of the modern Olympic Games, the French Baron Pierre de Coubertin, is buried. There, a further appeal was made to Zeus for the success of the Winter Olympics in Lillehammer. The torch was then carried, among other means, by a relay of runners across Germany and was greeted by thousands of people. The Norwegians already had their own flame, but this was not permitted to be mixed with the Greek flame, as had been allowed at the Olympic Games in Norway in 1952. Instead, the Norwegian flame was kept hidden until it was brought out for the opening of the Handicapped Olympics. There had not been such care taken to preserve the purity of the Greek 'strange fire', unmixed with flame from any other source, since the 1936 Games in Berlin when Hitler had recently come to power. Anti-Christian personalities are helped to come to power through occult ceremonies.

A minority of Christians protested at the singing of a hymn to Zeus at the opening ceremony. The Norwegian Lutheran Church was divided. The majority of the bishops said: 'There is only one God. Zeus does not exist, nor do any of the other gods. Therefore it does not matter if you sing a hymn of praise to a god who is not there.' But that was not the way that the first Christians thought; they chose to be martyrs rather than to sing the praises of Zeus.

The leader of the Norwegian Church's Olympic Games Committee, Bishop Georg Hille, answered the criticism against the hymn to Zeus by showing that the opening ceremony was an entertainment and not a religious service, and therefore it did not matter that it contained pagan elements. Other Christians said: This is worshipping a pagan god. In the fourth century, the Roman Emperor forbade the Olympic Games because he perceived them as pagan. The Christian martyrs were thrown to the wild beasts in the Colosseum in Rome for the purposes of entertainment. Before they were led in to their deaths, they were invited to deny their faith by sacrificing to Zeus, but they refused.

A few days before the beginning of the Winter Olympics, sixteen Christian leaders wrote a letter to the Olympic Games president Gerhard Heiberg, asking him to remove the Olympic Hymn from the Games programme:

> 'We wish to express our concern that the Olympic Games has an ideological purpose that promotes multi-faith religion with roots in Greek mythology.'

The historian Edvard Karstensen went even further and said, 'The Olympiad is an anti-Christian phenomenon.'

By giving homage to the Greek gods in the Olympic Games, it became obvious both in Barcelona and in Lillehammer that the opening and closing ceremonies were full of occult content. In Lillehammer, creatures dressed as forest-spirits and trolls oozed up from the underworld, and in the closing ceremony, the evil-looking black forest-spirits came up from the abyss and performed a weird dance.

When I visited Lillehammer after the Olympics had ended, people said to me: 'We had more trouble with the living gods than with the old Greek ones.' The members of the Olympic Committee behaved as if they were gods. None of the furniture in Lillehammer was up to their standard; they had special rococo furniture flown in from Italy to furnish their rooms. If anyone had to be admitted to the hospital in Lillehammer, they were frightened that they might contract Aids from blood transfusions, so they had their own supply of blood flown in as a precaution. They wanted to be treated as if they were gods. Those who were guarding the honour and traditions of the Greek gods themselves became gods, just as the Roman Emperors had done.

New Age and the Greek tradition

In New Age bookshops, a rich variety of literature about the Greek gods can be seen, explaining how the Greek tradition can be followed today, and how to conduct rites and prayers, so as to become one with the god or goddess and to 'feel' the touch or receive a visitation from one's favourite god. New Age people take the Greek gods seriously. I believe that behind the Greek gods there are demonic powers and that those who honour the gods come into contact with those powers.

In the Greek myths, it is told how men could be taken up among the gods on Olympus. Hercules was one who, from having been once a man, became a god. In the Greek tradition men go the way of their hero, becoming dedicated step by step until they become one with their god-companion. So they are exhorted, 'Choose one of the gods or goddesses as your companion and spiritual teacher.' Choosing a god is not something to be taken lightly.

> 'It is rather a question of "Man, know thyself", because in knowing yourself ... you will become aware of your spiritual ancestry or cosmic roots.'

After choosing your Greek god comes the next step: the mystical identification with him or her. To enter into this identification with your god is to become the god yourself.

> ' "Enter thou into my spirit and my thoughts my whole life long, for thou art I and I am thou; thy name I guard as a charm in my heart." In a similar prayer we read: "I know thee, Hermes, and thou knowest me, I am thou and thou art I." '
>
> 'We are all gods in the making and we will achieve the Olympian heights only when we have overcome our mortality or conquered death through the Path of Initiation.' [15]

As we read how the Greek god tradition is being carried further by the New Age movement, and how by worshipping his god and by mystical identification with him a person can himself seek to become a god, we can easily understand how a Roman Emperor could be ambitious of becoming a god and ruling through the power of his god. We Christians have our own identification with Christ, and therefore there is a direct confrontation in our spirit when we meet those who have become one with other gods.

Prayer action in the cave, the birthplace of Zeus

In December 1993 I led a prayer team to Crete. In Crete in the time of the first Christians, there was a church in every town. Paul instructed Titus to *'appoint elders in every town'* in Crete (Titus 1:5). Today there are only a few small churches.

Our international team with two Israeli intercessors went to the cave that was supposed to be the birthplace of Zeus, the Dikteon cave, to pray. Zeus is the father figure among the Greek gods, and we saw him as a world ruler.

According to the Greek legend, Zeus was born in the cave of Dikteon in Crete. It was also the place where he took Europa, the daughter of the king of Tyre. He took the form of a bull and attracted Europa's attention. As she rode on the bull, he leapt down into the sea and swam over to Crete with Europa on his back. There in the cave of Dikteon Zeus made love to Europa, and she bore him three sons, one of whom was King Minos who ruled over the Mediterranean from his palace at Knossos.

As we made our way as a team to the cave, I thought of another team that had been to the same cave. Plato sets out his book *The Republic* in the form of a conversation between three characters on their way to the cave, the birthplace of Zeus, in Crete. In the introduction, the Athenian asks who stands behind the law that governs society, and the Cretan replies that it is the god Zeus. Every ninth year, King Minos used to go and seek counsel from his father Zeus, and would then bring into effect the laws that Zeus had proclaimed.

We discerned that the cave of Dikteon was a stronghold of satanic power which exercised an influence not only over Crete but over all the nations. During our prayer warfare against Zeus and the other gods that were holding Israel and the other nations in their grip, we named nation after nation until we counted 153 of them.

Afterwards it was disclosed that Zeus' birthplace was a centre for Satan-worshippers who had used the caves around Heraklion and Hania for their ceremonies. I have learnt from experience that one sign of making a direct hit in prayer is that there is a disclosure of what the enemy has been doing in the dark. For us on that occasion it was the disclosure that the worship of Zeus was close to Satan-worship. Our team received a letter of thanks for our prayer effort in Crete; the following is an extract:

Satan-worship disclosed in Greece

'The major theme in Greece these days is satanism. The whole nation has been really shattered and people are shocked as they watch in the mass media reports on the deeds of a group of very young satanists that have been caught by the police. These young kids, 18–21 years old, have really performed shocking actions including drinking blood of young girls which during the rituals [they] would get from them with syringes. But even worse 3 homicides that took place in the past two years have been confessed by them as sacrifices they had conducted to offer to the ancient evil spirit. And it is only the beginning of the interrogations. It is very obvious that such young boys and girls cannot be the leaders of satanic worship and so the police are investigating and so [are] reporters. Up till now a lot of old buildings and caves where satanic rituals were taking place have been located.

'We wish to thank Kjell Sjöberg and the team who prayed in Crete and conducted spiritual warfare against the spirit that asked for human sacrifices. It is interesting that in Crete alone fifteen caves have been identified as centres of satanic rituals. Ten were found in the area of Chania and five in Iraklion. I must say though that this has been the best and clearest teaching on the Devil that the Greeks could get.

'We are praying ... that the Body of Christ will stand strong as they are now called to present the answer of the Lord to their fellow citizens.'[16]

The fallen angels and the legends of the Greek gods

In the Greek myths, it is often described how the gods had sexual relations with the daughters of mortals, who bore children to the gods. Zeus stole Europa, the king's daughter, who bore him three sons. The great heroes in the legends always had a god for a father and a mortal mother. Hercules was the son of Zeus and the princess Alkmene.

The Bible says that the fallen angels (sons of God) went to the daughters of men and had children (giants) by them. *'They were the heroes of old, men of renown'* (Genesis 6:1–7). This great evil among men caused God to repent that he had created mankind, so that he decided to bring the Flood, and to shorten the length of man's life on earth.

The revelation of God's Word that there were giants on earth gives us a true picture of that which Greek mythology was trying in vain to say to us. The version given in God's Word is divinely inspired. Mythology has grown out of tradition and story-tellers' legends about the deeds of supernatural men and their offspring – the fact that giants had fallen angels as fathers made it easy for men to look on them as gods.

In the rabbinic Jewish legends it is related that the angels Asa and Azael reproved God for his folly in creating man who so quickly provoked him. He answered them that if they had been on earth, they would have sinned exactly as mankind did. After that he let them come down to earth, but they also sinned with the daughters of men. When they wanted to return to heaven, they could not, for they had been banished from their former existence, and they were carried to the dark mountains of the earth.

I suggest that the Greek gods and their families are the fallen angels and their offspring from the daughters of men. What became of the giants who were half fallen angels and half men? There was no salvation for them, nor any resurrection: they were spiritual powers of evil, rulers and authorities. It was these powers that rebelled against God, invaded the earth and robbed us of the first millennial kingdom. It was the Greek gods who caused mankind to lose his original divine wisdom and who limited him to only a small part of his full capacity. These powers offered mankind demonic wisdom instead of God. The well-known wisdom of the Greek culture is not the wisdom of God but that of the fallen angels. If we want to see the millennial kingdom restored, we must take up the battle against the powers that caused us to lose it. It is entirely logical that the last battle of this age will take place on this same battlefield.

Hercules, one of the mighty men of old

I would love to know the names of those *'mighty men which were of old'* who were so well known according to Genesis 6:4. I wonder whether Hercules was not one of them. He is well-known from stories from Babylon and from all the Mediterranean area.

There are many tales of Hercules and his twelve labours, all of which took place in the Eastern Mediterranean. In Crete he caught the wild bull, and the town of Heraklion was called after him (Herakles, as he is called in Greek). It would be easy to believe that these Greek tales are harmless, but they lead to a kind of role-playing. We know how young people today become caught up in a role-playing game such as Dungeons and Dragons. They become one with their heroes. Those in earlier times who wanted to excel in contests of strength lived in the role of Hercules. Today, people achieve various grades in fighting sports. The twelve labours of Hercules became initiation ceremonies for those who wished to become heroes or gods or to win victories in the Olympic fighting contests. Hercules was the hero who was taken up to be among the gods on Olympus. The initiation ceremonies of the Freemasons are built around what the legends tell of Hiram of Tyre; and there are indications that the labours of

Hercules also enter into the initiation rituals of secret societies.

The Pillars of Hercules and the entrance to the Mediterranean

The two great rocks that stand one on each side of the Straits of Gibraltar are called the Pillars of Hercules. According to the legend, Hercules set up these two rocks or pillars at Gibraltar and Ceuta in order to guide himself home. They lie at the entrance to the Mediterranean, but the Spanish associate them with two bronze pillars at the town of Gades (Cadiz). The Pillars of Hercules appear on Spain's coat of arms, and are also depicted on Spanish coins. On the pillars there is an inscription reading 'Here but no further'. The former Greek colonies founded in Spain, Gaul and Italy had Hercules as their protector. In these areas there were temples dedicated to the hero-god Hercules. The fact that the Pillars of Hercules stand at the gate to the Mediterranean means that Hercules is the watchman guarding the gates. Which god, then, controls the Mediterranean? It seems likely that it is the power that stands behind Hercules.

The King of Tyre was told by an oracle, a kind of fortune-teller, that he would found a trading colony near the Pillars of Hercules. He sent out three expeditions to carry out this task, and the third expedition founded the city of Gades, where a temple was built in honour of Hercules.

Hercules and the United States dollar

The American dollar is tied up with the Pillars of Hercules in the following way. The dollar sign is the letter S with two vertical lines through it. This dollar sign was from its origin closely connected with the Spanish king Philip IV (1683–1746). The sign represents the king's shawl draped over the Pillars of Hercules. The name 'dollar' comes from the *thaler* coin used in Germany. Silver was mined to make the coins in Joachimsthal, the valley of Joachim, in Bohemia. The coins were at first called Joachimsthaler, later shortened to thaler, a 'valley-piece'.

Whence then does the dollar derive its strength? On the one-dollar bill is written the motto 'In God we trust'. But which God is it that men have trusted in, to make the dollar strong? According to the symbolism in the dollar-sign, their trust has been in the strength of the hero-god, Hercules. As we join in battle against the demonic powers that stand behind Hercules, the strength will gradually seep out of the dollar. Some have prophesied that the dollar will collapse completely, and I can understand that, if its strength derives from Hercules.

Hercules and the power of the Pope

For centuries the Roman Catholic Church has understood itself as the owner of the chair of Peter, the one he sat on when he preached in Rome. But Peter would not have felt at home on the chair that is now connected with him. On the front of the chair there are woodcarvings of mytho-logical animals and of the twelve labours of Hercules. The position of power that has been built up around the Popes is supported by the hero-god Hercules.

The sons of Zion and the Lord's judgment over the Greek gods

The judgment of God must come on the gods of Greece, before God's kingdom can be restored. Greek mythology has influenced the whole of Western culture. It represents the fallen angels' rebellion and invasion of our world. The saints in the End Time will judge angels, the fallen angels. When Moses and Aaron were God's instruments to bring Israel out of Egypt, they pronounced judgment and punishment on the gods of Egypt. The Lord judged the gods of Egypt as a group; there were about 2,000 gods in

Egypt. It is hard to keep them all in order, but the Lord dealt with them collectively. The gods of Greece are likewise numerous, and sometimes we have to deal with them one by one, but the Lord can pronounce his judgment on the entire pantheon of gods collectively.

The Greek gods have world-wide ambitions, and therefore we need a global network of intercessors to defeat them. I have given examples of intercessors in Nashville ('Athens of the South') and in Edinburgh ('Athens of the North') realizing that they had their own Athens right at hand. We need to take up the prayer battle on the local front against humanism and the local expressions of the Greek gods.

It is important that the Lord should awaken a will to fight among the intercessors in Greece itself. They have the principal responsibility for their country and their culture, and for the launching-platform which their land affords to the Greek gods. They are not going to win the victory in their own land unless they break down the high places of sacrifice on Olympus, in Delphi and on the Acropolis.

My Israeli brothers know that when that confrontation comes, they have a calling to be involved. Israeli believers and Greek intercessors have already made a small-scale beginning in this prayer battle.

The Lord himself will fight on the battlefield for his people against the sons of Greece, according to Zechariah 9:14:

> '*Then the Lord will appear over them; his arrow will flash like lightning. The Sovereign Lord will sound the trumpet; he will march in the storms of the south.*'
> (Zechariah 9:14)

I have learnt by experience that the Lord fights for a people who are awake, who have seen the enemy and have sounded the alarm. He does not fight for a people who are asleep, who are unconcerned about humanism and the false gods. When the Lord himself comes out to do battle against the enemies of his people, he will require a response from us.

The Greek gods present themselves as protectors. Poseidon (Neptune) is the protector of seafarers, and people crossing the Equator by sea are 'baptized' in his name. Hermes is the protector of businessmen. The statue of Athena stands high upon a bank building in Edinburgh and is presented as a protector of various sectors of society such as trade, shipping, art and agriculture. We need to break down this false protection in prayer. Isaiah speaks of those who have made a lie their refuge (Isaiah 28:15). The Lord will cut down their false refuge and teach them that Jesus is the only true refuge. People who go to false gods for protection find that all they are given is lawlessness, corruption and fraud. If we proclaim Jesus as our protector, however, the evil things are revealed, that which Jesus cannot protect, so that we come to learn what it is that he can truly protect.

The confrontation with the Greek gods needs to be taken by intercessors on those places where future Olympic games are to be held. George Otis Jr has shown how annual carnivals and festivals give the opportunity to Satan to renew his lease so that he can reign for a further year. Zeus renews his lease for world domination as he receives maximum TV publicity and worship through the Games.

Co-operation with the harvesting angels

When the harvest time comes, the command will go out to the harvesting angels to clear the harvest-field of all weeds and to burn them. Intercessors are aware of a great responsibility for controlling the weeds on the harvest-field.

The final harvest is so important that it must be brought in on a harvest-field that has been cleansed, so that the harvest will not be destroyed. We have seen many harvests destroyed by weeds. I believe that the intercessors will co-operate with the harvesting angels. The Lord is the God of hosts. He is the commander of the army of angels in the same way as he is the commander-in-chief of the prayer army. He is responsible for the co-ordination of all operations on the harvest-field. I believe that by prayer we target the weeds and obstacles that need to be removed from the harvest-field – as a result the Lord will send out the angels to carry them away. I have been very conscious, when praying, of co-operating with the great angels.

We can see an example of this co-operation between angels and people praying, in the account of the church in Jerusalem praying while Peter was kept in prison under Herod's persecution of the church (Acts 12:1–2, 5, 21–23). The Lord sent out an angel to free Peter from the prison; but it was also an angel who struck Herod with the disease from which he died, when his rebellion against God had reached its maturity. That happened when he made himself into a god. He would not give honour to the true God. It was a kind of blasphemy, a mortal man taking the place of God before the people. Jesus taught us that the harvesting angels only step in when the weeds, the children of the evil one, have reached their full growth. This action also shows the co-operation between intercessors and harvesting angels who are sent to carry out the clearing of the harvest-field. After Herod's death, we are told that the word of God continued to increase and spread (Acts 12:24). This expression occurs each time that an obstacle is cleared away from the harvest-field.

The task of clearing the weeds is not given to the harvesting angels alone in the end time, but is also given to one of the prophets:

> *'See, today I appoint you over nations and kingdoms to uproot and tear down, to destroy and overthrow, to build and to plant.'* (Jeremiah 1:10)

The prophet Jeremiah was given authority to uproot so

that later he could build and plant. John the Baptist set an axe to the root of the trees in his preaching for repentance (Luke 3:7–9). Jesus said, *'Every plant that my heavenly Father has not planted will be pulled up by the roots'* (Matthew 15:13). Jesus had in mind the traditions of the elders (Matthew 15:2). The teachers of the law had established their teaching, the commandments of men, as something higher than the commandments of God.

The final battle before God's kingdom comes on earth will be the struggle against humanism and the Greek gods. We have now begun to declare war against the Greek gods on all fronts. Humanism is *'arguments and every high thing that exalts itself against the knowledge of God,'* but we have spiritual weapons that are *'mighty in God for pulling down strongholds'* (2 Corinthians 10:4–5, NKJV). The Lord has begun to do battle for us. Make yourself ready for the battle on the day of the Lord. We have a responsibility as the Lord's servants to prepare God's people for the battle on the day of the Lord.

> *'You have not gone up to the breaks in the wall to repair it for the house of Israel so that it will stand firm in the battle on the day of the Lord.'* (Ezekiel 13:5)

Notes

1. George Otis Jr, *The Last of the Giants*, Chosen Books, Grand Rapids, Michigan, 1991.
2. The Humanist Manifesto, 1973, quoted in Harry Conn, *Four Trojan Horses of Humanism*, 1978, revised edition, Mott Media Inc, Milford, Michigan, 1982, pp. 123–131.
3. Hugo Odeberg, Commentary on 1 Corinthians, in *Pauli brev till Korintierna*, Svenska Kyrkans Diakonistyrelses Bokförlag, Sweden, 1944.
4. Ralph Stob, *Christianity and Classical Civilization*, Wm. B. Eerdmans, Grand Rapids, Michigan, 1950, p. 49, quoted in Marvin R. Wilson, *Our Father Abraham*, Wm. B. Eerdmans Publishing Company, Grand Rapids, Michigan, 1989, p. 167.

5. Marvin R. Wilson, *Our Father Abraham*, Wm. B. Eerdmans, Grand Rapids, Michigan, 1989, p. 167.

6. John Selby Spong, 'The continuing Christian need for Judaism', *Christian Century*, 26 September 1979, p. 918, quoted in Marvin R. Wilson, ibid. p. 167.

7. Norman Snaith, *The Distinctive Ideas of the Old Testament*, Schocken Books, New York, 1964, quoted in Marvin R. Wilson, ibid. p. 289.

8. Stephen Mansfield, *Releasing Destiny*, Nashville, Tennessee, 1993, p. 36.

9. Stephen Mansfield, ibid. pp. 33–34.

10. Tony Walker, 'The Greek influence on Edinburgh', from notes prepared for a conference of intercessors in Edinburgh, September 1993.

11. Harry Conn, ibid. pp. 45–46.

12. *Gods Within Us*, a paper issued by the Centre for Jungian Psychology, 1993.

13. Peter Beyerhaus, *Shaken Foundations*, The Zondervan Corporation, 1972, p. 17. Used by permission of Zondervan Publishing House.

14. Greek words by Costis Palamas, 1896. Free translation from Greek to English supplied by the International Olympic Committee, Lausanne. Quoted by permission.

15. *Elements of the Greek Tradition* by Murry Hope. Element Books, Shaftesbury, Dorset, 1989, pp. 89–90. The second of the three paragraphs is quoted from *The Rites and Symbols of Initiation* by M. Eliade, Harper & Row, New York, 1975.

16. From a letter to the author from Sophia Avtzoglou of the Orthodox Christian Apostolic Brotherhood, Thessaloniki, dated 12 January 1994.

Chapter 10

Come, Lord Jesus!

The hope of Jesus' coming is a bright one. The world is not going to end in chaos and destruction, but in a restoration of all things. God has not created the world so as to be deserted and empty, but to be a place filled with God's righteousness and glory.

We have been born again to a living hope. We wait for the fulfilment of our blessed hope, and for the glorious appearing of our great God and Saviour, Jesus Christ (Titus 2:13).

> *'When the Lord restored the fortunes of Zion, we were like men who dreamed. Our mouths were filled with laughter, our tongues with songs of joy.'*
>
> (Psalm 126:1-2, marginal reading)

The return of Jesus is the most vivid dream of restoration, and the one that excites us most greatly.

As soon as I was saved, I discovered at once that we have tasted the powers of the age to come, and therefore I belong to that age to come, the age when Jesus will have returned and restored his kingdom. I walk here as a foretaste of the age that will break in when he comes. When it happens, I will enter into that for which I am intended and created.

There was a Muslim who worked in a petrol station in Rawalpindi who said to me, 'There will never be any order on this earth until Hazrat Isah comes back.' Hazrat Isah is a name the Muslims use, with all respect, of the revered Jesus. This Muslim man told me that his comrades, who worked with him at the petrol station, sold drugs, but that he himself did not wish to take part in that kind of lawlessness; he was waiting for the coming of the Messiah.

A Jewish rabbi in Israel said to my brother Stanley: 'Imagine that your daughter is expecting a baby. The time has come when she is going to give birth. She has already gone into hospital and labour has begun. At a time like that, you do not move far away from the telephone. You go around in excitement and anticipation. It can ring at any time, and then the message will come to say that your grandchild has been born. That is how expectantly I am waiting for the coming of the Messiah.'

About fifteen years ago I heard a prophetic message in a worship service at the church on the outskirts of Stockholm of which I was the pastor: 'I, the Lord, have chosen you to do the works that will bring my son back as king over all the earth.' No other prophecy has moved me so deeply. For a week I went about as if in a dream, carried away, and seeking to know the works that should be done in order to bring Jesus back to earth. This is the reason why I have been engaged in helping Russian Jews to return to Israel. When Messiah comes, all the Jews will be gathered back in Israel to welcome him home. I lead prayer teams to unreached peoples and closed lands in order, through prayer, to prepare the way for mission workers and new churches. Jesus will not come until the Gospel has reached to every people and tribe. I pray and work for the establishment of a church in Mecca in Saudi Arabia before the coming of Jesus.

Prayer is a way of welcoming the coming of Jesus

The door into prophetic intercession is praying for the coming of Jesus. The Spirit and the bride say, *'Come!'* It is the deepest desire of the bride, completely in agreement with the Holy Spirit, welcoming the Lord Jesus back to earth. The last prayer in the Bible is, *'Amen. Come, Lord Jesus.'* That prayer became a greeting among the first Christians. They greeted one another with, *'Maranatha, come, Lord Jesus!'* The prayer for the coming of Jesus is found in one sentence in the Lord's Prayer: *'Your kingdom come.'* When we pray for the kingdom, we are praying for the coming of the King.

When I first decided to pray for the coming of Jesus, I did not feel any inner acceptance. I had to overcome my fear of the End Time. When I was a child, I was frightened about the coming of Jesus, because the evangelists of my childhood were skilful in depicting the experience of those who would be left behind. In praying for the coming of Jesus, there is no fear. I prayed that prayer once in Pakistan as I lay in a trench listening to bombs exploding, in the middle of the war between India and Pakistan. My prayer at that time was an expression of fear, not of love for the Lord. The true prayer for the coming of Jesus is born out of the deepest love in the heart of the bride, longing to be able to stand face to face with her bridegroom. 'I love you with the most fervent love; come soon, so that I may be near you. Is there anything that you want me to do in order to hasten your coming?'

Once when I was leading a Communion celebration during the Feast of Tabernacles in Jerusalem under the auspices of the International Christian Embassy, I asked all who would be taking part to come dressed as bride and bridegroom to the Lord's supper, the women in white and the men in black. I said to the four or five thousand Christians from all over the world, in preparation, that we would have a dress-rehearsal for the marriage supper of the Lamb: 'Come dressed in white, with a bridal bouquet in your hand.' We are together the bride of Jesus, and the bride has made herself ready. Jesus is coming soon, and the marriage of the Lamb is approaching. Jeremiah prophesied:

'There will be heard once more the sounds of joy and gladness, the voices of bride and bridegroom.'

(Jeremiah 33:11)

Preparing for the coming of Jesus is to prepare yourself for a marriage feast.

I had a dream-vision once about the coming of Jesus which made me curious. I saw Jesus coming back to the Mount of Olives. There were crowds of people there already who had gone out to greet him. They followed him down the slope of the the Mount of Olives, across the Kidron valley and up towards the Temple area. The eastern gate, which I had seen walled-up, was now open directly to the Temple platform. There was a continuous roar of praise to him, just as there was when he rode into Jerusalem amid the shouts of 'Hosanna' and the crowds of people waving palm branches. Jesus gladly received all the praises for a long time, but then a moment of resolution came when he seemed to say, 'That will do for the praises, but now I have some important matters to deal with.' He made a sign with his hand and said, 'Now I must meet the bankers and financial people in Jerusalem.' The key people of the financial world were called together into a conference hall. I watched him go up to the podium in a hall filled with economic experts. He began his speech by saying, 'Now I want to explain how my economic programmme and the constitution of my kingdom are built on the teaching of God's word about the year of jubilee. I want to explain to you bankers and finance people how the economy of the jubilee year is going to influence your work in my kingdom.' Then the door was closed, and I could follow no more of what went on in the conference hall.

One of the founders of the New Age movement, Alice A. Bailey, wrote a book called *Glamour – a World Problem*.[1] In this book she teaches how, by means of group meditation, the obstacles can be cleared away so that the masters of the New Age movement in their great

White Brotherhood can come forward and be revealed on the world scene. The most difficult obstacle to clear away must be the zeal and fervour of the Christians who are awaiting the return of the Messiah. If I can stop the masters of the New Age movement from appearing, then I want to stand firm in my spirit as a blockade barring their way. Perhaps I have not fully known what a major obstacle I can be to them, by living in joyful anticipation of the coming of Jesus. Now I realize how much Satan wants to extinguish the fires of passion within those who dream enthusiastically of the return of Jesus.

I look forward with the greatest joy and eagerness to Jesus coming back. I have already seen his coming with my inward eyes, and I can understand exactly what Peter meant when he wrote of the morning star that rises in our hearts (2 Peter 1:19). Peter had once been with Jesus on the Mount of Transfiguration. He had an inward picture of the glorified Jesus that gave him a foretaste of his coming. One day he will be seen by every one that waits for him. I interpret history in the light of the fact that Jesus is indeed coming back. Yet when I see the misery, the evil and the intrigues, I do not start singing songs about heaven; no, I develop a lust for battle. We do need to have our priorities right about this if we are going to be able to give him a worthy welcome. So I am not writing as a passive spectator of what is happening. When the King comes, I want to be able to give him a report that we have been working for the coming of his kingdom, and that we could never accept the kingdom of rebellion. We stood against it so that we could welcome as many as possible into Jesus' kingdom.

Jesus' return as the climax of a series of events

The hope of Jesus' coming is, for those who are called to prepare for it, a series of events whose climax comes when the King comes in the skies, returns to the Mount of Olives, and makes his entry into Jerusalem. We who are leaders will prepare the people of God for battle on the day of the Lord. The *'day of the Lord'* is the period in the intermediate stage between the two ages, when Antichrist appears, there is persecution of those who refuse to accept the mark of the beast, there is tribulation over the earth, the birth-pains are suffered, the final harvest is brought in, Israel are saved, and the battle on the Lord's day culminates in the King coming at the head of his heavenly armies.

To be ready for the coming of Jesus implies being ready to go through the whole of the End Time including the birth-pains and the tribulation, without being seized by panic or paralysis, so that we can complete all the tasks we have been given in bringing in the final harvest and leading the church into maturity. We wait for Jesus' coming, ready to suffer, ready to say 'no' to the evil one and never to compromise, ready to be tested in the time of trial that will cover the whole world. The coming is not a flight or an evacuation; it is taking responsibility and keeping the faith in a time of evil, and when we have accomplished everything and held the field, then we can stand victorious on the last day when he comes.

I can identify myself with Enoch's long walk with God, in which he is an example for us who follow the final stretch of the way in this age. Enoch had received a testimony that he would not see death, and God took him. Identifying myself with Enoch's walk means an increased alienation from the world, which is compensated by an increased sense of being at home in the presence of the Lord.

The return of Jesus is the Father's restoring of the Son on earth

The coming of Jesus is the climax of the Father's plan for restoring the Son. When the Father saw the Son's humility and suffering, and saw that he was obedient to death on the cross, he decided to exalt the Son.

> *'Therefore God exalted him to the highest place and gave him the name that is above every name.'*
>
> (Philippians 2:9)

God raised Jesus from the dead and restored him in heaven by setting him at his right hand. Jesus' return implies that the Father will give the Son full restoration on earth.

Restoration has two dimensions. One side of it is that God restores those who have fallen into sin, when they repent. But there is also a restoration for those who have suffered unjustly. Evil on earth was so great that the sinless one had to suffer. Many blameless people suffer; many are misunderstood. The Lord's messengers are ill-treated and killed. A prophet is not honoured in his own country.

In an evil world, the blameless are persecuted. The righteous are misunderstood and put under pressure and made to suffer for righteousness' sake. Therefore the Lord's servant must be the suffering servant.

> *'Blessed are those who are persecuted because of righteousness, for theirs is the kingdom of heaven. Blessed are you when people insult you, persecute you and falsely say all kinds of evil against you because of me. Rejoice and be glad, because great is your reward in heaven, for in the same way they persecuted the prophets who were before you.'* (Matthew 5:10–12)

Jesus' first coming was a humiliation. He had committed no sin, and had done only good for mankind, yet he was despised and rejected by men, betrayed and condemned to death by his own people to whom God had sent him. Still today, Jesus is cursed, rejected and blasphemed. People make blasphemous films about him. He is represented as a fornicator. The Father is never going to send the Son again into an evil world to be humiliated.

Every restoration begins from the lowest bottom level. Before the Father restores the Son on earth, the world will sink yet lower. Evil will reach its full maturity as the majority of mankind, of their own free will, welcome the lawless one, the man of destruction, the one who lifts himself up above everything that is holy, and shows all sorts of counterfeit miracles. People will come to honour the beast as their leader. They will choose to give him their loyalty by accepting his mark, which shows that they are his property, despite all the warnings from heaven. With the mark of the beast on their bodies, they are already lost.

Another group seek their identity with the Father, and will have the Father's name written on their foreheads.

As the distinction between the two groups becomes crystal-clear, the world matures until it is ready for God's judgment. When the angels go out to execute the judgments of God's wrath, they will have no difficulty in distinguishing those bearing the beast's mark from those who are the Father's possessions.

Then, when the people of the world have first tasted something of the régime of the beast, the time comes for the Son of man to appear in the skies. The people will begin to mourn (Matthew 24:30). They will see that they have chosen wrong. Those who remain after God's judgments of wrath will long for a world in which righteousness lives. That is when the time comes for God to restore his Son to his rightful position on earth. He who suffered unjustly, he who was meek and mild, will be honoured and exalted, and before him every knee shall bow.

The Father will not only restore the Son on earth, but will also restore all those who have suffered for righteousness' sake. All those who have been beheaded and given their lives for the testimony of Jesus and the word of God will be restored to life and will reign with Christ for a thousand years. The humble and the meek will inherit the earth; the saints will be given the kingdom. But before they can be restored, they must first be tested in the final persecution. In the tribulation, the evil forces will work by concentrating their attack on the prophets, the apostles and the Lord's messengers, and on all who have the testimony of Jesus and hold fast to the word of God in the last times. The kings of the earth, the soldiers, the merchants and the worshippers of false gods will be condemned to God's judgment of wrath if they persecute the saints. Because they persecute the blameless and the righteous, they will give God a free hand to clear them off the earth though his judgments of wrath.

> *'Since everything will be destroyed in this way, what kind of people ought you to be? You ought to live holy and godly lives as you look forward to the day of God and speed its coming.'*　　　(2 Peter 3:11–12)

Jerusalem will be called *'the City of Righteousness, the Faithful City'* (Isaiah 1:26). There will be *'a new earth, the home of righteousness'* (2 Peter 3:13). On the way towards the coming of Jesus, we must go through a fire of purification, the last great persecution before we come through as conquerors into the day of his coming. The victors must come out of great trials in order to be counted worthy of taking part in the kingdom of God.

> *'Therefore, among God's churches we boast about your perseverance and faith in all the persecutions and trials you are enduring. All this is evidence that God's judgment is right, and as a result you will be counted worthy of the kingdom of God, for which you are suffering. God is just: He will pay back trouble to those who trouble you and give relief to you who are troubled, and to us as well. This will happen when the Lord Jesus is revealed from heaven in blazing fire with his powerful angels. He will punish those who do not know God and do not obey the gospel of our Lord Jesus.'*
> 　　　(2 Thessalonians 1:4–8)

The Jews pray in synagogues for the Messiah to come

Twice a day, practising religious Jewish men gather in the synagogue and pray eighteen prayers called *shmonah esreh* ('the Eighteen').

In the tenth prayer, they pray for the regathering of the Jewish people from the four corners of the earth, back to the land of Israel.

In the fourteenth prayer, they pray for the return of the city of Jerusalem to the Jewish people.

In the fifteenth prayer, they pray for the coming of the promised Messiah.

In the seventeenth prayer, they pray for the rebuilding of the Temple with the restoration of the Temple worship system. [2]

These prayers have been prayed by religious Jews, morning and evening, for two thousand years. God has heard these prayers, and what has been prayed for will come to pass.

The risk of the Jews choosing the wrong Messiah

There is a serious risk that the Jews and the world may go wrong in their longing for a Messiah. How will they recognize him? The rabbis are going to be looking for a strong charismatic personality who fulfils all the needs of orthodox Jews so that they can accept him, someone who can reassemble a divided Israel into a political unity, at the same time demonstrating military skill in unusual measure by saving Israel from terrorism, attacks and boycotts from the enemies of Israel. If the rabbis were to find such a personality, he would be hailed as the Jewish Messiah. He would not need to distinguish himself by the holiness and righteousness in his character. To choose the right Messiah, they need to look and see whether his hands and his feet bear the scars of the nails.

The Jews have a key role in welcoming the Messiah. If they choose wrongly, they will lead the world astray. If they choose rightly it will be for the salvation of the world. It is the Jews who carry the principal responsibility for welcoming their own, and the world's, Messiah.

Many Jews have already made mistakes several times in history. Until his death in 1994, the aged Lubavitch rabbi from New York, Menahem Schneerson, had a large following of disciples who sincerely believed him to be the coming Messiah. I saw his picture on posters and banners on the walls of houses, on cars and on hoardings, with the text, 'Messiah is coming back'. He clung to life for a long time, but finally died, to the great distress of his followers. They say that in every generation there is an offer of a messiah, and that he comes if people just at that time are ready for him.

Israel will be restored and healed of her incurable wound

The Jews have a wound and an impediment. They cannot recognize God's son in the suffering servant. It is their own terrible sufferings that they went through during the time they were scattered among the peoples.

> *'This is what the Lord says: "Your wound is incurable, your injury beyond healing. There is no-one to plead your cause, no remedy for your sore, no healing for you."'* (Jeremiah 30:12–13)

> *'"But I will restore you to health and heal your wounds," declares the Lord, "because you are called an outcast, Zion for whom no-one cares." This is what the Lord says: "I will restore the fortunes of Jacob's tents and have compassion on his dwellings; the city will be rebuilt on her ruins, and the palace will stand in its proper place."'* (Jeremiah 30:17–18)

When the Lord restores Israel, he will heal them from their incurable wound. It is the wound inflicted on them by the peoples among whom they were scattered during the time of the dispersion. It is the memory of the Inquisition in Spain, the pogroms in Russia, Hitler's 'final solution'. The greatest wound is the six million Jews killed under the Nazis. Whenever anyone makes a public speech in Jerusalem, the subject of the Holocaust is expected to be mentioned in some way or other. When the Jews meet tourists in Jerusalem, they ask whether they have visited the Holocaust museum, Yad Vashem. The memory of the mass murder of Jews stays alive and must remain so, to ensure that it does not happen again. But it does not need to remain alive as a continuous, aching wound. The Jews' own suffering means that they cannot grieve about the suffering Messiah, God's only son, until their grieving is completed and they are healed from their own wound.

Comfort, comfort my people

'There is no-one to plead your cause, no remedy for your sore,' said the Lord through Jeremiah. God is calling his church to take their part in his healing of the Jewish people from their incurable wound. He wants to use Christians who can show their steadfast, persevering love to comfort them. Christians who love the Jews have two national flags in their homes: their own nation's and Israel's. One Jew working for the Jewish Agency told me how overwhelmed he was when he knocked on the door of a house in Finland to ask the way, and saw an Israeli flag. He had not known until then that there were Christians who loved Israel. We cannot convince them only by our words; we have to prove our loyalty when the time comes that the world turns against them. The International Christian Embassy was started in the year that a number of countries in the world removed their embassies from Jerusalem to Tel Aviv, because they did not recognize Jerusalem as the capital of Israel. So when Israel was

abandoned by the world, the Christians were able to show that they stood together with Israel.

> *'Comfort, comfort my people, says your God. Speak tenderly to Jerusalem, and proclaim to her that her hard service has been completed, that her sin has been paid for, that she has received from the Lord's hand double for all her sins.'* (Isaiah 40:1–2)

At last, national mourning for a beloved king

One day, national mourning will be proclaimed in Jerusalem and in Israel. There will be grief, as the people grieved for king Josiah when he fell in battle on the plain of Megiddo. All Judah and Jerusalem mourned Josiah, for he was a well-loved king. Jeremiah sang a lament for him. All the singers and choirs sang laments for Josiah, because the emptiness and sense of loss that followed his death were very great. Of all the kings in Jerusalem, he was the one whose loss was the most mourned. Jesus was never mourned in that way, but the Holy Spirit will eventually orchestrate national mourning for Jesus the king of the Jews. Even though two thousand years have passed since he visited Jerusalem and was crucified among them, the Holy Spirit will bring mourning and loss so close to every Jewish family that they will feel as if they had lost a close relative, even their only son, and as if the grieving family were themselves responsible for his wounds. It is not going to be a national mourning of despair and hopelessness. While the mourning is proceeding, people will remember that the Messiah's hands and feet were pierced, but at the same time a Spirit of grace and prayer will be poured out. The Jews will come to realize that there is grace, and that they can pray for forgiveness and restoration. As they pray, a cleansing stream will be opened up. Jesus will at last be restored among the Jews. The Koreans are a people who can express very strong feelings. North Korea showed this when they had a time of national mourning following the death of their President Kim Il Sung. The entire people wept and grieved. Policemen, soldiers, TV reporters, all wept just as much as the schoolchildren. In the same way, the Jews will mourn Jesus, God's son.

> *'For I tell you, you will not see me again until you say, "Blessed is he who comes in the name of the Lord."'*
> (Matthew 23:39)

Jesus will not come back until a Hosanna welcome is prepared for him in Jerusalem. At his first coming, he came to those who were his own, but his own did not receive him. The Father is not going to send the Messiah to be humiliated yet again in Jerusalem. Jerusalem is a city capable of rejoicing. Every year at the Feast of Tabernacles there is a Jerusalem march when tens of thousands walk in procession through Jerusalem, singing and dancing through streets lined with happy people.

Jesus' entry into Jerusalem will be repeated, and perfected, when the Jewish leaders have learnt the Hosanna lesson. Jesus was welcomed by the children, the disciples, and the ordinary people with shouts of 'Hosanna' and waving of palm leaves when he rode into Jerusalem. But the Hosanna welcome came to a dead stop. The chief priests and elders were enraged when they heard the children's shouts of praise, and they questioned Jesus' authority: *'By what authority are you doing these things? And who gave you this authority?'* (Matthew 21:23). Their anger and unbelief in the face of his authority caused his entry into the city to be cut short. If they had welcomed Jesus, the kingdom of peace might have started then and there; but now the entry has to begin over again. The Father is not going to send his Son unless the Jewish leaders are there to welcome him.

At the same time that we in the world-wide church are praying as we undergo the birth-pains, *'Maranatha! Come, Lord Jesus!'* the Jewish leaders will have reached the point where they can proclaim and sing, *'Baruch haba bashem*

Adonai' and address it to Jesus. 'Blessed are you who come in the name of the Lord! We no longer question why the children sing your praises. We do not question that the God of Israel has given you full authority to do all that you will, with us and with Israel. We give you power, we give you honour, we give you worship. You are our king and our Messiah.'

The revelation of Jesus' glory and his return

When the Jews repent and turn to God, times of refreshing will come. Then God will send the Messiah that he has appointed for the Jews, namely Jesus. He must remain in heaven until the whole stage of the restoration is completed: until Israel is ready to receive him; until the church has become a mature bride who can rule at Jesus' side, a church that has become a queen. The restoration will happen in parallel with sin reaching its maturity on earth. The purpose of Jesus' revelation of his glory, and his return, is that heaven should come to earth and that God's will should be done on earth.

We who are then alive will be caught up to meet the Lord (1 Thessalonians 4:17). We shall be transformed. The angels will be sent out with a loud trumpet call, and they will gather his elect from the four winds, from one end of the heavens to the other (Matthew 24:31). The rapture and the gathering in the skies are rapid transfers so that we can be right in the centre of operations above the Mount of Olives before Jesus begins his entry into Jerusalem. Jesus comes with all his saints. At the revelation of his coming, Jesus destroys the man of lawlessness with the breath of his mouth (2 Thessalonians 2:8). Jesus then comes, setting his feet on the Mount of Olives where he once left his disciples.

I see the rapture, the coming of Jesus and after this his continuing presence as a single event. At the same moment as the rapture and the transformation occur, I go into the time-dimension of eternity. We shall not be able to comprehend time as we have done on earth. The time taken up by the rapture and the gathering can be understood by us as a day in eternity, in which as much is accomplished as in a thousand years. Then begins the time when we shall be for ever with the Lord, whether it is in the skies, on the battlefield where Antichrist is destroyed, or at his side in Jerusalem. We shall be just as he is, because we shall be like him, and where he is, there shall we be also.

We are caught up straight from the persecution and suffering under Antichrist into the triumph of reigning as bride by the side of Jesus the king. We have the promise that we shall be saved from the judgment of wrath. God has arranged protection for us while the bowls of wrath are being poured out over the earth. The pouring-out of God's wrath is something so intensive that the earth cannot escape from it for some long period of time.

When we come together with Jesus into the new glorious freedom of the children of God, then we shall come dancing in our new resurrection bodies, like David, who danced with all his might before the ark on the road into Jerusalem. The whole creation stands on tiptoe in expectancy. At the same moment that we appear, a shock-wave of freedom goes through the creation, and it becomes free from the slavery that began with the Fall, when the ground was cursed because of Adam and Eve. Now the earth will be blessed, and will come into a new harmony with the rain and the perfect temperature, so that its fruitfulness increases. The ground will be healed from the destruction of the environment and the discharge of poisons, and far out in the atmosphere the ozone layer will be restored so that it gives its proper level of protection. The deserts will blossom. The instinct of animals to hunt and kill will be broken, and the wolf will lie down with the lamb, the lion will eat straw like the ox, and a little child will be able to play near a snake without risk of snakebite. Jesus comes in the revelation of his glory with his saints, and this is only the beginning of the kingdom of peace.

Jesus comes as king to restore the kingdom to Israel

After forty days' teaching on the kingdom of God with the risen Jesus, the disciples asked, *'Lord, are you at this time going to restore the kingdom to Israel?'* (Acts 1:6). The question was not wrongly put, but in his reply Jesus spoke of what must come first before the kingdom can be restored. First, the mission task must be finished, and the testimony carried forth in the power of the Holy Spirit to the ends of the earth. Then the kingdom can be restored; and this kingdom that will be restored will not only consist of Israel. It will be an international kingdom. By calling out a chosen company from every people and nation, who will be prepared for the kingdom and are intercessors for their land, a platform will be created so that Jesus can, from Jerusalem, assemble the nations of the world in a single kingdom.

When the disciples put their question to Jesus, they knew that David's kingdom, which had stood united and at its highest peak in Solomon's time, had been taken from Israel because Solomon had fallen into sin and turned his heart to other gods, led astray by all his many wives. Solomon's kingdom was one of peace, lasting for forty years without any war. The wisdom of Solomon was known internationally; Israel made treaties with her neighbours and the land experienced economic well-being during Solomon's reign. It was a foretaste of the kingdom of peace, but a prophet sent by God pronounced a judgment on it that has, even now, not yet been withdrawn.

The prophet who tore a cloak into twelve pieces

The judgment was pronounced, because of Solomon's worship of false gods, that the kingdom would be taken from him and split into two. The Lord spoke to Solomon and said, *'I will most certainly tear the kingdom away from you and give it to one of your subordinates'* (1 Kings 11:11). This message was repeated to him by the prophet Ahijah, who carried out a prophetic act when he met Jeroboam wearing a new cloak. The prophet took the cloak and tore it into twelve pieces. Ten of the pieces he gave to Jeroboam, and by this prophetic act he pronounced a judgment upon Israel. God condemned them to be a divided land, though he ended by saying, *'but not for ever'* (1 Kings 11:39).

This judgment was carried out when the people made a negative confession. They spoke to king Rehoboam, Solomon's son, and said:

> *'What share do we have in David, what part in Jesse's son? To your tents, O Israel! Look after your own house, O David!'*　　　　　　　　　　(1 Kings 12:16)

It is shaking to see what consequences a negative confession can have, even after the passing of thousands of years. They renounced their share of the inheritance in David and in Israel. They shouted out negative words, breaking up a united army and going off to their own tents, every man for himself. The division has continued in Israel from that day onwards, but God's word says that when the Lord restores Israel, just as dead bones are brought to life, then there will also be a reunification, so that they will no longer be two kingdoms, but will become one people.

As I read about this prophet who acted out a judgment by tearing a cloak into twelve pieces, with an effect that has persisted to this day, so the faith was born that we might carry out a prophetic act as part of our praying for Israel, for the reunification and restoration of the kingdom. The opportunity came when the International Christian Chamber of Commerce (ICCC) arranged a conference in Jerusalem in June 1992, and I was invited to speak. I asked Christine Snelson from England if she could make a cloak of twelve pieces. She was thrilled with the idea. She sewed together ten beautiful pieces of material and embroidered 'Ephraim' on them, then sewed together two more pieces and wrote 'Judah' on them. Then, while we all prayed and confessed the division between Judah and Ephraim, and sought to reverse the negative proclamations that encouraged the division to remain permanent, Christine sewed all the pieces together at the front of the platform by the reading-desk. The result was a broad, beautiful, colourful cloak, big enough to cover a Messianic Jew and a Gentile Christian together as we put it over them.

'He bowed down to the ground seven times as he approached his brother'

On the Wednesday evening of the same conference, Derek Prince was speaking about Jacob's troubles, basing his talk on the description of the struggle between Esau and Jacob. The conflict between the twins had begun when they were still in the womb. The babies jostled each other within their mother Rebekah, and the Lord said to her:

> *'Two nations are in your womb, and two peoples from within you will be separated; one people will be stronger than the other, and the older will serve the younger.'*
>
> (Genesis 25:23)

In the same way, we recognize in our innermost being the struggle between two peoples, Jews and Gentiles, Jews and Arabs, jostling each other. Jacob's troubles came to an end when he bowed down seven times to the ground and humbled himself before his brother Esau (Genesis 33:3). Israel will undergo the same troubles as Jacob, before they are saved. Derek Prince described all this so that we could truly see that when Israel's own power is utterly broken, they will fall on their knees seven times before the Arab world and the rest of the Gentiles. Derek ended by suggesting that two Messianic Jews and two Gentile Christians should publicly humble themselves and be reconciled to one another. So two Messianic Jews represented Israel and bowed down to the floor seven times, each time confessing the pride of the Jews, how they had despised the Gentiles, how they had neglected to give the Gentiles God's word and had denied the calling that God had given them to the world. This went on for some time, in the presence of the Holy Spirit. That evening, there were a number of Jews and Arabs who received Jesus as their Saviour, as the process of reconciliation continued.

The two sheepfolds become one flock under one shepherd

The prophet saw the stick of Ephraim and the stick of Judah become united as one stick in the hand of the Lord: *'... and they will become one in my hand'* (Ezekiel 37:19).

> *'I will make them one nation in the land ... There will be one king over all of them and they will never again be two nations or be divided into two kingdoms.'*
>
> (Ezekiel 37:22)

Jesus referred to Ezekiel's vision of the reuniting of Judah and Israel, when he said:

> *'And other sheep I have which are not of this fold; them also I must bring, and they will hear my voice; and there will be one flock and one shepherd.'*
>
> (John 10:16, NKJV)

Jesus was speaking to his Jewish disciples, telling them to bring in other sheep who were not of the Jewish fold. That means us Gentiles who have heard the voice of the Shepherd and have been called together into the church.

But the Shepherd will bring these two sheepfolds together, so that there will be one shepherd, one flock and one kingdom.

Jesus spoke about Israel and the church being reunited. We Christians can identify ourselves with Ephraim. He was the son of Joseph, born in Egypt, and his mother was the daughter of an Egyptian priest of the sun-god cult. Ephraim would never have been accepted as Jewish under the present-day immigration law in Israel; to be accepted as Jewish you have to have a Jewish mother. Although Ephraim was half foreign, he was included in the direct line of family blessing from Abraham through the patriarch Jacob, who uttered a very special blessing over Ephraim: *'His decendants shall become a multitude of nations'* (Genesis 48:19, NKJV). The Hebrew phrase *melo' hagoyim* (multitude of nations) can be translated *'fullness of the Gentiles'*, an expression found in only one other place in the Bible, where Paul says, *'... until the fullness* [the full number, NIV] *of the Gentiles has come in. And so all Israel will be saved'* (Romans 11:25, NKJV).

Christians and Jews are on the way to becoming reunited. A spiritually born-again Israel is going to be joined with a restored church and become one flock and one kingdom under Christ the shepherd. Ezekiel saw that the miracle of unity would take place in the Lord's hand, as the two sticks became one in the Lord's hand. The expression 'the Lord's hand' in the Bible generally means an occasion when God intervenes and acts in history. For example, the Lord brought the children of Israel out of Egypt *'with a mighty hand'* (Deuteronomy 6:21), and *'The Lord's hand was with them, and a great number of people believed'* (Acts 11:21). The meeting-places for Christians and Jews are where God acts in history and fulfils the prophetic word; and supremely in reconciliation, when Jews and Gentiles meet at the Cross, where the dividing wall of hostility is broken down and both become joined in one body. The new citizen of the kingdom of peace is one in whose heart the reconciliation between Jews and Gentiles has been realized.

Jerusalem as an international centre

God's plan is that Jerusalem should be restored so as to become an international spiritual, cultural and economic centre. We have a calling to prepare for the coming of Jesus. The city to which the Messiah will come must be prepared. I have heard the former mayor of Jerusalem, Teddy Kollek, say to a gathering of Christians, 'We are working to make Jerusalem a beautiful city before the coming of Messiah. It is for this reason that we want all the houses to be clad in white limestone – have you noticed that most of the houses in Jerusalem are white? It is for this reason that we are laying out beautiful parks in Jerusalem. We believe that he is coming for the first time. You Christians believe he is coming for the second time.'

We study the prophetic word, and we ask God how we can pray and work so as to be in the place where he wants us, walking in the direction shown to us by the prophetic word. We believe that we are part of a prophetic people who are making ready. We are a part of those who have gone before us and of those who follow after us in preparing for the coming of Jesus, and we want to help Israel to build up Jerusalem so as to prepare the way for Jesus' return. *'For the Lord will rebuild Zion and appear in his glory'* (Psalm 102:16).

Building up Jerusalem as a spiritual centre

God's Word says that Jerusalem will become an international spiritual centre:

> *'Many peoples will come and say, "Come, let us go up to the mountain of the Lord, to the house of the God of Jacob. He will teach us his ways, so that we may walk*

*in his paths.'' The law will go out from Zion, the word
of the Lord from Jerusalem.'* (Isaiah 2:3)

For a number of years now, intercessors have been
coming each year to Jerusalem from many different countries to pray together with Jews who believe in the
Messiah. In this way they work together to build up Jerusalem as an international prayer centre. Jesus quoted the
word of Isaiah about the temple in Jerualem, *'My house
will be called a house of prayer for all nations'* (Isaiah 56:7;
Mark 11:17). Jerusalem will be the centre of a global
network of prayer:

*'And many peoples and powerful nations will come to
Jerusalem to seek the Lord Almighty and to entreat
him.'* (Zechariah 8:22)

Jerusalem as a centre of worship and culture

Since the beginning of the 1980s, Christians have come
each year from many countries of the world to celebrate
the Feast of Tabernacles in Jerusalem at the same time as
the Jews are also celebrating. This is part of the preparation for the great Hosanna-feast when the people of the
city will welcome their Messiah and hail their King in
Jerusalem.

*'Then the survivors from all the nations that have
attacked Jerusalem will go up year after year to
worship the King, the Lord Almighty, and to celebrate
the Feast of Tabernacles.'* (Zechariah 14:16)

We prepare for the coming of Jesus by working together
to cause the worship of Jesus to increase in Jerusalem. At
the first celebration in 1980, the Chief Rabbi in Jerusalem
said to the Christians, 'Your presence here with us during
the Feast of Tabernacles is for us Jews a sign that we
are approaching the time of Messiah.' The Mayor of

Jerusalem had a similar message: 'We have an old traditional saying among the Jews that when the Gentiles come up to Jerusalem to celebrate this feast, then the coming of Messiah is near.'

Jerusalem as a world-wide financial centre

So that Jerusalem can be prepared for the coming of the King, we pray and work for the city to become an international financial centre. At the ICCC conference in Jerusalem in June 1992, some 500 businessmen from 29 countries gathered with their stated object 'to link together in a new business perspective with the purpose of providing work opportunities for Jewish immigrants.'

The African countries were well represented. In that year, 15 African countries had re-established diplomatic relations with Israel. As well as the businessmen, about 100 came as intercessors. The Christian businessmen linked together in a matchmaking process with 600 Israeli businessmen in co-operation with the Israeli Import and Export Council.

President Chiluba of Zambia, who is an ardent Christian (see Chapter 2), restored his nation's diplomatic relations with Israel and sent his minister and second Vice-President, Brigadier G. Miyanda, who had recently been baptized in the Holy Spirit, to our conference. He came to establish contacts with solar energy experts in Israel. The theme of the conference was Isaiah's prophecy:

> *'Foreigners will rebuild your walls, and their kings will serve you ... so that men may bring you the wealth of the nations – their kings led in triumphal procession.'*
>
> (Isaiah 60:10–11)

The Brigadier was a firstfruits of the Heads of State who will come to build up Jerusalem. The Jewish Rabbi David Hartman spoke on 'Prophetic Israel'. He said in his introduction that if we had been a group of Christian preachers he would never have agreed to come and speak to us. But because it was a group of Christian businessmen who had come to help Israel in obtaining job opportunities, he had gladly agreed to come. 'Because you first help us with our bodies, one day we will listen when you speak to us about our souls,' said the Rabbi.

Jesus comes to restore David's fallen tent

> *'In that day I will restore David's fallen tent. I will repair its broken places, restore its ruins, and build it as it used to be, so that they may possess the remnant of Edom and all the nations that bear my name.'*
>
> (Amos 9:11–12)

God has promised that he will restore David's fallen tent. His tent is, first and foremost, David's family. God gave David a promise that his royal throne would remain for ever:

> *'Your house and your kingdom shall endure for ever before me; your throne shall be established for ever.'*
>
> (2 Samuel 7:16)

This promise was reinforced by God through Jeremiah:

> *'This is what the Lord says: "If you can break my covenant with the day and my covenant with the night, so that day and night no longer come at their appointed time, then my covenant with David my servant ... can be broken and David will no longer have a descendant to sit on his throne." '*   (Jeremiah 33:20–21)

David wanted to build a house for God, but he was not able to build the temple; instead, his son Solomon was the one who built it. But the Lord said that he would build a house for David, meaning that he would build up David's family from generation to generation so that it would last for ever. Yet David's family did not remain on the throne in a continuous line of descent in Israel. The prophet Hosea foretold:

> *'For the Israelites will live for many days without king or prince ... Afterwards the Israelites will return and seek the Lord their God and David their king.'*
>
> (Hosea 3:4–5)

When Peter spoke on the day of Pentecost, he demonstrated that Jesus was the anointed king of David's line, whom God had raised up so that, as Messiah, he could sit on the throne of David. When the people of Israel turn to God, then they will have their king back again.

The restoration of David's fallen tent is also a restoration of the unbroken song of praise that went on for forty years in Jerusalem. David brought the ark of the covenant back to Jerusalem and set it in the tent of meeting, the tabernacle. The singers and musicians ministered day and night and praised the Lord. David himself wrote songs and played a musical instrument, and he established an order for the services with instructions as to how the praise should be conducted. The worship continued in David's tabernacle without ceasing, until Solomon built the temple. Solomon's temple was richly built, but the worship never reached the level it had attained in David's time.

If you travel to South Korea, you can go at any time of the day or night to one of the prayer mountains, and find thousands of Christians gathered in prayer. This prayer continues twenty-four hours in the day without a break. We can imagine then what it was like in David's Jerusalem. You could come there at any time of the day or night and if you stood outside the tabernacle, even in the middle of the night, you could hear the blowing of the trumpets before the ark, and the Levites singing: 'Give thanks to the Lord, for he is good; his love endures for ever.' 'Give to the Lord glory and strength. Give to the

Lord the glory due his name; worship the Lord in the beauty of holiness!'

The restoration of David's tabernacle is a restoration of the highest, clearest and richest worship that the world has ever experienced. David's instrument was tuned to the scale used in the worship of heaven. Imagine the difference. First, what is offered from Broadway: from nightclubs and discotheques comes the sound of rock music. We are influenced by the output from our culture, and there is a culture that gives life and inspiration to rebellion against God. In contrast, David's tabernacle manifested the Hosanna culture, which exists to welcome God's glory. My vision is that David's tabernacle should be restored in my own capital city: that there should be a culture centre of the Kingdom of God right in the middle of the city, where people can come at any time of the day or night and see the dance of worship, hear the music of praise and take part in honouring and worshipping the King. On a few occasions I have taken part in arranging for 24 hours of continuous worship during a conference. We drew up a list of worship leaders and worship teams who were each responsible for their particular hour. It was as if the worship went through a purifying process. After 24 hours it was no longer an effort. We were humbled, so that there was no longer a need to be seen or to push ourselves forward. During the final hour, God was all in all.

Notes

1. Alice A. Bailey, *Glamour – A World Problem*. Lucis Publishing Company, New York, 1950.
2. The significance of these prayers came to my attention through reading Dan Juster and Keith Intrater, *Israel, the Church and the Last Days*, Destiny Image Publishers, Shippensburg, Pennsylvania, 1990, p. 240, and the summaries of the prayers are quoted from their book by permission.